The Plot the White House

The Shocking TRUE Story of the Conspiracy to Overthrow FDR

Jules Archer

Introduction by Anne C. Venzon

Skyhorse Publishing

Visit our website at www.skyhorsepublishing.com.

10 9 8 7 6

The Library of Congress Cataloging-in-Publication Data.
Archer, Jules.
The plot to seize the White House / by Jules Archer. — 1st Skyhorse Pub. ed.
p. cm.
Originally published: New York : Hawthorn Books, [1973].
Includes index.
1. United States—Politics and government—1933-1945. 2. Fascism—United
States.
3. Subversive activities—United States. 4. Butler, Smedley D. (Smedley
Darlington), 1881-1940. I. Title.
E806.A663 2007
322.4'20973—dc22

Print ISBN: 978-1-63220-358-8
Ebook ISBN: 978-1-63450-024-1

Printed in China

To
reporters George Seldes and John L. Spivak
for their courageous dedication to the
truth, wherever it led

CONTENTS

INTRODUCTION

Few, if any, events jeopardized the stability of the United States more than the Great Depression, which dominated the entire decade of the 1930s. Bread lines, bank failures, tramps riding the rails, the Dust Bowl, hopeless Okies praying they'd find work in California, and suicides from Wall Street skyscrapers were all realities of the era. The Crash of Black Tuesday, October 29, 1929, was no respecter of class. Everyone was affected, from Main Street to the Main Line. In July 1932, veterans of World War I, desperate for the Bonus promised to them at the close of the conflict, but not payable until 1945, marched on Washington to demand an early payout. President Herbert Hoover—the same man who fed starving children in Belgium during World War I and brought aid to a devastated Europe after the Great War—seemed helpless in the face of such unprecedented economic devastation.

The election of Franklin D. Roosevelt in 1932 brought a new approach, a "New Deal," aimed at pulling the country back from the edge of the abyss. FDR's programs, which he set into motion in the famous 100 Days, included a bank holiday to determine the solvency of the remaining institutions as well as establishment of the FDIC and SEC. At the time, these programs seemed quite literally revolutionary as they placed unmatched oversight on economic institutions. However, it was the President's desire to abandon the gold standard that stunned both the super-rich, who had felt fairly insulated from the Depression, and a significant number of average Americans who believed that Roosevelt was flirting with Bolshevism.

The U.S. was not alone in its economic desperation. Governments the world over were collapsing, often replaced with equally feeble regimes which just offered more of the same. The only nations which seemed to provide a degree of order and stability for their people were Italy and Germany, but they were under the thumb of Fascist dictatorships. In the early days of both regimes, outsiders only saw improved employment figures and growing economies. Opponents of Roosevelt's New Deal began to wonder if they might find a "man on horseback" who could rally a force to oust the administration and replace it with a regime similar to Italy's corporate state. Nothing like that had ever happened in U.S. history, but conditions had never been so bad. The conspirators faced two questions. Where would they find such a man, and where would he find his troops?

Thoughts immediately turned to the 20,000-man Bonus Army—veterans who knew how to fight and had already expressed their desperation and extreme discontent with the status quo. Would they be enough? Probably not. However, the recently founded American Legion, with over 500,000 members, might. But it would take an extraordinary event or individual to persuade them to take up arms against the country which they had fought for in the trenches of the Western Front. The leader would have to be charismatic and utterly fearless, a soldier's general with a national reputation. Who better than retired Marine Major General Smedley D. Butler?

Butler dropped out of his Quaker high school in 1898 and joined the Marines at age sixteen to fight in the Spanish American War. He prided himself on being a "roughneck," happier marching with his men than walking the halls of power. Many of the veterans knew Butler from their time at Camp Pontenazen where they waited to be transported home from France. Others remembered his exploits in the Nicaragua, Haiti, the Philippines, Mexico, and China, where he earned two

Medals of Honor and countless other decorations. Still others had seen or heard him on the lecture circuit after his retirement. Butler was discontent in his own right, having been passed over for the post of Commandant of the Marine Corps in 1931. He had gradually concluded that the State Department had used "his" Marines in Central America to further so-called Dollar Diplomacy. But most important to those considering a coup d'état was his impassioned speech to the Bonus Marchers on July 19, 1932. Whipping off his jacket in the sweltering, sticky July heat of Washington, D.C., he rolled up his sleeves and stomped back and forth across the platform. In his raspy voice with his signature staccato delivery that mimicked bursts from a machine gun, he told the Marchers to follow the law, but expressed his support for their cause with the passion of a revivalist preacher and the "hells" and "damns" of a drill sergeant. Who better to lead the ouster of FDR and the New Deal?

In the pages that follow, Jules Archer weaves a tale of intrigue, clandestine meetings, wealthy interests who remained in the shadows, the formation of the Congressional Special Committee on Un-American Activities (the McCormack-Dickstein Committee) and an outraged general who may have been convinced that war is a racket, but would do everything in his power to expose the plotters because he believed in the Constitution and the oath he had taken to defend it.

—Anne C. Venzon, 2014

FOREWORD

This is the true story of a remarkable American who, during the early New Deal years, was sought by wealthy plotters in the United States to lead a putsch to overthrow the government and establish an American Fascist dictatorship.

According to retired Representative John W. McCormack, former Speaker of the House, if the late Major General Smedley Butler of the U.S. Marine Corps had not been a stubborn devotee of democracy, Americans today could conceivably be living under an American Mussolini, Hitler, or Franco.

An ironic aspect of the conspiracy General Butler unmasked is that few Americans have ever heard about it, or even know anything about the general. As children all of us were taught about the treason of Aaron Burr and Benedict Arnold, whose betrayals were safely cobwebbed by the distant past. But school texts that deal with the New Deal are uniquely silent about the powerful Americans who plotted to seize the White House with a private army, hold President Franklin D. Roosevelt prisoner, and get rid of him if he refused to serve as their puppet in a dictatorship they planned to impose and control.

There is strong evidence to suggest that the conspirators may have been too important politically, socially, and economically to be brought to justice after their scheme had been exposed before the McCormack-Dickstein Committee of the House of Representatives. The largely anti-Roosevelt press of the New Deal era scotched the story as expeditiously as possible by outright suppression, distortion, and attempts to ridicule General Butler's testimony as capricious fantasy.

Smedley Butler's whole life, however, was proof that he was a man of incorruptible character, integrity, and patriotism, with a deserved reputation for bluntly speaking the whole truth at all times, regardless of consequences. He was named by Theodore Roosevelt "the outstanding American soldier." The official Marine Corps record calls him "one of the most colorful officers in the Marine Corps' long history" and "one of the two Marines who received two Medals of Honor for separate acts of outstanding heroism." He was decorated no fewer than twenty times.

Former Speaker McCormack told the author, "In peace or war he was one of the outstanding Americans in our history. I can't emphasize too strongly the very important part he played in exposing the Fascist plot in the early 1930's backed by and planned by persons possessing tremendous wealth."

The crucial events of the plot to seize the White House unfolded between July and November, 1933, with hearings before the McCormack-Dickstein Committee begun in New York City on November 20, 1934. On November 26 the committee released a statement detailing the testimony it had heard, and its preliminary findings. On February 15, 1935, the committee submitted to the House of Representatives its final report, verifying completely the testimony of General Butler.

This book may help break some of the seals of silence that have kept Americans from knowing the truth about that conspiracy. As the first effort to tell the whole story of the plot in sequence and full detail, it may serve as a fresh reminder of Wendell Phillips's warning about the price of liberty.

No American was ever more dedicated to eternal vigilance in preserving our freedom under the Bill of Rights than the remarkable war hero, pacifist, and Republican democrat—Smedley Darlington Butler.

ACKNOWLEDGMENTS

I am deeply indebted first and foremost to the immediate family of the late Major General Smedley D. Butler—daughter Mrs. Ethel Peters Wehle and sons Smedley Butler, Jr. and Thomas Richard Butler—for their generous cooperation; for use of the general's private and military papers, scrapbooks, memorabilia, recordings, and photos; and for vivid personal recollections of their father.

Sincere gratitude is also expressed to the following persons and institutions for their contributions to my research:

Former Speaker of the House of Representatives John W. McCormack, who headed the McCormack-Dickstein Committee and who answered all my questions about the hearings he held during which General Butler testified about the conspiracy.

General David M. Shoup, retired commandant of the United States Marine Corps, who served under General Butler in China and who shared some of his reminiscences with me.

George Seldes, whose newsletter *In Fact* and books *1000 Americans* and *Facts and Fascism* gave me my first inklings of the conspiracy many years ago and who generously helped me with my research efforts.

John L. Spivak, former foreign correspondent for International News Service, who rendered invaluable cooperation by answering all my questions and generously permitting me to quote from his own fascinating reminiscences, *A Man in His Time*, in which he relates how he was able to thwart efforts to suppress important names involved in the conspiracy.

Senator Jacob Javits and Representative Hamilton Fish, Jr., who assisted me in obtaining copies of the testimony at the conspiracy hearings of the McCormack-Dickstein Committee.

E. Z. Dimitman, former executive editor of the Philadelphia *Inquirer* and close friend of General Butler's, who shared his reminiscences of the general.

Jerry Doyle, Philadelphia *Daily News* staff artist, who helped me locate old friends of the general's.

Jesse Laventhol, Philadelphia newsman, confidant, and press secretary for the general's Senate campaign, now retired, who explained some of the behind-the-scenes political factors.

Tom O'Neil, former city editor of the Philadelphia *Record* at the time of the conspiracy, who helped put some of the pieces of the puzzle together.

William J. Stewart, Acting Director, National Archives and Records Service, Franklin D. Roosevelt Library, who guided me through the Roosevelt papers in locating material pertaining to General Butler and helped me identify sources.

Mary Schutz and Charlotte Wright, of the Mid-Hudson Library System, Poughkeepsie, New York, who obtained for me rare and hard-to-get research on the conspiracy from universities and public libraries all over the East Coast; James Brock, Ethel Tornapore, and Jane McGarvey, of Adriance Library in Poughkeepsie; the Starr Institute Library, Rhinebeck, New York; Neda M. Westlake, Curator, Rare Book Collection, Charles Patterson Van Pelt Library, University of Pennsylvania; and Mary Lou Alm, of the Pine Plains, New York, Library.

Colonel F. C. Caldwell, U.S. Marine Corps (retired), director of Marine Corps History, Historical Division, who gave me valuable research leads and provided me with helpful articles and public records from Marine Corps sources.

Warrant Officer D. R. Aggers, U.S. Marine Corps, Head, Administrative Section, Director of Information, for providing certain Marine Corps photos of General Butler.

Catholic University of America, Washington, D.C., which permitted me to study a 1962 master's thesis in library science by Eunice M. Lyon, *The Unpublished Papers of Major General Smedley Darlington Butler, United States Marine Corps: a*

Calendar, based on files turned over by the Butler family to the Marine Corps.

Robert B. Pitkin, editor, *American Legion Magazine,* who gave me statistical information about past Legion commanders.

Donald R. McCoy, historian, University of Kansas, for granting permission to quote from his book, *Coming of Age: The United States During the 1920's and 1930's.*

Assistant Professor Dane Archer, of the University of California, Santa Cruz, who originally researched the conspiracy for me eight years ago in old newspaper files at Yale University's Sterling Library.

My wife, Eleanor E. Archer, who aided me in interviews with Speaker McCormack, General Shoup, and General Butler's family as well as serving as adviser, critic, indexer, and proofreader.

Time magazine, for permission to quote from its article, "Plot Without Plotters," December 3, 1934.

Susan Berkowitz and Joan Nagy, whose brilliant editorial help aided me in sifting and organizing the elements in this book to let what remained stand out like gold dust in a prospecting pan.

JULES ARCHER

Pine Plains, New York

PART ONE

The
Plot

1

Perspiring on the raw-wood platform in the broiling heat of a July day in Washington, Major General Smedley Darlington Butler, retired, took off his coat, rolled up his sleeves, and opened his collar. His violent deep-set eyes surveyed ten thousand faces upturned among the lean-tos, shanties, and tents on Anacostia Flats.

Bums, riffraff, drifters, and troublemakers—those were some of the descriptions being applied to the Bonus Army. Many of the ragged veterans who had marched on the Capital had been sleeping in doorways and under bridges, part of the vast army of twelve million unemployed. Some were the same men who had fought under Smedley Butler in the Spanish-American War, the Philippines campaign, the Boxer Rebellion, the Caribbean interventions, the Chinese intervention of 1927–1928, and World War I.

Butler had come to Washington in 1932 at the urging of James Van Zandt, head of the Veterans of Foreign Wars, to lend moral support to veterans at a crucial moment. Congress had just voted down the Patman Bonus Bill to pay veterans the two-billion-dollar bonus promised them in bonus certificates payable in 1945. Bonus Army Commander Walter W. Waters, a former army sergeant, and other leaders feared that their discouraged followers would now give up and return home.

When Waters introduced Smedley Butler to the huge crowd of veterans gathered along the Anacostia River to hear him, he was greeted with an enthusiastic roar of acclaim that echoed through Washington like thunder. They all knew Old Gimlet Eye, one of the most colorful generals who had ever led troops into battle. He was even more famous and popular among rank-and-file leathernecks, doughboys, and bluejackets for the fierce battles he had fought against the American military hierarchy on behalf of the enlisted man. He was also admired, respected, and trusted because of his one-man fight to compel Americans to remember their tragic war casualties hidden away in isolated veterans' hospitals.

Smedley Butler was a wiry bantam of a man, shoulders hunched forward as though braced against the pull of a heavy knapsack, his hawk nose prominent in the leathery face of an adventurer. Silhouetted against a flaming sunset, he made a blazing speech of encouragement in the blunt language that had kept him in hot water with the nation's highest-ranking admirals and generals, not to mention Secretaries of State and Navy.

"If you don't hang together, you aren't worth a damn!" he cried in the famous hoarse rasp that sent a thrill through every veteran who had heard it before. He reminded them that losing battles didn't mean losing a war. "I ran for the Senate on a bonus ticket," he said, "and got the hell beat out of me." But he didn't intend to stop fighting for the bonus, and neither should they, he demanded, no matter how stiff the opposition or the names they were called.

"They may be calling you tramps now," he roared, "but in 1917 they didn't call you bums! . . . You are the best-behaved group of men in this country today. I consider it an honor to be asked to speak to you. . . . Some folks say I am here after something. That's a lie. I don't want anything." All he wanted, he told the cheering veterans, was to see that the country they had served dealt with them justly. He concluded his exhortation by urging, "When you get home, go to the polls in November and lick the hell out of those who are against you. You know who they are. . . . Now go to it!"

Afterward he was mobbed by veterans eager to speak to him. Until 2:30 A.M. he sat sprawled on the ground in front of his tent, listening sympathetically to tales of lost jobs, families in distress, and troublesome old wounds. He slept three hours, then woke to resume talks with the veterans.

Sharing a Bonus Army breakfast of potatoes, hard bread, and

coffee, he learned that the food was running out, and veterans were muttering about rioting against Congress if it did. Before he left for his home in Newtown Square, a small town outside of Philadelphia, he warned the Bonus Marchers, "You're all right so long as you keep your sense of humor. If you slip over into lawlessness of any kind, you will lose the sympathy of a hundred twenty million people in the nation."

It was the government, however, that unleashed the violence. Under orders from President Herbert Hoover, General Douglas MacArthur led troops in driving the Bonus Army out of Washington at bayonet point and burning down their shacktowns.

By August 1 rumors spreading from the last stronghold of the veterans, an encampment at Johnstown, Virginia, indicated that the infuriated Bonus Marchers were determined to organize a new nonpartisan political organization of veterans and wanted General Butler to lead it. Reporters pressed him to comment.

"I have heard nothing about it at all, although I was in Washington about two weeks ago to address the veterans," he replied with a shrug. "I have neither seen nor heard from Mr. Waters or any of the other leaders of the Bonus Expeditionary Force."

Meanwhile he phoned the governors of a number of states and won their agreement to provide relief for those of their veterans who wanted to return home. He phoned Waters in Washington to urge that the remnants of the Bonus Army break camp and start back home under this plan, and he issued a blast at the Hoover Administration as heartless for its treatment of the veterans and its failure to help them, their wives, and their children return home without further humiliation.

That November lifelong Republican Smedley Butler took the stump for Franklin D. Roosevelt and helped turn Herbert Hoover out of the White House.

2

On July 1, 1933, General Butler's phone rang soon after he had had breakfast. Calling from Washington, an American Legion official he had met once or twice told Butler that two veterans were on their way from Connecticut to see him about an important matter and urged him to make time for them.

About five hours later, hearing a car pull up into his secluded driveway at Newtown Square, Butler glanced out the porch window. His lips pursed speculatively as two fastidiously dressed men got out of a chauffeur-driven Packard limousine.

At the door the visitors introduced themselves as Bill Doyle, commander of the Massachusetts American Legion, and Gerald C. MacGuire, whom Butler understood to have been a former commander of the Connecticut department.

Butler led the visitors into his study at the rear of the house, and they took chairs opposite his desk. MacGuire, who did most of the talking, was a fat, perspiring man with rolls of jowls, a large mouth, fleshy nose, and bright blue eyes. He began a somewhat rambling conversation during which he revealed that he, too, had been a Marine, with a war wound that had left a silver plate in his head. Doyle established his combat credentials by mentioning that he also had a Purple Heart.

Butler's compassion for wounded veterans made him patient as MacGuire encircled the subject of their visit in spirals that only gradually narrowed until their apex pierced the point. The point, it seemed, was that MacGuire and Doyle, speaking for a coterie of influential Legionnaires, were intensely dissatisfied with the current leadership of the American Legion. Considering it indifferent to the needs of rank-and-file veterans, they revealed that they hoped to dislodge the regime at a forthcoming Legion convention to be held in Chicago. They urged

Butler to join them and stampede the convention with a speech designed to oust the "Royal Family" controlling the organization.

. Their dissatisfaction with the leadership of the American Legion did not find Butler unsympathetic. He had long been privately critical of the organization's close ties with big business and its neglect of the real interests of the veterans it presumably represented. These convictions were to be made dramatically public before the year was out, but now he declined his visitors' proposal on grounds that he had no wish to get involved in Legion politics and pointed out that, in any event, he had not been invited to take part in the Legion convention.

MacGuire revealed that he was chairman of the "distinguished guest committee" of the Legion, and was on the staff of National Commander Louis Johnson, a former Secretary of Defense. At MacGuire's suggestion Johnson had included Butler's name as one of the distinguished guests to be invited to the Chicago convention. Johnson had then taken this list to the White House, MacGuire said, and had shown it for approval to Louis Howe, Roosevelt's secretary. Howe had crossed Butler's name off the list, however, saying that the President was opposed to inviting Butler. MacGuire did not know the reason, but Bill Doyle assured Butler that they had devised a plan to have him address the convention anyhow.

Butler remained silent. He was used to oddball visitors who called with all kinds of weird requests. Curiosity, and the leisure afforded by retirement, often led him to hear them out in order to fathom their motives.

He thought about his visitors' finely tailored suits and the chauffeur-driven Packard and their claim to represent the "plain soldiers" of the Legion. The story about the rejection of his name on the Legion convention guest list by the White House struck him as more than peculiar, in view of the fact that the President had gratefully accepted his campaign help in a "Republicans for Roosevelt" drive eight months earlier. Why should F.D.R. suddenly be so displeased with him?

It crossed his mind that the purpose of the story, true or false, might be intended to pique him against the Roosevelt Administration, for some obscure reason. Keeping his suspicions to himself, he heard out his visitors in the hope of learning why they were so anxious to use him.

They explained that they had arranged for him to attend the convention as a delegate from Hawaii, which would give him the right to speak. When he still declined, they asked whether he wasn't in sympathy with their desire to oust the "Royal Family." He was, he said, because the leadership had simply been using the organization to feather their own nests, but he had absolutely no intention of attending the convention without an invitation.

His disappointed visitors took their leave but asked permission to return in a few weeks.

3

A month later Doyle and MacGuire returned. Without waiting to inquire whether Butler had changed his mind, MacGuire quickly informed him that there had been a change of plans. The general had been right to object to coming to the convention as just another delegate, MacGuire acknowledged. It would have been ineffective, and a waste of the general's immense prestige.

MacGuire outlined a new plan in which Butler would gather two or three hundred Legionnaires and take them to Chicago on a special train. They would be scattered throughout the audience at the convention, and when Butler made an appearance in the spectators' gallery, they would leap to their feet applauding and cheering wildly. The proceedings would be stampeded with cries for a speech that would not die down until Butler was asked to the platform.

Incredulous at the audacity with which this scheme was being unfolded to him, Butler asked what kind of speech his visitors expected him to make. MacGuire produced some folded typewritten pages from an inside jacket pocket. They would leave a speech with him to read. MacGuire urged Butler to round up several hundred Legionnaires, meanwhile, to take to Chicago with him.

Holding on to his fraying temper, Butler pointed out that none of the Legionnaires he knew could afford the trip or stay in Chicago. MacGuire quickly assured him that all their expenses would be paid. But Butler, who was constantly being approached with all kinds of wild schemes and proposals, was not prepared to take the plotters seriously until they could prove they had financial backing. When he challenged MacGuire on this point, the veteran slipped a bankbook out of his pocket. Without letting the name of the bank or the account be seen, he flipped over the pages and showed Butler two recent deposits—one for $42,000 and a second for $64,000—for "expenses."

That settled it. No wounded soldiers Butler knew possessed $100,000 bank accounts. His instincts sharpened by two years' experience, on loan from the Marines, as crime-busting Director of Public Safety for Philadelphia, warned him that there was something decidedly unsavory about the proposition.

He decided to blend skepticism, wariness, and interest in his responses, to suggest that he might be induced to participate in the scheme if he could be assured that it was foolproof. He would profess himself interested, but unconvinced as long as he suspected that there was more to be learned about the scheme. So far they had told him practically nothing except what was barely necessary for the role they wanted him to play. He determined to get to the bottom of the plot, while trying not to scare them off in the process.

After they had left, he read over the speech MacGuire had left with him. It urged the American Legion convention to adopt a resolution calling for the United States to return to the gold standard, so that when veterans were paid the bonus promised to them, the money they received would not be worthless paper. Butler was baffled. What did a return to the gold standard have to do with the Legion? Why were MacGuire and Doyle being paid to force this speech on the convention—and who was paying them?

4

Butler detected an odor of intrigue. Some kind of outlandish scheme, he was convinced, was afoot. Knowing little about the gold standard, why Roosevelt had taken the country off it or who stood to gain by its restoration and why, he began thumbing through the financial pages of newspapers and magazines—sections of the press he had never had any occasion to read.

The first important fact he learned was that the government no longer had to back up every paper dollar with a dollar's worth of gold. This meant that the Roosevelt Administration could increase the supply of paper money to keep its pledge of making jobs for the unemployed, and give loans to farmers and homeowners whose property was threatened by foreclosure. Banks would be paid back in cheapened paper dollars for the gold-backed dollars they had lent.

Conservative financiers were horrified. They viewed a currency not solidly backed by gold as inflationary, undermining both private and business fortunes and leading to national bankruptcy. Roosevelt was damned as a socialist or Communist out to destroy private enterprise by sapping the gold backing of wealth in order to subsidize the poor.

Butler began to understand that some wealthy Americans might be eager to use the American Legion as an instrument to pressure the Roosevelt Administration into restoring the gold standard. But who was behind MacGuire?

A short while after MacGuire's second visit, he returned to see Butler again, this time alone. MacGuire asked how he was coming along in rounding up veterans to take with him to the convention. Butler replied evasively that he had been too busy to do anything about it. He then made it clear that he could have no further interest in the plan unless MacGuire was willing to be candid and disclose the sources of the funds that were behind it.

After some hesitation MacGuire revealed that they had been provided by nine backers, the biggest contributor putting up nine thousand dollars. Pressed to explain their motives, MacGuire insisted that they were simply concerned about helping veterans get their bonus and a square deal.

People who could afford such contributions, Butler reflected ironically, were hardly the type who favored a two-billion-dollar bonus for veterans.

When he prodded MacGuire further, the fat veteran revealed that one of his chief backers was a wealthy Legionnaire he worked for, Colonel Grayson M.-P. Murphy, who operated a brokerage firm at 52 Broadway in New York City. Butler pointed out the contradiction between MacGuire's claim that his group was concerned with the problems of the poor rank-and-file veteran and the fact that his backers were all obviously wealthy men. MacGuire simply shrugged and frankly admitted that as far as he personally was concerned, he was primarily involved in the transaction as a businessman and was being well taken care of for his efforts. It would be equally profitable for Butler, he hinted, if the general were disposed to cooperate.

Butler pumped him about Colonel Murphy's connection with the plan. Murphy, MacGuire revealed, was one of the founders of the Legion and had actually underwritten it with $125,000 in 1919 to pay for the organizational field work. He had been motivated by a desire to see the soldiers "cared for."

That was too much for Butler, who sardonically pointed out that wealthy men had been using the Legion ever since to break strikes. MacGuire hastily assured him that Murphy had had nothing to do with *that* aspect of the organization.

When Butler questioned Murphy's motive in wanting the gold-standard speech made at the convention, MacGuire explained that he and the other backers simply wanted to be sure that the veterans would be paid their bonus in sound gold-backed currency, not in "rubber money."

He showed Butler several checks for large amounts signed by Murphy and two other men—Robert S. Clark and John

Mills. Clark's name rang a bell with Butler. He had known a
Second Lieutenant Robert S. Clark in China during the Boxer
Campaign who had been called "the millionaire lieutenant."

The money, MacGuire said, would be used to open an expense
account for Butler in Chicago. He hoped that the general
would now get busy rounding up veterans to take to the convention.

Butler remained noncommittal. He intended to procrastinate
as long as he could, continuing to pump MacGuire until he had
enough information to make a complete report to the government. The President, he felt, ought to know what schemes his
rich opponents were up to to overturn New Deal policies.

After the visit, Butler brooded over the implication of Mac-
Guire's revelation that his employer, key founder and sponsor
of the American Legion, was involved. Tall, heavyset, Grayson
Mallet-Prevost Murphy * not only operated one of Wall Street's
leading brokerage houses but was also a director of Guaranty
Trust, a Morgan bank, and had extensive industrial and financial
interests as a director of Anaconda Copper, Goodyear Tire, and
Bethlehem Steel. A West Point graduate, Murphy was a veteran
of the Spanish-American War and World War I with the rank
of colonel. Butler's bushy eyebrows rose when he also learned
that the financier had been decorated by Benito Mussolini, who
had made him a Commander of the Crown of Italy.

Butler found out that he had been one of twenty American
officers who had met in Paris in February, 1919, reportedly on
orders from the commanders of the A.E.F., to counter revolutionary unrest in Europe following the end of World War I, by
forming a veterans' organization with the alleged purpose of
looking after veterans' welfare and uniting them to defend
America at home as they had abroad.

Murphy had put up $125,000 to get the American Legion
going, and it had been organized in the spring with a caucus of
about a thousand officers and men. The Legion had then solic-
ited funds and support from industrialists. Swift and Company
executives had written other firms, "We are all interested in the

---

* The Grayson Mallet-Prevost Murphy referred to here and throughout
the book died on October 19, 1937.

Legion, the results it will obtain, and the ultimate effect in helping to offset radicalism."

The average veteran who joined the Legion in the 1920's had been unaware that big-business men were backing it to use it as a strikebreaking agency. When workers struck against wage cuts, Legion posts were informed that the strikers were Communists trying to create national chaos so that the Reds could take over. Legionnaires were given baseball bats to break up strikes and civil rights demonstrations. The American Civil Liberties Union later reported, "Of the forces most active in attacking civil rights, the American Legion led the field."

The rank and file, however, had grown increasingly restless and impatient with the "Royal Family" that ran the Legion, especially after the Depression had left so many jobless. Veterans forced to sell apples on street corners were angered by a Legion leadership that opposed the bonus and government spending as inflationary. That was why so many thousands had bypassed the Legion to join the Bonus March on Washington.

Adding up the facts, Butler was struck by a startling contradiction. MacGuire had claimed to speak for rank-and-file discontent with the Legion's bosses and professed to want to oust them, yet he was an agent for a top founder of the Legion who was obviously one of the powers behind the throne. MacGuire had revealed that the Legion still owed Murphy part of the $125,000 foundation money he had provided and had tacitly acknowledged that Murphy "makes the kings."

MacGuire obviously had to be lying in his claim that he—or Murphy—wanted to topple the present leadership. Why? Perhaps it was a ruse to channel and control popular discontent in the Legion, hopefully with Butler's help, for the purposes of the nine wealthy men behind MacGuire. Butler awaited MacGuire's next move with deep interest.

5

In September Butler was asked to address a convention of the Legion's 29th Division at Newark, New Jersey. On the Sunday morning he was in the city, the phone rang in his hotel room. It was MacGuire, who was in the lobby and asked to see him.

Invited to Butler's room, MacGuire reminded the general that the time for the American Legion convention was rapidly approaching. Was Butler finally ready to take a contingent of veterans to Chicago and make the gold-standard speech?

Butler displayed increasing skepticism about the whole plan. In a gruff voice he challenged MacGuire's proposal as a bluff without any real money behind it. His visitor whipped a fat wallet out of his hip pocket, extracted a mass of thousand-dollar bills, and scattered them all over the bed. The eighteen thousand dollars, he said smugly, would amply cover the expenses of Butler and the veterans he led to Chicago.

The gesture caught Butler by surprise; losing his temper, he accused MacGuire of trying to give him thousand-dollar bills whose numbers had been recorded, so that once he cashed them, the plotters would have proof of his complicity. MacGuire hastily assured him that he could have smaller denominations.

In his vexation Butler snapped at the bond salesman to take back the money immediately, as he had no intention of getting involved in MacGuire's scheme. But then, as he regained control of his anger, he sought to make it appear that he was merely indignant at being forced to deal with an emissary. He would negotiate, he told MacGuire firmly, only with principals.

After some hesitation MacGuire agreed to have him contacted by Robert S. Clark, a banker who had inherited a large fortune from a founder of the Singer Sewing Machine Company.

One week later Clark phoned Butler at his home. They arranged a meeting at the railroad station. Butler instantly recognized the tall, gangling man, hair now steel-gray, who stepped off the train as the lieutenant he had known thirty-four years earlier.

Butler drove him home for lunch, during which they exchanged memories of the Boxer Campaign. Afterward they adjourned to the spacious, glassed-in porch, and Clark got down to the business of his visit. He was going to the American Legion convention in a private car attached to the Pennsylvania Limited, he told Butler. He planned to have the train stop at Paoli to pick the general up, and they would continue on to Chicago together. A suite of rooms had already been reserved for Butler at the Palmer House.

Clark would see to it, he told the general, that Butler was calling for a resolution demanding restoration of the gold standard. In discussing the speech, the millionaire was induced to reveal that the author was none other than John W. Davis, the 1924 Democratic candidate for President, and now chief attorney for J. P. Morgan and Company.

Butler pointed out to Clark that the speech did not seem to have anything to do with the soldiers' bonus, which was presumably the purpose of his trip to Chicago. Shrugging, Clark blandly repeated MacGuire's assurance that those supporting the speech simply wanted to be sure that the bonus would be paid in gold-backed currency, not in worthless paper.

Butler decided to draw blood and observe Clark's reaction. Sharp eyes honed on his visitor's face, he suggested that the speech had all the earmarks of big-business propaganda. The banker, taken aback, did not reply for a moment. He seemed to be debating with himself whether to deny the allegation or take Butler into his confidence. Then he astonished the general by a sudden burst of candor.

He had a personal fortune of thirty million dollars, he revealed, and he was greatly worried about losing it to a Roosevelt inflation—runaway government spending unbridled by the need to back each paper dollar with gold. He was willing to spend fully half his fortune if that would save the other half. He was confident that if Butler made the speech at Chicago, the Legion would go on record as demanding a return to the gold standard.

That would be an important step toward organizing the veterans of America to put pressure on Congress and the President for such a bill.

Why, Butler asked him curiously, did he think the President would allow himself to be pressured by such tactics? Clark expressed confidence that Roosevelt would yield because he belonged, after all, to the same social class that was solidly behind the gold standard. Once he had restored it, his fellow patricians would rally around him and defend his position against criticism.

Butler was shocked by Clark's blatant snobbery, but even more by the millionaire's assumption that the wishes of economic royalists should—and would—prevail over the democratic processes of government. Once more his anger boiled over. In a voice that cracked with indignation, he exploded that he wanted nothing to do with a scheme to exploit veterans. Furthermore, he rasped, he intended to see to it that the veterans of the country were not used to undermine democracy but to defend it.

Clark's face turned crimson. Chagrined, he reproached Butler for being stubborn and "different," hinting that such things as the mortgage on Butler's house could be taken care of for him, and in a fully legal fashion.

This crude attempt to bribe him was too much for the dumbfounded general. Bellowing his indignation, he roared an order at the millionaire to follow him into the living room. Clark meekly trailed him into a large hall resplendent with flags, banners, decorations, plaques, scrolls, citations, and other symbols of esteem that had been presented to the general during his long career in the Marines. The hall was flanked at both ends by huge canopies on tall poles—"Blessings Umbrellas" awarded by unanimous vote of the people of Chinese cities only to their greatest benefactors.

Quivering with rage, Butler pointed out to Clark that most of the awards in the hall had been given to him by poor people all over the world, and he vowed that he would never betray their faith. Ordering Clark to inspect them until he understood the enormity of his mistake, Butler stormed off to his study, pacing back and forth in an effort to simmer down.

In a few minutes a chastened Clark joined him and meekly

asked permission to make a phone call to MacGuire at the Palmer House in Chicago. As Butler listened stony-faced, Clark informed MacGuire that for "excellent" reasons the general would not be coming to the convention. MacGuire was reminded that he had money enough to do the job alone and could "send those telegrams." At the completion of the call, Clark then apologized so contritely that his host, mollified, forgave him.

To lighten the strained atmosphere, the conversation now returned to the Boxer days until it was time to drive Clark to the station to catch a six o'clock train from Paoli.

Butler felt ambivalent about having revealed his true feelings. On the one hand, it made him feel better to get them off his chest; tact and restraint and subterfuge were alien to his nature. On the other hand, it seemed hardly likely that after his explosion the plotters could possibly believe they could persuade or buy him. He would have no further opportunity to ferret out their plans.

A few days later he carefully studied a newspaper account of the proceedings of the American Legion convention in Chicago. The story revealed that a huge flood of telegrams had poured into the convention urging delegates to endorse a return to the gold standard. A resolution to this effect had been proposed and carried.

Butler felt mingled amusement and disgust.

6

To the general's surprise MacGuire stopped off to see him, this time in a hired limousine, on the way back from the convention. The man said nothing about the contretemps with Clark, although Butler was certain he must have heard about it, and his manner was as buoyant and friendly as ever. He boasted to Butler about having put over the gold-standard resolution.

The general pointed out wryly that no action had been taken at the convention to endorse the soldiers' bonus. MacGuire airily repeated his contention that there was no point in that until the country had sound currency.

Shortly afterward MacGuire came to Newtown Square again and surprised the general with the news that a dinner had been arranged by Boston veterans in his honor. He was promised transportation in a private car, and, MacGuire beamed, Butler would be paid a thousand dollars to speak at the dinner—in favor of the gold standard, of course.

Butler was dumbfounded at MacGuire's incredible persistence. Surely the indefatigable bond salesman had realized by this time that he was barking up the wrong tree! But perhaps, the general speculated, MacGuire felt challenged to "make the sale," in much the same manner that he undoubtedly sought to overcome the sales resistance of reluctant prospects for his bonds. And apparently MacGuire was convinced that only Smedley Butler had the prestige and popularity among veterans that his coterie needed to put over their scheme.

Irked by the new attempt to bribe him, Butler rasped that he had never been paid a thousand dollars for any speech and had no intention of accepting such a sum to let words be put in his mouth. Chagrined but undiscouraged, MacGuire cheerfully promised to come up with some other more acceptable plan to utilize the general's talents as a public speaker.

In October a former Marine running for office in Brooklyn, New York, begged Butler to make some campaign speeches in his behalf. Butler was hesitant because he was about to leave on a tour of the country for the Veterans of Foreign Wars, speaking for the bonus and for membership in the V.F.W. as the best way to get it. But loyalty to the men who had served under him took him first to Pennsylvania Station.

To his astonishment he was met by MacGuire. The bond salesman somehow knew where he was headed and asked to accompany him. Butler consented, more and more intrigued by the ubiquitous MacGuire who kept turning up everywhere he went like a bad penny. He found himself even growing perversely fond of MacGuire for his stubborn refusal to take No for an answer. In the Marines Butler had always had a soft spot for incorrigible rascals who brightened up monotonous routine by their unpredictable shenanigans.

Besides, he was still curious to learn more about what the plotters in the gold scheme were up to. MacGuire now revealed a new plan to involve the general through his impending lecture tour for the V.F.W. Wasn't he, MacGuire probed, going to use the opportunity to speak out on public issues important to the veterans? Butler wasn't sure whether this was simply a shrewd guess or whether MacGuire somehow had eyes and ears all over the country.

Butler declared that he believed that democracy was in danger from growing antidemocratic forces within the country and that he planned to appeal to the nation's veterans to unite against this threat. At the same time he wanted to alert them to the risk of being dragged into another war by the propaganda of organizations camouflaged with patriotic trappings.

MacGuire looked thoughtful. Then he asserted that the group he represented really had the identical objectives. He urged Butler to let him go along on the tour. He would stay in the background, enlisting veterans in "a great big superorganization to maintain our democracy."

Butler lost no time in squelching that idea. He admitted that he couldn't keep MacGuire off any train he rode, but made it firmly clear that he would not be associated with the plans of MacGuire and his rich friends in any way. He softened the reprimand by saying that he did not want to hurt the feelings of a wounded veteran, but MacGuire would have to understand that he could not be used to aid money schemes.

MacGuire said peevishly that he couldn't understand why Butler refused to be a businessman like himself. The general expressed blunt suspicions of MacGuire's real reasons for wanting to trail in the wake of his V.F.W. tour. MacGuire protested that he had no intention of doing anything subversive.

Then he made the general a new offer. If Butler would merely insert in each of his V.F.W. speeches a short reference to the need for returning to the gold standard, in order to benefit veterans when a bonus bill was passed, MacGuire and his backers would pay him $750 per speech—three times what the V.F.W. was paying him. Butler replied emphatically that he would refuse to abuse the veterans' trust in him even if the offer were for $100,000.

Frustrated, MacGuire took his departure abruptly.

Soon afterward Butler began his swing around the country for the V.F.W. He was no longer bothered—for the moment— by the persistent attentions of Jerry MacGuire, who left for Europe on December 1, on a mission for his backers.

MacGuire took his departure against the background of a steadily rising chorus of hatred for "that cripple in the White House" by big-business leaders. It was reflected in the anti-Roosevelt slant of both news and editorials in the business-oriented press. In the eyes of America's industrialists and bankers, the President, if not an actual secret Communist, was dedicated to destroying the nation's capitalist economy by the New Deal, which they labeled "creeping socialism."

Many believed that unless F.D.R. were stopped, he would soon take America down the same road that the Russians had traveled. They were horrified by his recognition of the Soviet Union on November 16, 1933, seeing it as a sinister omen. They were equally appalled by his speech six weeks later promising that the United States would send no more armed forces to Latin America to protect private investments.

Some business leaders envied their counterparts in Italy, who had financed Mussolini's rise to power. Il Duce's efficiency in "making the trains run on time" was highly lauded, along with the dictatorial control of labor unions by his corporate state. Thomas Lamont, a J. P. Morgan partner, praised the dictator for his methods of providing low-paying jobs, cutting the public debt, and ending inflation.

"We all count ourselves liberal, I suppose," Lamont told the Foreign Policy Association. "Are we liberal enough to be willing for the Italian people to have the sort of government they apparently want?"

Butler, who had not known that MacGuire had left for Europe, received a postcard from him from the French Riviera, reporting only that he and his family were having a wonderful time. Another card came from MacGuire in June, 1934, this time from Berlin. Butler surmised that the bond salesman's long stay in Europe had to be on business, paid for by his boss or all his backers. But what kind of business? More shenanigans in connection with the gold standard?

Continuing his tour for the V.F.W., Butler observed more and more storm signals flying in the United States as he traveled around the country. The nation was rapidly becoming polarized between the forces of Left and Right. Demagogues with apparently inexhaustible funds for propaganda and agitation led "patriotic" crusades against Communists, Jews, and "Jewish bankers," who were alleged to be behind the New Deal.

That June Roosevelt further inflamed big business by a whole new series of New Deal acts that crippled stock speculation, set up watchdog agencies over the telephone, telegraph, and radio industries, stopped farm foreclosures, prevented employers from hindering unionization and compelled them to accept collective bargaining. As an epidemic of turbulent strikes broke out, the orchestration of Roosevelt hatred in the nation's press rose to a fresh crescendo.

To Herbert Hoover the New Deal represented "class hatred . . . preached from the White House," "despotism," and "universal bankruptcy." Butler was intrigued by the July, 1934, issue of *Fortune*, the Luce magazine read by America's leading industrialists and bankers, which devoted a whole edition to glorifying Italian fascism.

It was produced by Laird S. Goldsborough, foreign editor for *Time*, who asked *Fortune*'s wealthy readers "whether Fascism is achieving in a few years or decades such a conquest of the spirit of man as Christianity achieved only in ten centuries." He concluded, "The good journalist must recognize in Fascism certain ancient virtues of the race, whether or not they happen to be momentarily fashionable in his own country. Among these are Discipline, Duty, Courage, Glory, Sacrifice."

In that summer of 1934 it was not difficult to detect the acrid smell of incipient fascism in the corporate air. Smedley Butler's large hawk nose was soon to detect more than a mere whiff of it.

7

Resting at home after his exhausting V.F.W. tour, which had included emotionally draining visits to the casualties hidden away in eighteen veterans' hospitals, Butler received a phone call from a familiar voice. Jerry MacGuire insisted that he had to see the general immediately because he had "something of the utmost importance" to impart.

Butler and his wife had planned to drive into Philadelphia that afternoon, so, curiosity aroused, he agreed to meet Mac-Guire at the Bellevue Hotel. It was August 22, 1934, three days after a German plebescite had approved vesting sole executive power in Adolf Hitler as führer of Nazi Germany.

Shortly before three o'clock Butler entered the empty hotel lobby, where he found the pudgy bond salesman waiting for him. MacGuire wrung his hand enthusiastically as though they were long-lost comrades from Butler's old 4th Battalion in Panama. Leading the way to the rear of the lobby, MacGuire took him into the hotel's empty restaurant, which was not operating for the summer.

They took a table in a secluded corner of the room, and Mac-Guire began describing how enjoyable his trip to Europe had been. Butler patiently waited for him to get down to business. He wondered, not without sympathy, whether it was the silver plate in MacGuire's head that made him so prolix.

MacGuire finally asked whether the general planned to attend the forthcoming American Legion convention in Miami. Butler replied curtly that he did not. He felt irritated by MacGuire's arrogant assumption that the stale scheme of using the Legion for his gold clique's propaganda was a matter of the "utmost importance" to Butler.

MacGuire then insinuated that it was time to "get the soldiers together." Butler agreed grimly, but his cryptic tone, he was sure, implied a considerably different purpose for organizing the veterans than MacGuire had in mind.

MacGuire revealed what he had been up to on the Continent during the previous seven months. His backers had sent him abroad to study the role that veterans' organizations had played in working for and bringing about dictatorships. In Italy Mac-Guire had found that Mussolini's real power stemmed from veterans organized in his Black Shirts; they had made him dictator and were the chief protectors of his regime.

Beginning to suspect what MacGuire had in mind, Butler tried to seem matter-of-fact as he asked whether MacGuire thought Mussolini's form of government was a good example for American veterans to work toward. MacGuire didn't think so.

His investigations on the Continent, he revealed, had convinced him that neither Mussolini nor Hitler, nor the kind of paramilitary organizations they had built, could be made attractive to the American veteran. But he *had* discovered an organization that could be, he revealed in elation.

He had been in France during a national crisis brought about by nationwide wage slashes. Riots had erupted in Paris early in February, ending in the calling of a general strike that had paralyzed the country. Civil war had been averted only by the formation of a National Union ministry made up of all parties except Socialists, Communists, and Royalists.

A key role in ending the crisis had been played by a right-wing veterans' organization called the Croix de Feu. It was a superorganization, MacGuire explained, an amalgamation of all other French veteran organizations, and was composed of officers and noncoms. The Croix de Feu had 500,000 members, and each was a leader of ten others, so that their voting strength amounted to 5,000,000.

It occurred to Butler that if MacGuire's description was accurate, the Croix de Feu was an elitist outfit minus the democratic voice of the greatest majority of veterans—the buck privates, who were expected only to follow and obey, exactly as they had been ordered to do in wartime.

MacGuire now told Butler that his group planned to build

an American version of the Croix de Feu. Asked its purpose, the fat man hesitated, then replied that it was intended to "support" the President. Butler asked wryly why Roosevelt should need the support of 500,000 "supersoldiers" when he had the whole American people behind him.

Looking petulant and impatient, MacGuire ignored the question, pointing out that the crux of the matter was Roosevelt's dilemma in not having enough money to finance the New Deal, and the danger that he might disrupt the American system of finance to get it. MacGuire and his group were firmly determined that the President would not be allowed to do it.

Despite MacGuire's exasperating circumlocution and the twists in his logic, a fresh pattern was becoming clear to Butler. Far from "supporting" Franklin Delano Roosevelt, MacGuire and the interests behind him were obviously planning to compel the President to yield to their demands about American finances. The American version of the Croix de Feu was intended to be a powerful paramilitary organization to enforce those demands.

But when Butler pressed him on its purpose, MacGuire denied emphatically any intention to frighten the President. In fact, he explained, the whole idea was really to support and help Roosevelt, who was obviously overworked, by providing him with an "Assistant President" to take details of the office off his shoulders. It was quite constitutional, MacGuire insisted. The aide would be called a Secretary of General Affairs.

According to MacGuire, the President himself had been grooming an aide for such a role—General Hugh S. Johnson, controversial administrator of the National Recovery Administration (N.R.A.). But, MacGuire confided, Johnson had been too loose-lipped to suit Roosevelt, and as a result was slated to be fired within three or four weeks.

Pressed to explain how he acquired this information, MacGuire assured Butler that his group was close to the White House and had advance information on all such secret matters. Confused, Butler didn't know quite what to make of these oddly faceted revelations, but he was subsequently reminded of MacGuire's prediction when Johnson resigned in pique from the administration soon afterward and began attacking Roosevelt and the New Deal in a syndicated column for the Scripps-Howard press.

Butler did not have to feign new interest in MacGuire's proprosals; obviously much more was now involved than simply lobbying efforts for restoration of the gold standard. MacGuire, interpreting the general's absorption as an omen of cooperation, grew more candid about the plan of his group.

They would work up public sympathy for the overburdened President, he explained eagerly, by a campaign explaining that Roosevelt's health was failing. The "dumb" public would accept the need to give him "relief" by having a Cabinet official take the chores of patronage and other routine worries of the office off his shoulders. Then the President's status would become like that of the President of France, a ceremonial figurehead, while the Secretary of General Affairs ran the country.

Thus, at one stroke, the country would be rid of Roosevelt's misrule and would be put back on the gold standard. And now, MacGuire concluded triumphantly, how did the general feel about heading the new "superorganization" that would be the power behind bringing about these sweeping changes?

Unable to contain himself any longer, Butler exploded that if MacGuire and his backers tried to mount a Fascist putsch, he would raise another army of 500,000 veterans to oppose them—and the nation would be plunged into a new civil war.

Upset, MacGuire hastily assured the general that he and his group had no such intentions, but only sought to ease the burdens of the Presidency. Butler sarcastically expressed doubt that Roosevelt would appreciate their concern and turn his executive power over to their "Secretary of General Affairs," while limiting himself to ceremonial functions. Besides, Butler pointed out tersely, any attempt to build a huge paramilitary army of half a million men would require enormous funds.

MacGuire revealed that he now had $3 million in working funds and could get $300 million if it were needed. He added that in about a year Butler would be able to assemble 500,000 veterans, with the expectation that such a show of force would enable the movement to gain control of the government peacefully in just a few days.

Butler was stunned. Either MacGuire was a madman, psychotic, or fantastic liar, or what he was describing was a treasonous plot to end democracy in the United States.

He demanded to know who was going to put up all the money. MacGuire replied that Clark was good for $15 million and that the rest would come from the same people who had financed the "Chicago propaganda" about the gold standard at the American Legion convention, and who were now behind the planned march on Washington.

What plans, Butler wanted to know, did they have to take care of the veterans? The "superorganization," MacGuire said, would pay privates ten dollars and captains thirty-five dollars a month for one year, and after that it would no longer be necessary. But how did the plotters plan to manage the legal aspects of setting up an Assistant President in the White House? MacGuire explained that the President would be induced to resign because of bad health. Vice-President Nance Garner, who didn't want to be President, would refuse the office. By the rule of succession, Secretary of State Cordell Hull was next in line, but he was far too old and could easily be set aside to make way for a Secretary of General Affairs to take Roosevelt's place as President.

MacGuire again urged Butler to head the paramilitary army.

The scale of the plot, as it was unfolding to him, took Butler's breath away. It occurred to him now that MacGuire's backers had been contemplating the creation of a Fascist veterans' army at the time MacGuire had first approached him to "get the soldiers together" behind their gold-standard campaign. That explained why MacGuire had wooed him so persistently, despite the general's obvious reluctance and outbursts of temper when patriotic indignation overcame his attempts to play along and learn what the plotters were up to.

No false modesty prevented Butler from recognizing that he was perhaps the best-known, and certainly the most popular and charismatic, military figure in the United States. He also suited the plotters' plans perfectly because he was noted for a brilliant, hard-hitting style of oratory that, they undoubtedly reasoned, could be put to the service of demagoguery in the same spellbinding way Hitler and Mussolini had magnetized millions into following them. His rasping voice and fiery spirit captured audiences and held them hypnotized.

His reputation for fearless honesty, for speaking his mind bluntly no matter whose corns he trod on, also made him the ideal candidate to sell the plotters' propaganda to the nation's veterans, if he could be persuaded to view their scheme as ultra-patriotic. A combination of these reasons had unquestionably inspired Jerry MacGuire's insistent campaign to win him as the head of the putsch. It explained why MacGuire had refused to take No for an answer, counting on his persuasive powers as a bond salesman to break down Butler's sales resistance by camouflaging the raw nature of the conspiracy, and tempting him into the plot with the biggest bribe ever offered to any American—the opportunity to become the first dictator of the United States. In a word, MacGuire was convinced that with Smedley Butler as their Man on the White Horse, the plotters would have their greatest chance of success.

Increasingly uneasy and on guard, Butler now resolved to play along carefully until he had penetrated the full secret blueprint of the conspiracy. Keeping his voice cordial, he expressed interest in MacGuire's scheme, but exhibited enough doubts to induce him to reveal more in the effort to reassure Butler and win him over.

Butler became convinced that if MacGuire was telling the truth, far richer and more powerful men than just Robert S. Clark had to be involved. Clark had told Butler that he had been willing to spend $15 million of his fortune in the plotters' schemes to restore the gold standard. But MacGuire had revealed that the people behind him could, and would if necessary, raise $300 million for the putsch.

Butler determined to find out who they were. He demanded assurances from MacGuire that reputable and important people were really behind the plan to create an American Croix de Feu, pointing out that he could not afford to risk his reputation by getting involved in any second-rate adventure.

Convinced that at last he was on the verge of winning the general's support, MacGuire eagerly sought to impress him with the caliber of the influential movers and shakers of America who were involved in the plot. He revealed that in Paris he had made his headquarters at the offices of Morgan and Hodges. Butler tried to conceal his astonishment.

There was only one Morgan in the financial world—J. P. Morgan and Company. MacGuire left no doubt in his mind that the nation's biggest financiers were, indeed, involved. According to the bond salesman, there had been a meeting in Paris to decide upon the selection of the man to head the superorganization. MacGuire and his group had held out for Butler, but the Morgan interests distrusted the general as "too radical," preferring Douglas MacArthur instead.

MacArthur's term as Chief of Staff expired in November, and the Morgan interests felt that if Roosevelt failed to reappoint him, he would be bitter enough to accept their offer. Butler observed that MacArthur would be likely to have difficulty in lining up veterans behind him, because his dispersion of the Bonus Army had made him highly unpopular.

MacGuire indicated that the Morgan coterie's second choice was Hanford MacNider, an Iowa manufacturer who was a former commander of the American Legion. But MacGuire emphasized that his own group was still insisting that Butler was the only military leader in the country capable of rallying the veterans behind him. The Morgan interests had acknowledged Butler's immense prestige and popularity, he revealed, but were apprehensive that as head of the paramilitary force Butler might lead it in the "wrong direction."

Butler observed that MacNider would have no more popular appeal than MacArthur because he had gone on record as opposing the bonus. MacGuire then revealed that MacNider would be cued to change his stand, and would do so. Butler remembered this prediction when, three weeks later, MacNider suddenly reversed his position and came out in support of the bonus.

If Butler could not be persuaded to head the new superorganization, MacGuire said, the offer would definitely be made to MacArthur, whether or not the latter was reappointed Chief of Staff. He confided that there would be an administration fight over MacArthur's reappointment, but he would get it because he was the son-in-law of Philadelphian Edward T. Stotesbury, a Morgan partner.

It was a bold prediction, since never before in American history had a Chief of Staff been allowed to succeed himself. Butler was all the more startled and impressed with MacGuire's sources of information when his prediction came true several months later.

MacGuire also informed Butler that James Van Zandt, the national commander of the V.F.W., would be one of those asked to serve as a leader of the new superorganization. He would be approached by one of MacGuire's envoys at the forthcoming V.F.W. convention in Louisville, Kentucky.

Butler asked when the new superorganization would surface and begin functioning, and what it would be called. MacGuire said that he didn't know the name of it yet but that the press would announce its formation in two or three weeks and that the roster of its founders would include some of the most important men in America. One of them, MacGuire revealed, would be none other than former New York Governor Al Smith, who had lost the 1928 presidential race to Hoover as the candidate of the Democratic party.

Butler raised his bushy eyebrows in astonishment. It seemed incredible that the derby-hatted "happy warrior," who had grown up in New York's East Side slums, could be involved in a Fascist plot backed by wealthy men. But he knew that Smith was now a business associate of the powerful Du Pont family, who had cultivated him through Du Pont official John J. Raskob, former chairman of the Democratic party. Under their influence, Smith had grown more and more politically conservative following his defeat, while still remaining a Democrat.

Could it really be possible that a leading standard-bearer of the Democrats was committed to help overthrow the chief Democrat in the White House? In slight shock Butler asked MacGuire why Smith was involved. MacGuire replied that Smith had decided to break with the Roosevelt Administration and was preparing a public blast against it which would be published in about a month.

Pressed for more information about the new superorganization,

MacGuire told Butler that it would be described publicly as a society "to maintain the Constitution." Butler observed dryly that the Constitution did not seem to be in any grave danger, then he bluntly asked what MacGuire's stake was in the enterprise. MacGuire shrugged that he was a businessman, and besides, he, his wife, and his children had enjoyed a long, expensive stay in Europe, courtesy of his backers.

Taking his leave, MacGuire said that he was going to Miami to agitate again for the gold standard, as well as to get the new paramilitary organization rolling. He promised to contact Butler again after the Legion convention.

After he had gone, the bemused general was almost tempted to dismiss the whole plot as the product of a disordered imagination—his or MacGuire's. But a grim sense of foreboding told him that he was in the eye of a gathering storm.

8

There were too many things that MacGuire had told him that rang true, and could not possibly have been invented. Even as Butler brooded over the affair and wondered what to do about it, another of MacGuire's uncannily accurate predictions materialized two weeks after their talk.

In September, 1934, the press announced the formation of a new organization, the American Liberty League, by discontented captains of industry and finance. They announced their objectives as "to combat radicalism, to teach the necessity of respect for the rights of persons and property, and generally to foster free private enterprise."

Denouncing the New Deal, they attacked Roosevelt for "fomenting class hatred" by using such terms as "unscrupulous money changers," "economic royalists," and "the privileged princes of these new economic dynasties."

Butler's eyes widened when he read that the treasurer of the American Liberty League was none other than MacGuire's own boss, Grayson M.-P. Murphy, and one of its financiers was Robert S. Clark. Heading and directing the organization were Du Pont and J. P. Morgan and Company men. Morgan attorney John W. Davis was a member of the National Executive Committee—the same Davis that Clark had identified as author of the gold-standard speech MacGuire had tried to get Butler to make to the American Legion convention in Chicago.

Heavy contributors to the American Liberty League included the Pitcairn family (Pittsburgh Plate Glass), Andrew W. Mellon Associates, Rockefeller Associates, E. F. Hutton Associates, William S. Knudsen (General Motors), and the Pew family (Sun Oil Associates). J. Howard Pew, longtime friend and supporter of Robert Welch, who later founded the John Birch Society, was a generous patron, along with other members of the Pew family, of extremist right-wing causes. Other directors of the league included Al Smith and John J. Raskob.

Two organizations affiliated with the league were openly Fascist and antilabor. One was the Sentinels of the Republic, financed chiefly by the Pitcairn family and J. Howard Pew. Its members labeled the New Deal "Jewish Communism" and insisted "the old line of Americans of $1,200 a year want a Hitler."

The other was the Southern Committee to Uphold the Constitution, which the conservative Baltimore *Sun* described as "a hybrid organization financed by northern money, but playing on the Ku Klux Klan prejudices of the south." Its sponsor, John H. Kirby, collaborated in anti-Semitic drives against the New Deal with the Reverend Gerald L. K. Smith, leader of the first Silver Shirt squad of American storm troopers.

"The brood of anti-New Deal organizations spawned by the Liberty League," the New York *Post* subsequently charged, "are in turn spawning Fascism."

Butler was stunned by this fulfillment of MacGuire's prediction. As he later testified, just at the time MacGuire had said it would, the American Liberty League had appeared and was all that MacGuire had said it would be. And it was obviously no coincidence that Grayson M.-P. Murphy, Robert S. Clark, and the Morgan interests were deeply involved.

Even yet another of MacGuire's predictions came true a fortnight later, when Al Smith published a scathing attack on the New Deal in the *New Outlook*, breaking publicly with the President over economic policies. If Butler had had any lingering doubts about the authenticity of MacGuire's claim to have inside knowledge of what American big-business leaders were up to, the appearance of the American Liberty League on schedule, and Al Smith's break with the White House, convinced him that MacGuire's revelations of a plot to seize the White House were no crackpot's fantasy. MacGuire had called the shots every time.

Butler was now genuinely alarmed. For the first time it dawned upon him that if the American Liberty League was, indeed, the "superorganization" behind the plot that it seemed to be, the country's freedom was in genuine peril. Such money and power as the men behind the League possessed could easily mobilize a thinly disguised Fascist army from the ranks of jobless, embittered veterans and do what Mussolini had done in Italy with the financial support of the Italian plutocracy.

Getting in touch with Van Zandt, Butler told the V.F.W. commander that he had been approached to lead a coup as head of a veterans' army. He warned that the conspirators intended to try to involve Van Zandt, too, at the V.F.W. convention in Louisville. Thanking him for the warning, Van Zandt assured Butler that he would have nothing to do with the plotters.

Butler was tempted to leave for Washington immediately to warn the President or his advisers. He now knew enough to expose the whole plot. But he was pragmatist enough to realize that on his unsupported word, without the slightest shred of evidence, he was likely to be greeted with polite skepticism, if not ridicule. Heads would shake. Poor Smedley Butler. How sad—a fine, brave Marine general like that, losing touch with reality. Too many campaigns, too many tropical fevers.

At best they might believe that MacGuire had, indeed, told him all those fantastic things, but then MacGuire, obviously, had to be some kind of psychotic nut. And Butler would have to be an idiot to have taken him seriously, to have believed that many of the nation's greatest leaders of the business and financial world would get involved in a conspiracy to depose the President and take over the White House!

MacGuire, of course, would deny everything. So would Robert S. Clark. So would everyone connected with the American Liberty League—if this was, indeed, the superorganization Mac-Guire had revealed was behind the plot.

The enemies Butler had made among the military brass during his colorful career would help the press ridicule his revelation. "Old Gimlet Eye," they would scoff, "is at it again—stirring up a storm, making headlines. Worst publicity hound that ever wore a uniform!"

But Smedley Butler had never in his life backed off from his duty as he saw it. Convinced that the democracy he cherished was in genuine danger, he steeled himself for the ordeal of public mockery and humiliating attacks that he knew would follow his exposure of the conspiracy. He was enough of an expert tactician, however, to know that he couldn't win his battle without supporting troops. He would need corroborative testimony by someone whose word, when combined with his own, would have to be respected and force a full-scale investigation.

Butler confided in Tom O'Neil, city editor of the Philadelphia *Record*. Observing that the whole affair smacked of outright treason to him, he asked O'Neil to assign his star reporter to dig into the story. O'Neil agreed, and reporter Paul Comly French, whose news features also appeared in the New York *Post*, was instructed to seek confirmation of the plot. Butler knew and respected French, who had done an intelligent and honest job of covering his fight against crime and corruption in Philadelphia ten years earlier.

French set about determining whether MacGuire and his group were operating some kind of racket to extort money out of the rich by selling them political gold bricks, or whether a cabal of rich men, enraged by the President and his policies, was putting up big money to overthrow F.D.R. with a putsch.

In view of the powerful people the general had named in connection with the plot, French knew that his assignment was a keg of dynamite. Even if he could somehow confirm the existence of the plot and identify the conspirators, he and the general were bound to meet with incredulity when they sought to expose the blueprint for treason and the traitors.

Much would depend upon establishing and documenting the credibility of Smedley Butler, the chief witness. If the general's career showed him to be given to gross exaggeration or chronic lying, or to be an officer of dubious character whose word could not be trusted, then his sworn testimony against those he charged with treason would be held worthless.

If, on the other hand, an examination of his life and career proved that he was a man of incorruptible character, integrity, and patriotism, then his testimony would have to be given the gravest consideration, especially when supported and corroborated by the findings of French's investigation.

Whatever the outcome, the reporter knew that the denouement would be a stormy one. To Butler's enemies he was a highly controversial, unorthodox fighting man whose irrepressible temper and tongue kept him in the headlines. To his friends he was a patriotic war hero with strong convictions about democracy and a deserved reputation for bluntly speaking out the truth, regardless of consequences.

What kind of man, actually, was the Marine general who was accusing many of America's leading financiers and industrialists of seeking him as the indispensable man for their Fascist plot to seize the White House?

PART TWO

The Indispensable Man

1

Smedley Darlington Butler was born July 30, 1881, in West Chester, Pennsylvania, the first of three sons. Both his parents came from old and distinguished Quaker families. Some of his forebears included pacifists who had operated an underground railroad station for runaway slaves, and grandparents who had joined the Union Army to defend Gettysburg against Robert E. Lee's army.

On his mother's side he was descended from the Hicksite branch of the Society of Friends and Congressman Smedley Darlington, the grandfather for whom he was named. His paternal lineage traced back to Noble Butler, who came to America shortly after William Penn.

His father, Thomas S. Butler, was a bluntly outspoken judge who spent thirty-two years in Congress, where he wielded great influence as chairman of the House Naval Affairs Committee. Once when he had advocated a large Navy, a close Quaker friend reproached him, "Thee is a fine Friend!"

"Thee," the fine Friend snorted, "is a damn fool!"

The Quaker archaisms *thee, thy,* and *thine* were used only within the family and sometimes to intimate friends. The Quakerism of both Thomas Butler and his son Smedley was of that order of earlier hot-tempered Quakers who belabored each other with wagon tongues, while pausing between the hearty blows they exchanged to invoke divine forgiveness.

Smedley picked up some of his father's uninhibited language as early as age five, inviting maternal chastisement until his father went to his defense by roaring, "I don't want a son who doesn't know how to use an honest *damn* now and then!"

37

Reared in upper-class comfort with a politically prominent father, grandfather, and uncles, it was taken for granted that he was marked for prominence. Subtle pressures were exerted by four maiden aunts who adored and fussed over their first nephew, keeping him in golden curls and dressing him in a Little Lord Fauntleroy suit. Jeering peers who mistook the clothes for the boy found his fistwork as fancy as his finery.

Stirred by tales of both his grandfathers in the Union Army, he developed a passionate love for tin soldiers, toy cannon, and books with pictures of battles. His mother, Maud Darlington Butler, sought to inculcate peaceful doctrines in her son by taking him to Hicksite Quaker meeting twice a week and sending him to the Friends' grade school in West Chester.

However, his early fascination with things martial persisted. When he was twelve, he joined a West Chester branch of the Boys' Brigade, a preparedness youth movement that went in for military drills. His father had no objection and even bought his son the first uniform Smedley ever wore. He felt proud.

At Haverford Preparatory School near Philadelphia, a popular choice of old Quaker families, he joined both the baseball and the football teams. Although he was younger and lighter than his teammates, his fighting spirit, qualities of leadership, candor, and fair dealing made him highly popular and won him the captaincy of both teams.

He was only a little over sixteen and a half on February 15, 1898, when the U.S. battleship *Maine* blew up in Havana Harbor at 9:40 P.M. Americans began chanting, "Remember the Maine, to Hell with Spain," around public bonfires, and volunteer companies marched happily off to war singing, "We'll Hang General Weyler to a Sour Apple Tree."

Young Butler found himself swept up by the excitement. Struggling with math and English seemed a hopelessly insipid pursuit, with the newspapers full of blazing accounts of the terrible brutality of Spanish masters of the little Caribbean island they had enslaved. Smedley yearned to join the noble crusade to liberate Cuba in the company of the fine fellows he saw marching off from West Chester daily.

Fearful of revealing his aspirations to his parents, he attempted a fait accompli by seeking to enlist with the 6th Pennsylvania Volunteers in his hometown. Rejected as under age, he braced himself to corner his father in the sunlit library of their house on Miner Street one morning.

"Father," he said, "I want to enlist. Thee could get me into the Navy, as an apprentice, if necessary."

Thomas Butler tugged at his thick handlebar moustache with stubby fingers, regarding his slender son skeptically. "I have known of thy desire to go to war. But thee is too young."

Smedley's jaw jutted. "If thee won't help me, I'll run away and join the general army!"

"If thee does, it will avail thee nothing," his father said quietly. "I will see that they discharge thee."

One night the crestfallen youth overheard his father tell his mother privately that Congress had authorized an increase of the Marine Corps by two thousand men and twenty-four second lieutenants for the duration of the war. "The Marine Corps is a finely trained body of men," his father said. "Too bad Smedley is so young. He seems determined to go."

A new idea took root. Smedley had seen a Marine in West Chester—a young god in a magnificent uniform of dark blue coat decorated with many shiny buttons, and light blue trousers with scarlet stripes running down the seams. Wouldn't a fellow cut a fine figure in *that!* That night he fell asleep with visions of himself as a faultlessly tailored Marine charging up a Cuban hill, his Mamluk hilt sword pointed forward, inspiring the men behind him in a victorious charge.

At breakfast, heart pounding, he gave his mother an ultimatum. "I'm going to be a Marine. If thee doesn't come with me and give me thy permission, I'll hire a man to say he is my father. And I'll run away and enlist in some faraway regiment where I'm not known!"

His mother reluctantly agreed to accompany him by train to Marine Corps headquarters in Washington, without telling his father. In the competitive examination for Marine lieutenants he ranked second among two hundred applicants. Joyfully he heard the gates of childhood close behind him; ahead beckoned the exciting world of manhood and adventure. But he swallowed hard when he had to face his father and admit that he had won acceptance in the Marine Corps by adding two years to his age.

"Well," his father sighed. "if thee is determined to go, thee shall go. But don't add another year to thy age, my son. Thy mother and I weren't married until 1879!"

He could scarcely contain his pride when his lean, wiry frame was encased in a crisp new uniform. Only average in height with sloping shoulders, one higher than the other, the new second lieutenant nevertheless managed to look properly fierce because of a long, large nose and a pair of blazing, protruding eyes that gave him the bold look of a young adventurer. Huge-handed, he had a husky voice that quickly developed into a leatherneck growl, and a lively sense of humor that appealed to his fellow Marines.

His first glimpse of war came the day he arrived at Santiago, Cuba, on July 1, 1898, past a Spanish cruiser still burning in the harbor. Rigid with excitement, he boarded another ship that took him to Guantánamo Bay, where he joined the Marine Battalion of the North Atlantic Squadron.

Next day Mancil C. Goodrell, the captain of Butler's company, took him on a two-man reconnaissance of enemy positions. As they moved along a mountain trail, a shot rang out, and a bullet whizzed past Butler's head. He flung himself prone and hugged the earth, his heart beating wildly.

"What in hell is the matter?" Goodrell demanded.

"That was a . . . bullet."

"Well, what if it was? A little excitement now and then keeps you from going stale."

Soldiering under Goodrell, who had had no formal military education, Butler became infused with the spirit of the Corps. He relished the bonds of comradeship, the fierce loyalties, the cool courage, the pride in being a Marine that united men who considered themselves a fighting elite.

The officers were all professional soldiers who chewed tobacco, drank raw whiskey, cursed a blue streak, drilled the tails off their troops in garrison, and were experts on the Lee straight-pull 6-mm. rifle, Gatling gun, and Hotchkiss revolving cannon. Thoroughly unorthodox, wild in their humor, they were fierce

warriors who set an example for their men in battle by often
fighting on after they were wounded.

In young Butler's eyes they were heroes all.

He was enormously proud of his first two decorations—the
Spanish and West Indian Campaign medals. But he was even
prouder simply of being a full-fledged leatherneck who had
shared the bonds of a campaign with the Marines of Guantánamo. By the time his battalion returned home, he and two
other young Marine officers—John A. Lejuene and Buck Neville—
had become an inseparable trio. Lejuene and Neville were each
destined to rise to the rank of commandant of the Marine Corps.

"The Spanish-American War was a high point in my life when
I went to it at the age of sixteen," Butler later reminisced wryly,
"to defend my home in Pennsylvania against the Spaniards in
Cuba."

2

Commissioned a first lieutenant on April 8, 1899, Butler left
four days later with a battalion of three hundred Marines bound
for the Philippines. Emilio Aguinaldo had begun a revolution
against American occupation of the islands following Spain's
surrender.

He led his company at the head of a battalion attack on Noca-
leta, a fiercely defended rebel stronghold that the Spaniards had
never been able to take. Stumbling onto concealed trenches and
rifle pits, his company met with a blanket of heavy fire. The
men went prone, waiting for his orders.

Desperation overcoming fright, Butler sprang to his feet,
waving the company to charge and open fire. The battle drove
the insurgents back from the trench. He pursued them through
waist-high rice paddies until they turned and fled.

He grew increasingly confident of his ability to survive after several more skirmishes had driven the Aguinaldo forces north to mountain strongholds. His pride in the Corps kept growing. When a Japanese tattoist turned up in the Navy yard at Cavite, he had an enormous Marine Corps emblem tattoed across his chest. Infection from the tattoist's needle brought him down with a raging fever.

In June, 1900, he was ordered to a new Asian outpost of trouble under Major Littleton Tazewell Waller, a crusty bantam of a man with a fierce moustache. The Marines sailed for China to rescue the American legation, which had been imperiled by the Boxer uprising. The expedition numbered only a hundred Marines, but by the time they arrived in China, the situation had reached crisis proportions.

All of North China was now up in arms against the foreign powers who had carved the country into colonial spheres of influence. The Chinese bitterly resented the alien flags that flew over the imperialist compounds and the foreign ships that dominated Chinese ports, flooding the country with Western goods. Most infuriating of all were entrance signs the foreign legations had posted at their luxurious clubs: "Forbidden to dogs and Chinese." Eventually the allied nations had to send over 100,000 troops to protect their nationals.

The eighteen-year-old Butler, who had no understanding of the political causes of the Boxer Rebellion, saw his role simply as that of a Marine doing his duty to protect American citizens on foreign soil. Waller received word that the legation compound at Tientsin, twenty-five miles inland, was in desperate straits. A small defending force of allied soldiers was trying to hold off fifty thousand attacking Boxers.

Waller, Butler, and their ninety-eight men were joined by a column of four hundred Russians also en route to relieve the siege. At a gray mud village later known as Boxertown, bursts of heavy fire suddenly exploded from trenches on all sides. The Russians, who received the brunt of it, fell back swiftly through the lines of the Marines. Waller's men flattened on the plain, returning the fire.

Three Marines were killed, nine wounded. Ordered to withdraw, Butler counted noses and found a private named Carter missing. With a lieutenant named Harding and four privates, he ran a gauntlet of fire to search for him. Locating Carter in a ditch, Butler found that his leg had been broken. While the four privates fought off Boxers, Butler and Harding removed their shirts to bandage Carter's legs together, carrying him off between them. It took them an excruciating four hours to fight seven miles through the whine of persistent bullets to catch up with the company. Tripped several times by his sword, Butler unbuckled it in exasperation and flung it away.

During the weary retreat of the Marines, Butler constantly fought off an urge to collapse and give himself over to sleep or death, without caring too much which. Suddenly the crack of a bullet was followed by a dull sound right next to him. Startled, he looked up to see a stream of blood flowing down the face of a grizzled sergeant. The veteran Marine made no sound, just scowled, pulled his hat over the wound, and continued the pace of the march. It was an image of tough Marine courage that engraved itself on Butler's memory.

Stumbling on through a fierce North China dust storm with a raging toothache, his heels rubbed raw by marches that began at 2:30 A.M., famished by hunger, Butler was so miserable that Boxer gunfire seemed the mildest of his torments.

The Marines finally joined forces with a newly arrived column of three thousand international troops and fought their way through to the Tientsin compound. Routing a Chinese cohort, they broke the siege as overjoyed women and children rushed out to hug their rescuers.

The international troops defending the Tientsin compound were soon reinforced by an allied army of seven thousand men. On July 13, 1900, they attacked the native walled city of Tientsin to rout the Boxers from their stronghold. Butler was in the forefront of the assault, which required breaking through an outer mud wall twenty feet high and crossing fifteen hundred yards of rice paddies to an inner high stone wall.

Leading his company through a hail of Chinese shells and snipers' bullets, he climbed over the mud wall only to find himself dropping into a moat. The Chinese had flooded the paddies between the walls. He and his men splashed through the morass, slipping and lurching in waist-high muck as they sought to fire their weapons. When they approached the inner wall gate, thousands of Chinese on the wall poured down a withering fire, forcing Butler to order a retreat.

A tall private next to him named Partridge was hit and seriously wounded. Butler and two Marines carried him above water level through the rain of bullets splashing around them.

A burning sensation in his right thigh puzzled Butler momentarily until he realized he had been shot. Ignoring his wound, he continued to help carry Partridge until they reached some high ground. There he applied first aid to the private's wounds, then limped off in search of a medic for him.

By the time he found a Marine doctor, blood was pouring copiously out of his own wound. He protested volubly when the doctor, who outranked him, insisted on treating him first. By the time he got the doctor back to Partridge, the private was dead. Grieved and angry, he refused to leave when the doctor ordered him to the rear with the other wounded.

His first lieutenant, Henry Leonard, and a sergeant insisted on dragging him off to the other side of the mud wall. Here he was joined by a Marine lieutenant who had been wounded in the left leg. Tying their disabled legs together, they hobbled three-legged back to the nearest first-aid station. When they had been treated and bandaged, they helped dress the wounds of hundreds of casualties now pouring in.

Recommending Butler for promotion, Major Waller declared, "I have before mentioned the fine qualities of Mr. Butler in control of men, courage, and excellent example in his own person of all the qualities most admirable in a soldier."

On July 23, 1900, a week before he turned nineteen, Butler was made captain while recuperating in the hospital. The enlisted men who had helped him rescue Private Carter at Boxertown received Medals of Honor which, until 1914, were not awarded to officers. But Butler's promotion took cognizance of his heroism, citing his "distinguished conduct and public service in the presence of the enemy."

Insisting that his leg was fully healed, he painfully concealed a limp until he had nagged the doctors into getting rid of him with a hospital discharge so that he could lead his men on a march to relieve the siege of Peking. They were part of a large, colorful international army that included French Zouaves in red and blue, Italian Bersaglieri with plumed helmets, Royal Welsh Fusiliers with ribbons down their napes, Bengal cavalry on Arab stallions, turbaned Sikhs, Germans in pointed helmets, and flamboyantly uniformed troops of half a dozen other countries.

Butler's leg wound throbbed painfully, and he suffered spells of sickness from polluted water and food. His stomach was not soothed by sights en route to Peking: two Japanese soldiers, eyes and tongues cut out, nailed to a door; an old Chinese mandarin pinned to his bed by a huge sword; village streets strewn with fly-covered corpses, their skulls smashed in. The Boxers were just as ruthless with Chinese "traitors" as with luckless foreigners.

In one village a Chinese family, frightened by the allied army's approach, jumped into a canal and tried to drown themselves. Butler and his men rescued them and pinioned them firmly while an interpreter explained that the troops would not harm them. After some animated conversation, the interpreter told him, "Captain, these people say that since you have saved their lives, you are responsible for them as guardians and must now take care of them."

"Good-bye!" yelled Butler, racing off with his men.

Reaching the outskirts of Peking, they ran into blistering fire from the top of the city's stone and mud wall. They joined a combined five-thousand-man American and British force hastily digging a trench before the city.

One British private left the trench in an attempt to wipe out a Chinese strongpoint at one gate but was hit between the trench and wall. Butler's friend, Henry Leonard, sped out to rescue him but was shot and badly wounded. Clearing the trench at a bound, Butler raced through fire to reach him, but Leonard proved able to scramble back on his own, so Butler lifted the wounded Tommy on his back instead and staggered back to the trench with him.

Just as he eased the British soldier over the parapet, a stunning blow hit him in the chest. Whirling and falling, he lost consciousness briefly.

When he recovered, he heard one Marine say he'd been shot through the heart. He tried to speak but found he had no breath to vocalize. His shirt was torn open, and it was discovered that a bullet had struck the second button of his military blouse, flattening it and driving it into his chest. The button had gouged a hole in the eagle of the Marine Corps emblem he had had tattooed on his chest in the Philippines. The wound was not serious, although for weeks afterward his bruised chest ached painfully, and he spat blood when he coughed.

He was later congratulated by General A. R. R. Dorward, commanding general of the British contingent, who called Butler's rescue of the wounded Tommy the bravest act he had ever seen on the battlefield and recommended him for the Victoria Cross. But the American Government in those days did not permit an American officer to accept foreign decorations of any kind.

By August 14 Peking was in the hands of the allies, and the Boxer Rebellion was crushed. Butler's company of Marines, the longest in China, had suffered the greatest casualties in the fighting—twenty-six killed or wounded. Exhausted, Butler now came down with a bad case of typhoid fever that wasted his already spare frame down to a skeletonized ninety pounds.

3

The ailing captain was shipped to a naval hospital at Cavite, from which he was invalided home to San Francisco. Arriving on December 31, 1900, he was embraced at the port by his worried father and mother, who had rushed to the West Coast to meet him. But during his convalescence he had gained thirty pounds and was almost fully recovered. He returned home with his parents resplendent in his dress blues with two new decorations—a Marine Corps Brevet Medal for "eminent and conspicuous personal bravery" and a China Campaign Medal.

The town of West Chester gave him a hero's reception attended by the Secretary of the Navy and the commandant of the Marine Corps. It was a heady tribute for a boy not yet twenty.

His parents now suggested that since his enlistment period was about up, and he had done more than his duty in serving his country, he might want to return to his Quaker heritage in civilian life. As a boy he had sometimes talked of becoming a civil engineer. Why not go to college and study for it?

He found himself powerless to explain why he felt bound to the blue brotherhood; to make his parents understand his deep pride in the Corps, the warm bonds of solidarity that united Marines, the enjoyable excitement of danger, the honor of being foremost in defense of the nation and its citizens. Any other way of life seemed pale and drab by comparison.

"I'm reenlisting," he told them.

On October 31, 1902, he was put in command of a company of 101 men and shipped to the island of Culebra twenty miles east of Puerto Rico. There was trouble in Panama, and Butler's company was part of two battalions being stationed in reserve on Culebra while the fleet, under Admiral George Dewey, conducted maneuvers offshore.

Living on field rations and fighting scorpions, centipedes, and tarantulas, the Marines built docks and other naval constructions. In the midst of their perspiring labors Squadron Admiral Joe Coghlan sent 125 Navy gunnery experts ashore to challenge Butler and his men to a race in dragging five-inch coastal guns up four-hundred-foot hills. Admiral Dewey sent word that a victory shot was to be fired from the first gun mounted.

Stripped to the waist, Butler worked like a madman alongside his men to prove the superiority of leathernecks over bluejackets. At sunrise a jubilant Butler ordered his men to fire a victory shot. The shell sailed over Admiral Dewey's flagship, landing a mile beyond. Instead of congratulating the winners, the furious hero of Manila Bay sent Butler an icy reprimand for "reckless firing."

Their reward was an order to dig a canal. The work was backbreaking, with the ground solid rock in many places, marshland in others, all tenaciously guarded by a ferocious mosquito army. And the Navy insisted that they had to work under the broiling tropic sun in full uniform with leggings.

Unwilling to inflict any ordeal upon his men that he was not willing to endure himself, Butler wielded a shovel in the ditch beside them. Soon their ranks began to be decimated by tropical fever. A Marine major asked the Navy flagship, which had an ice machine aboard, for ice to bring down their fevers. His request scornfully refused, he returned to camp to find Butler unconscious. The major ordered him rowed immediately across the bay to a temporary Navy hospital.

Indignant at the Navy's treatment, the major wrote to Butler's father in Washington to tell him what was happening at Culebra. Thomas Butler let out an angry roar in the House Naval Affairs Committee. Secretary of the Navy William H. Moody sent swift orders to Admiral Dewey that no more Americans were to be used as forced labor on the miserable canal. The Navy brass fumed, convinced that it had been Captain Smedley Butler who had complained to his father. As soon as he was off the sick list, Admiral Coghlan put him in charge of sixty-five natives hired to finish the canal. Two weeks later, the canal finished, he collapsed with a relapse of tropical fever.

While Butler was in the hospital, a belated award of the Philippine Campaign Medal made him think about his old battalion under Major Waller, who was now back in the Philippines under Army General Adna Chaffee fighting rebels. He was stunned when an uproar in the American press compelled Waller's court-martial for killing ten Filipino native carriers who had balked at orders during a march. Waller had been acquitted, however, on grounds that he had merely been obeying "kill and burn" orders relayed from General Chaffee.

Butler was distressed by the news. Having served under both Waller and Chaffee, he admired them as courageous officers whose code called for protecting, first, American civilians wherever they might be; then the men under them; then their comrades-in-arms. From his own experience in the Philippines and China, Butler guessed that Waller had suspected the carriers of being rebels. It was impossible to tell apart insurrectionists and noncombatant natives.

The twenty-one-year-old Marine captain was not yet troubled by doubts as to what the Marines were ordered to do in the service of their country, or why. He shared the easy condescension of most Marines of that swashbuckling era toward people of underdeveloped countries as naïve natives who had to be patronized, directed, and protected by Americans.

The Marines were an elite gendarmerie entrusted with the duty of maintaining international law and order on behalf of civilization. A Marine's only concern was carrying out his orders as expertly as possible, without questions. It was only later, as he gradually came to know native peoples better and learned to admire their age-old customs and traditions, that Smedley Butler felt impelled to question his role as an instrument of American foreign policy.

4

When a revolution broke out in Honduras early in 1903, Butler's battalion was dispatched there aboard an old banana freighter, the *Panther*, as part of a squadron under Admiral Coghlan.

On the second day out the ship's commander summoned all hands to the quarterdeck to complain that someone had been using profane language near his cabin. "I know the guilty party cannot be one of these fine men," he declared, indicating the sailors, "therefore it must have been one of these men enlisted from the slums of our big cities." Pointing to the Marines, he restricted their use of the deck. Butler restrained an impulse to apply the tip of his boot to the seat of the commander's naval rectitude.

"Then and there," he recalled later, "I made up my mind that I would always protect Marines from the hounding to which they were subjected by some of the naval officers."

At the end of his duty in Culebra, his father had reproached him for not having kept him better informed as to what was going on in America's naval outposts. Now Butler did not hesitate to write his father field reports in the Plain Language, sometimes asking him to use his influence on the House Naval Affairs Committee on behalf of the Marine Corps. Thomas Butler did not always consent, but did serve informally as the Marines' court of last resort against Navy hostility.

In Honduras Smedley was vague as to what the trouble was all about, noting, "It all seemed like a Gilbert and Sullivan war." He led a force ashore at Trujillo between government and rebel forces who were firing at each other to rescue the American consular agent.

After seeing some duty in Panama, for which he won an Expeditionary Medal, he returned to the Philadelphia Navy Yard in 1905. A pretty Georgia-born girl named Ethel Conway Peters, some of whose family had been prominent in the affairs of Philadelphia since Colonial times, helped him make good use of his leave time. They were married on June 30 at Bay Head, New Jersey, in a military wedding. Commented the Philadelphia *Inquirer*: "Cupid and Mars in a wedding by the sea at high noon today."

Their honeymoon was a world trip made possible by orders assigning him to the Philippines as captain of Company E, Second Regiment. Arriving with his bride by way of Europe, India, and Singapore, he was stationed at a small naval base on Subic Bay, sixty miles north of Manila. Here, in November, 1906, his daughter Ethel was born. Butler's popularity led to her adoption by the regiment. Giving a dinner for the enlisted men, he carried her to the table on a pillow as guest of honor. Not surprisingly, she grew up a "Marine brat" and years later married a Marine lieutenant, John Wehle.

With a detachment of fifty men Butler spent several months

dragging six-inch guns up mountaintops to defend Subic Bay against possible attack by Japan, an attack that did not materialize for another thirty-six years. He and his men lived ruggedly on hardtack, hash, and coffee. A Navy supply tug, which never brought them supplies or rations, continued to ignore them even when they signaled that they had run out of hash.

Butler decided to sail to the Navy supply base across the bay. With two volunteers he set out in a native outrigger. A typhoon blew up suddenly behind them, ripping away their sail and snapping their paddles. For five hours they fought to keep from drowning until the storm finally blew the seafaring trio ashore at the supply base.

Soaked and chilled, Butler lost no time in arranging to have the supply tug carry beef and vegetables back to his men. The hungry Marines cheered his return on the tug. The camp dock had been swept away by the typhoon, so they splashed out into the bay to form a chain that passed the food from tug to shore. Butler was a hero to his men, but not to the Navy brass who heard about his bypass of official channels.

A Navy board of medical survey decided that his taking the outrigger into a typhoon, and use of the tug to take supplies back to his men, indicated signs of an "impending nervous breakdown." He was ordered home.

In October, 1908, despite the dim view of him taken by the Navy brass, he was promoted to the rank of major. His fitness reports submitted by his commanding officers could not be ignored; all unanimously rated him "outstanding," commending him as a strict disciplinarian impatient of inefficiency, laziness, or cowardice.

His contempt for red tape and his personal bravery were acknowledged to have made him one of the most popular and successful officials in the Corps. His units were distinguished by a high esprit de corps because of his devotion to his men, his concern for their welfare and pride in their accomplishments, and his democratic insistence upon rolling up his sleeves to work beside them physically.

Soon after his second child, Smedley, Jr., was born, July 12, 1909, Butler was put in charge of the 4th Battalion, 1st Marine

Regiment, and sent to Panama. Although he was stationed on the Isthmus for four years until the Panama Canal was opened, he was temporarily detached three times to command expeditions into strife-torn Nicaragua.

Washington had decided to intervene openly in the internal affairs of that Central American country. Butler's orders each time were "to protect American lives and property." He soon realized that this general order involved propping up Nicaraguan governments or factions that were favored in Washington for business reasons.

The Conservative party was seeking to drive the Liberals out of power. Their revolt was led by Adolfo Diaz, secretary-treasurer of the La Luz Mining Company, in which Secretary of State Philander C. Knox was said to own stock. The Liberal Government had smashed Diaz's forces and pinned 350 survivors at Bluefields, where Butler had been sent with the 4th Battalion. The American Consul at Bluefields made it clear to Butler that the State Department wanted Diaz to prevail.

Two Liberal generals prepared to take Bluefields with fifteen thousand well-armed men. Before the shooting could start, Butler sent them a message. The Marines were there only as neutrals protecting American residents, he told the attackers. The government forces could take the town but must leave their guns outside the city so that no Americans were accidentally shot. Marine guards would be posted outside the city to collect all weapons from Nicaraguans entering it.

How could they take the town, the dismayed generals protested, without arms? And why weren't Diaz's forces inside the town also being disarmed? Butler thought fast.

"There is no danger of the defenders killing American citizens, because they will be shooting *outward*," he replied blandly, "but your soldiers would be firing *toward* us."

The ploy compelled the government forces to retract, giving the Conservative forces time to regroup and mount a counter-attack that soon overthrew the Liberals. Juan Estrada became the new President, with Diaz as Vice-President.

Butler felt somewhat uneasy about the role the Marines had been compelled to play in this coup, especially since he knew that the American people had no idea of how Secretary of State Knox was using the armed forces in Central America, or why. But as a Marine officer he did not feel responsible for foreign policy. He saw his role simply as implementing that policy by dutifully carrying out his country's orders as he was sworn to do.

Before the Marines returned to Panama, he was confronted by a host of Bluefields shopkeepers who presented him with unpaid bills signed by members of his battalion, including George Washington, Abraham Lincoln, and Yankee Doodle. From the handwriting Butler deciphered the true identity of these pseudonyms and saw to it that they paid up. The first to defend his men against injustices, he also insisted that they scrupulously honor their word to tradesmen in whatever foreign land they were stationed, to protect the Corps's good name.

One month later the Nicaraguan revolutionary pot boiled over again. General Luis Mena, the Conservative party's Minister of War, had overthrown Estrada as President and had been overthrown in turn by Diaz. Mena went into rebellion with government troops loyal to him and had returned to attack Managua, the capital. Butler was rushed to Managua with a force of 350 men and ordered to prop up the faltering Diaz government.

Finding Diaz in the field and government forces in the capital in chaos, he took command of them. The American minister informed him that American banking interests had taken over the national railroad as security for a loan to the Diaz government, so that it must now be protected as "American property." But it ran through territory controlled by three thousand of Mena's troops, who had captured a train and held it against a small Marine force sent to retake it.

Nicaraguan newspapers mocked the Americans' rout. Mena's forces refused to let any other trains through, cutting off supplies from the port.

On August 25, 1912, Butler was ordered to retake the captured train and open the railroad line. Angry that a Marine officer had failed in the task and made the Corps "a laughingstock," he wrote his wife, "The idea prevails *very strongly* that Marines are not soldiers, and will not fight. I cannot stand any slur on our Corps and I will wipe it off or quit."

5

With a hundred Marine volunteers behind him, Butler located the train and approached the rebel forces guarding it with two heavy cloth bags in his hands. His way was barred by machetes and bayonets, and he was warned to retreat or have his small force annihilated. Through an interpreter he informed the rebels that the bags in his hands held dynamite, and he intended to blow them off the map if they did not back off and let his men repossess the train.

The rebel commander hesitated, then glumly ordered his men to yield. The Marines manned the train, and as it pulled away, Butler calmly emptied the two bags out of a rear window in sight of the rebels. They contained sand.

Checking a bridge to make sure it was safe for the train to cross, he was suddenly confronted by a rebel general with an enormous moustache who whipped out a huge pistol and shoved it against Butler's stomach. If the train moved forward one inch, the rebel officer yelled to Marines clustered around the locomotive, he would pull the trigger.

The slender Marine major suddenly sidestepped, simultaneously tearing the pistol out of the Nicaraguan's hand. Emptying the cartridges out of the barrel, he calmly returned the gun to the crestfallen general and drew his own revolver. The vanquished rebel leader meekly marched back to the train as a hostage, and the train went through.

Butler discovered that most Nicaraguans were supporting the rebellion against the Diaz government, which had hired brutal Honduran mercenaries to crush it. The people themselves had slain many mercenaries, who looted, raped, and murdered. Unfortunately for American prestige, a few Americans had been conspicuous among them. Butler's hundred Marines aboard the train were regarded with general hostility as similarly vicious instruments of the Diaz regime.

Butler and his men succeeded in opening the line between Managua and the port at Corinto. On the way back they had to build three new bridges and several miles of track. Returning to Managua after a fifteen-hundred-foot descent with the train's brakes gone, Butler collapsed into bed and pulled the covers over his face. During the whole week-long trip he had had just seventeen hours' sleep.

By now the cynicism of the American presence in Nicaragua was becoming depressingly obvious to him. "I expect a whole lot more rot about the property of citizens of ours . . . which has been stolen by the rebels and which I must see restored to their owners," he wrote his wife on September 13, 1912. The following day he complained of orders from Admiral William H. H. Southerland, who headed the fleet at Corinto, "virtually changing our status from neutral to partisanship with the government forces."

He was next ordered to open the railroad south to Granada, Mena's rebel headquarters. Another malaria attack delayed the expedition. Always restless and unhappy when illness forced him to be idle, Butler held ice in his mouth and drove down his temperature until the doctor reluctantly let him out of bed. Weak and haggard with 104° fever, he had to lie on a cot in a boxcar as his troop train pulled out of Managua. His eyes were so bloodshot and glaring that his men began calling him Old Gimlet Eye, a nickname that stuck.

Under constant harassment by guerrilla forces, Butler finally sent word ahead to Granada to warn General Mena that the Americans were prepared to attack him if he ordered any further assaults on the train. Mena replied that he was sending a peace delegation. Hoping to impress the emissaries with his military power, Butler ordered poles put in the muzzles of two small field guns on flatcars and covered them with tents to give them the appearance of fourteen-inch guns. He further awed the emissaries by receiving them seated on a wooden camp chair mounted on stilted legs like a primitive throne.

Glaring down at them, he warned that unless Mena signed an agreement surrendering the railroad property and moving his troops out of the railroad area, Marine "regiments" would attack Mena's two-thousand-man force in Granada.

His bluff worked so well that Mena not only agreed but, to Butler's amazement, also offered to surrender himself and his army if the Americans would provide a warship to take him safely to exile in Panama. The jubilant Marine major notified Admiral Southerland and the admiral at once agreed.

Butler was made temporary governor of the District of Granada until elections could be held. He promptly released all political prisoners Mena had thrown into dungeons and returned all the property that had been confiscated from them. He next issued a proclamation ordering all loot taken from the people by both rebel and government forces to be restored.

The astonished Granadans hailed him as a liberator.

On September 30, 1912, Butler was dismayed when the admiral transmitted cabled orders from Secretary of the Navy George von L. Meyer to side openly with the Diaz regime and turn over to it all captured rebels. Apologetically he disarmed Mena and his troops, confining them in their barracks under guard.

"I must say," he wrote his wife, "that I hated my job like the devil . . . but orders are orders, and of course, had to be carried out." But he protested bitterly to Admiral Southerland at the betrayal of his promise to Mena. Southerland finally agreed to stand behind his pledge and explain to Meyer.

Local Granadan politicians, deprived by Butler of their customary loot, loudly complained to the admiral that he was interfering in local affairs. Southerland felt compelled to relieve him as governor, sending him to crush the final remnants of the revolution. Zeledon's force of two thousand rebels was dug in at a fort on top of the Coyatepe Mountain, a stronghold that had never been taken in Nicaragua's stormy history.

On October 4 Butler and Colonel Joe Pendleton charged up the Coyatepe leading an 850-man Marine force. In a forty-minute battle twenty-seven rebels were killed in their trenches, nine captured, and the rest put to flight. Two Marines were killed.

The fall of Coyatepe put the town of Masaya, the last rebel outpost, in Marine hands. As they occupied it, some four thousand government troops celebrated by entering the town, looting it, and getting drunk. Incensed, Butler expressed his bitterness in a letter to his wife, decrying "a victory gained by us for them at the expense of two good American lives, all because Brown Brothers, bankers, have some money invested in this country."

6

Resting in Masaya, the major began longing to see his family. "I feel terribly over missing my son's most interesting period of development, but . . . this separation can't last forever," he wrote Ethel on October 9. "I get so terribly homesick at times that I just don't see how I can stand it."

The Taft Administration had another unpleasant assignment for him—rigging the new Nicaraguan elections to make certain that Diaz was returned to power. Checking on the country's election laws, Butler found that the polls had to be open a sufficient length of time ("at least that's the way we translated it") and that voters had to register to be able to vote.

He ordered a canvass of the district to locate four hundred Nicaraguans who could be depended upon to vote for Diaz. Notice of opening of the polls was given five minutes beforehand. The four hundred Diaz adherents were assembled in a line, and two hours later, as soon as they had finished voting, the polls were closed. Other citizens had either failed to register or didn't know balloting was going on.

"Today," Butler wrote Ethel sardonically, "Nicaragua has enjoyed a fine 'free election,' with only one candidate being allowed to run—President Adolfo Diaz—who was unanimously elected. In order that this happy event might be pulled off without hitch and to the entire satisfaction of our State Department, we patrolled all the towns to prevent disorders and of course there were none."

He consoled himself by reflecting that the constant revolutions in Central American politics did not represent a struggle for power by the people themselves, but were most often simply attempts by rascals out of office to overthrow rascals in office. He had a high regard for the Nicaraguan people and genuine compassion for their suffering.

On November 13, 1912, over five thousand Nicaraguans turned out in Granada to present him with a gold medal for saving them from troop disorders and looting. They also gave him a scroll signed by Granada's leading citizens, expressing gratitude for his "brave and opportune intervention" that "put an end to the desperate and painful situation in which this city was placed—victim of all the horrors of an organized anarchy."

They told him, "From this terrible situation and from the anguish that the future held for us, we passed as by magic to a state of complete guarantee for life, property, and well-being for all, as soon as the American troops entered the city. The tact and discretion with which you fulfilled your humane mission, so bristling with difficulties, was such that your name will be forever engraved in the hearts of the people."

There were fireworks and a fiesta. "The whole thing was very impressive and made me feel quite silly," he wrote sheepishly to his wife, "but rather proud for my darlings' sakes."

A people's committee urged him to stay on as police commissioner of the district. The twenty-nine-year-old major found himself intrigued by the prospect of introducing honest law enforcement in Granada. "What would thee think," he wrote Ethel, "of my accepting a $15,000 job as Chief of this Police down here, not to leave the Marine Corps, but to have a three-years' leave?" But he finally decided against it.

Despite his reservations about the ethics of the Nicaraguan campaign, it had filled him with exhilaration of adventure. "This is the end of the expedition," he wrote his wife. "Would like to have some parts of it over again; the excitement was fine." He indicated an early awareness that he was destined to play a meaningful role in American history: "Be sure to keep all my letters as they are a diary of my life, and may be useful sometime in the future."

With a second bronze star added to his Expeditionary Medal and a new Nicaraguan Campaign Medal, the indefatigable young campaigner returned to Panama and his family. His second son, Thomas Richard, was born in October, 1913.

With Woodrow Wilson in the White House, war clouds loomed with Mexico when bandit General Victoriano Huerta overthrew legally elected Mexican President Francisco Madero. In an angry exchange of notes, Wilson insisted that Huerta must hold new elections barring himself as a candidate. Wilson's choice was Huerta's rival for power, General Venustiano Carranza. Banning all arms shipments to Mexico, the President asked all Americans without urgent business there to leave the country and sent the fleet to cruise significantly in the Gulf of Mexico during a period of "watchful waiting."

Defying Wilson, Huerta began importing arms from Europe to crush Carranza. The President then violated his own embargo and rushed American arms to the Carranza forces. Full-scale fighting broke out all over Mexico, during which American industrial property was destroyed and United States businessmen were compelled to flee attacks against them from both sides.

In January, 1914, the Marines were ordered from Panama to the fleet standing off Vera Cruz. Ethel Butler took the children home to Pennsylvania, and her husband reported to the fleet flagship *Florida*, assigned to the staff of Admiral Frank Friday Fletcher. Welcoming him aboard, the admiral remarked on his courage and daring in the Chinese, Philippine, and Nicaraguan campaigns. He was just the man, the admiral thought, for a dangerous special mission for the War Department.

How did Butler feel about going into Mexico as a "civilian" spy to make an expert analysis of Huerta's fighting forces in and around Mexico City, as well as to gather general intelligence, in case war was declared? He would carry no official orders of any kind, of course, and if he were caught, the Navy would have to disavow any knowledge of either him or his mission.

"How soon can I start, Admiral?" he asked.

Beneath a night sky of swollen black clouds, as most of the crew aboard the *Florida* watched a Western movie starring Broncho Billy, a civilian-clad Butler dropped a small traveling bag out of his cabin port into a small boat, then slipped off the ship after it. His disappearance from the *Florida* was carried on the ship's rolls as "desertion."

Ashore in Vera Cruz, he decided to disguise himself as an Englishman. There were many English in Mexico at the time traveling on business. Attiring himself in a tweed suit, spats, deerstalker's hat, and a pair of gold-rimmed glasses with a black ribbon, he undertook a stage English accent. A fraudulent British passport and forged letters of introduction to important Britons in Mexico City completed his impersonation.

He left Vera Cruz aboard the private railroad car of the line's superintendent, a secret Carranza supporter cooperating with the Americans. The train rolled toward Mexico City along the road American troops would use if they invaded. The superintendent stopped the train several times en route, letting Butler inspect electric power plants and reservoirs by introducing him to leading citizens as "Mr. Johnson," a public utilities expert. Managing to stray inside some army forts on his own, he was apprehended several times but released.

"I carried a butterfly net and studied rocks," he grinned in recollection. "They thought I was a nut and let me pass."

In Mexico City he changed to American garb and posed as a private detective from the United States seeking a condemned murderer who had escaped and fled to Mexico. Mexican secret police escorted him to all the garrisons to help his search for the imaginary criminal. He soon had vital data on the troop strength and disposition of munitions dumps around Mexico City.

Making military maps of everything he had seen, Butler buried them in the false bottom of his bag and took the train back to Vera Cruz. He became aware that two Mexicans were following him. Apparently he had aroused suspicions, and the Mexican secret service was keeping an eye on him.

In the early morning when the train reached Vera Cruz, it paused temporarily to allow a rail switch to be thrown that took it into the station. During this pause Butler went to the washroom in pajamas, his bag concealed under his bathrobe. Locking the door behind him, he slipped out of the train window. He donned his clothes in the freight yard, then sped to the American consulate to contact Admiral Fletcher.

Two naval officers were sent ashore to the consulate. He turned over all his maps and data to them, then left separately, dressed once more in his British guise. Seeking to board a British steamer at the wharf to a port down the coast, from which he would secretly be picked up and brought back to the *Florida*, he was suddenly seized by a squad of police.

They considered it odd for a "British entomologist" to have been visiting the American embassy. His baggage was opened and searched thoroughly, but nothing incriminating was found. Threatening "you blighters" with official reprisals from the British Foreign Office, Butler bluffed them into letting him go. A few days later he was safely back aboard the *Florida*, where Admiral Fletcher warmly congratulated him on the success of his daring mission.

7

When war with Mexico seemed inevitable, on April 19, 1914, Admiral Fletcher put six companies of Marines ashore at Vera Cruz under Butler's old friend, Buck Neville, now a colonel.

At dawn when the six companies began marching through the city Mexican troops fired at them from rooftops and house windows, using machine guns as well as rifles. Marines rushed from house to house smashing in doors and searching for snipers.

The Marines Butler led were not his own command, and he

was not sure of their behavior under fire. To inspire coolness, he led them through Vera Cruz with no weapon of his own except a stick. The Marines, in two columns, kept close to the doorways for cover while he walked calmly down the center of the street for a better view of snipers in houses on both sides. Ignoring bullets spurting dust at his feet, he used the stick to point out snipers to his sharpshooters.

By nightfall the Marines had won control of the city, but at a cost of 135 Americans killed or wounded, 7 of the casualties Butler's men. Mexican casualties were four or five times as great.

Returning to Panama, Butler relieved tedious garrison duty by expending his inexhaustible energy in making Camp Elliott an exemplary Marine outpost. After a visit to the Panama Canal Zone, Secretary of War Lindley M. Garrison wrote him, "I was delighted . . . to observe the esprit de corps exhibited by your command. Their alertness, skill, and proficiency were models for military organizations."

Congress had by now authorized officers as well as enlisted men to receive Congressional Medals of Honor. One was now awarded to Butler for being "eminent and conspicuous in command of his Battalion. He exhibited courage and skill in leading his men through the action of the 22nd and in the final occupation of the city [Vera Cruz]."

"I've no more courage than the next man," he protested, "but it's always been my job to take my fellows through a mess the quickest way possible, with the loss of the fewest men. You can't do that from a distance. Besides, I was paid to do what I did. I've been scared plenty, but if I'd ever let my men know it, *they'd* have been scared. And soldiers who are scared aren't worth so much. They'll keep their lives, but the job won't get done."

To the astonishment of the Navy Department, he refused to accept his Medal of Honor, explaining that he did not consider what he had done at Vera Cruz worthy of the nation's highest military award. Admiral Fletcher, questioned by the Navy, replied that Butler was wrong; he had certainly merited the Medal of Honor not only for his courageous leadership in the Vera Cruz battle but also for his heroism as a spy.

The Navy Department thereupon sent the medal back to the reluctant hero with a terse order to keep it and wear it, but for Butler a matter of principle was involved. He was proud of his decorations and would wear none that he did not believe he fully deserved. He returned the medal to Secretary of the Navy Josephus Daniels, writing stubbornly, "I must renew my request that the Department reconsider its action in awarding this decoration." The matter was shelved by the outbreak of World War I in August, 1914, but Butler was later pressured into accepting the medal.

Wilson was keeping a careful and worried eye on Haiti. During 1914 four presidents of that volatile little republic were overthrown. The Germans were threatening to intervene to protect their economic interests. Wilson suspected that they wanted to use the volatile little republic as a naval base, which would put them within easy striking distance of the Panama Canal and the Florida coast.

Then in 1915 a new Haitian president, pursued by an angry mob, was forced to seek sanctuary in the French legation. The mob dragged him out and killed him. Now the angry French Government threatened intervention. Squirming in an agony of indecision, the anti-imperialist Wilson finally decided to put Haiti under American control to prevent any of the warring European powers from seizing it.

Besides, he told Secretary of State Robert Lansing, an American occupation would give him a chance to bring law, order, democracy, and prosperity to the wretched people of the misruled little country. Wilson's missionary impulse dovetailed neatly with less exalted plans by big-business interests. The National City Bank controlled the National Bank of Haiti and the Haitian railroad system. Dollar diplomacy also involved the sugar barons who saw Haiti's rich plantations as an inviting target for investment and takeover.

Rioting in the capital of Haiti in August, 1915, gave Wilson the excuse he needed to intervene with warships and Marines under Colonel Littleton Waller, Butler's commanding officer. Haiti was placed under an American commissioner who controlled the republic's affairs through the Haitian President. Cabinet ministers were puppets with only advisory powers. The government was not allowed to incur any "foreign obligations" without American consent, and an American customs official collected all money due Haiti. The Marines "pacified" the population and maintained the President's authority.

When the Haitian National Assembly met in Port-au-Prince, Marines stood in the aisles with bayonets drawn until Philippe Dartiguenave, the Haitian selected by the American minister, was "elected" President by the Assembly. He was the first Haitian President to serve out his full seven-year term, only because of the occupation of the Marines.

Under Dartiguenave American control of the island was assured by a treaty signed on September 16, 1915, which entitled the United States to administer Haitian customs and finance for twenty years, or longer if Washington saw fit. The Haitian constitution was revised to remove a prohibition against alien ownership of land, enabling Americans to purchase the most fertile areas in the country, including valuable sugar cane, cacao, banana, cotton, tobacco, and sisal plantations.

Northern Haiti, however, remained in the grip of rebels known as Cacos, whose chiefs Dartiguenave labeled bandits. Posing as nationalists, they were actually precursors of the brutal Tonton Macoutes of the later Duvalier regime, just as cruel to the peasants as the government's soldiers were.

Butler led a reconnaissance force of twenty-six volunteers in pursuit of a Caco force that had killed ten Marines. Like the Cacos in the mountains, he and his men lived for days off the orange groves. For over a hundred miles they followed a trail of peels, estimating how long before the Cacos had passed by the dryness of the peels. A native guide they picked up helped them locate the Cacos' headquarters, a secret fort called Capois, deep in the mountain range.

Studying the mountaintop fort through field glasses, Butler made out thick stone walls, with enough activity to suggest they were defended by at least a regiment. He decided to return to Cape Haitien for reinforcements and capture it. On the way back they were ambushed by a force of Cacos that outnumbered them twenty to one. Fortunately it was a pitch-black night, and

Butler was able to save his men by splitting them up to crawl past the Cacos' lines through high grass.

Just before dawn he reorganized them into three squads of nine men each. Charging from three directions as they yelled wildly and fired from the hip, they created such a fearful din that the Cacos panicked and fled, leaving seventy-five killed. The only Marine casualty was one man wounded.

When he was able to return with reinforcements, spies had alerted the Cacos, and Butler took a deserted Fort Capois without firing a shot. Only one last stronghold remained to be cleared —the mountain fortress at Fort Riviere, which the French, who had built it during their occupation of Haiti, considered impregnable. Butler was told it would be difficult to capture, even with a strong artillery battery.

"Give me a hundred picked volunteers," he said, "and I'll have the colors flying over it tomorrow."

8

Butler earnestly assured his volunteers that they could do the job. His pep talks were enormously persuasive because they were sincere—so sincere that after he gave one, he would often feel emotionally spent and limp. He refused to believe that any job was impossible for Marines and frequently hypnotized himself into believing it. His fervor made believers out of his men, who never hesitated to follow him against overwhelming odds.

His officers gave him unreasoning loyalty, even though he was a tough taskmaster and never played favorites. One captain, asked to explain his devotion to Butler, said, "Well, damn him, I don't know. I'd give him my shirt, and he would not only not thank me, but he'd probably demand that I give him my other one. I stick because—hell, I don't *know* why!"

What happened when Butler led his tiny force against Fort

Riviere was subsequently described in a memo by Franklin Delano Roosevelt, who visited Haiti in January, 1917, as Assistant Secretary of the Navy. The Congressional Medal of Honor could not be awarded to an officer unless a high official of the military branch concerned first made a personal investigation and authenticated the citation. When Butler was recommended for the award, Roosevelt went to Haiti to investigate.

He was taken by Butler on an inspection tour of Haiti and the ruins of Fort Riviere, which Butler had demolished with explosives after its capture to deny its reuse to the Cacos. In his memorandum Roosevelt wrote what he had learned from others about Smedley Butler's attack on the four-thousand-foot-high mountain fortress in November, 1915:

> This was the famous fortification captured by Butler and his 24 Marines in the Caco rebellion of a few months before. The top is a hog's back ridge a quarter of a mile long. Butler and his Marines left a machine gun at one end of the ridge while he and about 18 Marines crawled through the grass into the fort itself. Crawling down into a corner, they found a tunnel into the courtyard, serving as a drain when it rained.
>
> Butler started to crawl through it (about 2¼′ high x 2′ wide) and the old sergeant [Ross Iams] said, "Sir, I was in the Marines before you and it is my privilege." Butler recognized his right, and the sergeant crawled through first. On coming to the end within the courtyard, he saw the shadows of the legs of 2 Cacos armed with machetes guarding the place. He took off his hat, put it on the end of his revolver, and pushed it through. He felt the two Cacos descend on it and he jumped forward into the daylight.
>
> With a right and left he got both Cacos, stood up and dropped 2 or 3 others while his companions, headed by Smedley Butler, got through the drain hole and stood up. Then ensued a killing, the news of which put down all insurrections, we hope, for all time to come. There were about 300 Cacos within the wall, and Butler and his 18 companions killed [many] . . . others jumping over the wall and falling prisoner to the rest of the force of Marines which circled the mountain.
>
> I was so much impressed by personal inspection of the

scene of the exploit that I awarded the Medal of Honor to
the Marine Sergeant and Smedley Butler. Incidentally, Butler had received the Medal of Honor at Tientsin at the
time of the Boxer Rebellion.° He had been awarded a
second at the capture of Vera Cruz in 1914 but declined to
accept it. The third at Fort Riviere he did accept.

Butler saw pathos as well as bravery in the episode at Riviere.
"The futile efforts of the natives to oppose trained white soldiers
impressed me as tragic," he declared. "As soon as they lost their
heads, they picked up useless, aboriginal weapons. If they had
only realized the advantage of their position, they could have
shot us like rats as we crawled out one by one, out of the drain."

But the power of the Cacos was broken, and the revolution
was over. Surviving Cacos sought to keep the movement alive,
but their ancient horse pistols, Spanish cutlasses, Napoleonic
sabers, French carbines, and even flintlocks were futile against
the superior weaponry and training of the Marines.

President Dartiguenave awarded Butler the Haitian Medal of
Honor, with great praise for his dynamic personality, intense
determination, direct and unrelenting attacks against heavy odds,
and masterful ability to lead men.

Soon after peace was restored, Butler sent for his wife and
children. They had seen little of him since the beginning of his
tour in Panama, because of his three expeditions to Nicaragua
followed by the Mexican and Haitian campaigns.

They joined him at Port-au-Prince in a large, comfortable
house with white verandas and a pleasant, shaded garden, located on the outskirts of the town. Sumptuous by island stand-
ards, it nevertheless lacked indoor plumbing, and the family had
to share a two-hole privy.

A stern taskmaster in the Corps, Butler was a gentle and un-
demanding father. It was Ethel Butler who disciplined the
children, a matter of necessity because of his frequent absences.
The children loved the exotic flavor of the tropical republic.
Smedley, Jr. was sent to an integrated school with Haitian chil-

---

° Roosevelt's error; officers at the time of the Boxer Rebellion could not
win the Medal of Honor.

dren and a few other white youngsters. Young Ethel went to a convent taught by nuns in French and English.

Never allowed into town, as it was considered unsafe, they were accompanied everywhere by a gendarme. One night while the family was seated on the veranda, a Caco concealed somewhere on the hillside took a shot at their father, narrowly missing him.

Washington decided to reorganize the ineffective Haitian military, which had almost one general for every three privates in its thirteen-hundred-man army. Dartiguenave agreed to its replacement by a native constabulary of three thousand men to be trained and directed by Butler. Although still only a major, Butler's rank as head of the Haitian Gendarmerie was major general, and his power that of Minister of the Interior.

He was paid $3,000 a year as commandant of the Gendarmerie, which cost the American Government $800,000 a year. Ostensibly under the direction of the Haitian President, the new force was actually controlled by Washington. All of its officers were Marines.

Haiti's foreign minister demanded that the Gendarmerie be put under Haitian control. Butler refused, pointing out that according to an agreement signed by Dartiguenave, the commandant alone was made responsible for the force. The foreign minister angrily drew up a new constitution for Haiti that would force the Americans to relinquish their power over both the Gendarmerie and Haiti itself, and prepared to introduce it in the Haitian National Assembly.

Alarmed, Dartiguenave told Butler that the foreign minister had the support of a majority of the Assembly's legislators, who intended to ram the new constitution through the Chamber of Deputies and the Senate. Then they planned to vote to impeach Dartiguenave, ostensibly for violating the old constitution, in reality because they considered him an American pawn.

The American minister, A. Bailly-Blanchard, cabled a warning to Secretary of State Robert Lansing, who cabled back that since the new constitution was "unfriendly" to the United States, it must not be approved by the Haitian Legislature. Bailly-Blanchard was ordered to take any steps necessary to prevent its passage. He summoned Butler, Butler's regimental commander, Colonel Cole, and the top naval commander, Admiral Anderson, to a conference, and read them Lansing's cable.

It was decided that Americans would have no legal justification for interfering in Haiti's internal affairs, but that Butler, as major general of the Haitian Constabulary, did have that right. Commanded to carry out the State Department's orders, Butler went to see Dartiguenave, who urged him to use the Gendarmerie to dissolve the National Assembly.

But Butler had no relish for the role of dictator. If Dartiguenave and his cabinet wanted the Assembly suspended, he insisted, then they had to take full responsibility. He refused to act until they had apprehensively signed a decree ordering dissolution of the Assembly "to end the spirit of anarchy which animates it."

When Butler led his gendarmes to the National Assembly, he was greeted with loud, prolonged hissing. The gendarmes began cocking their rifles. Many, veterans of previous coups d'etat, were amazed at Butler's order to lower their guns.

He then handed the President's decree to the presiding Assembly officer to be read aloud to the chamber. Instead the latter launched into a wrathful tirade against the American occupation. His outburst threw the hall into an uproar.

Fearful of being charged, the gendarmes again threw up their weapons, and Butler once more snapped an order to ground arms. The reluctant presiding officer finally read Dartiguenave's decree and bitterly declared the Assembly dissolved. The gloomy legislators then filed into the street, and the gendarmes locked the hall behind them.

9

The Marine Corps promoted Butler to lieutenant colonel in August, 1916. Winning commendation as a capable administrator, he kept Haiti stable and at peace for the first time in half a century. He grew fond of Dartiguenave while acknowledging, "I knew he was an old political crook." Typical of the President's expenditures from the treasury was sixteen hundred dollars "to have the hole in a carpet mended."

Traveling all over Haiti without a gun, despite the Cacos, Butler established a postal service, a country school system, a network of telegraph lines, a civil hospital in Port-au-Prince, and a five-hundred-mile road system; he also restored lighthouses and channel buoys. Although these civic and economic improvements unquestionably benefited American investors, Butler's primary purpose was to improve life for the Haitians.

"I was, and have been ever since, very fond of the Haitian people," he wrote later, "and it was my ambition to make Haiti a first-class black man's country."

But no amount of Butler's "good works" could erase from Haitian minds the humiliating awareness that they had been robbed of their independence by a military occupation. Haitians had no shortage of legitimate grievances. The supreme power on the island was not Butler, who was preoccupied with the Gendarmerie, but the commanding officer of the Marines in Haiti, Littleton Waller, who was made a brigadier general in the fall of 1916. As the officer who had once been court-martialed for brutality toward Filipino natives, he did not inspire among his staff officers any vast respect for Haitian sensibilities.

In the interior they talked as casually of shooting "gooks" as sportsmen talked of duck-hunting. Patrolling against the Cacos, some Marine officers looted the homes of native families they were supposed to protect. Others talked of "cleaning out" the island by killing the entire native population. Prisoners were beaten and tortured to make them tell what they knew about Cacos' whereabouts. Some were allowed to "escape," then were shot as they fled.

Haitians in the interior were forced to carry *bon habitant* (good citizen) passes. Any native stopped by a Marine and unable to produce a *bon habitant* could be either shot or arrested. Understandably, many Haitians became convinced that all Americans were racial bigots who hated black men. And behind the Americans in uniform were the American businessmen, who plundered the wealth of the island with impunity.

Butler, now in his early thirties, did not take Haitian politicians very seriously. He viewed most of them as banana republic opportunists not too different from the crooked ward bosses who infested the American body politic. The ingenuity and pretensions of the shrewdest, like Dartiguenave, tickled his sense of humor, but he regarded the Haitian people themselves with respect and affection, if blind to the irony implicit in the presumption to offer superior government to a black republic by a nation that had signally failed to solve its own serious race problem.

His eyes opened increasingly, however, to the fact that he was being used by big-business interests to pacify the population in order to protect profitable American investments.

"The Haitian Government, such as it is, either yields perforce to American pressure," reported correspondent Herbert J. Seligmann in *The Nation*, "or finds itself in feeble and ineffectual opposition. . . . The present Government of Haiti, which dangles from wires pulled by American fingers, would not endure for twenty-four hours if United States armed forces were withdrawn; and the President, Dartiguenave, would face death or exile."

Butler protested to Washington about some of the injustices of the occupation. On April 9, 1916, he wrote to the State Department to point out that the Haitians logically objected to the retention of Marine officers in the Gendarmerie unless they were made subject to trial by Haitian courts. since otherwise the United States could mount a coup d'etat whenever it chose to order one. His protest fell on deaf ears.

By the spring of 1916 Haitian discontent was growing rapidly. Waller warned Butler to be on guard because Cacos, spreading the rumor that the Americans would soon pull out, were urging the people to rise and destroy them now.

Butler felt deeply discouraged. Despite everything he had tried to do for the people, the dollar sign behind the occupation had made all his efforts useless. In July he wrote to Lejeune, "All of us gendarmes are mighty tired, and I for one am going to ask to be relieved at the first opportunity presenting itself."

In August Waller ordered him into Santo Domingo, the Dominican Republic sharing the island with Haiti, to put down a revolt led by Celidiano Pantilion and "stabilize the economy." The Dominican Government had defaulted its obligations to American banks and paid for its sins with an American occupation to protect U.S. investments that lasted eight years.

When he returned from Santo Domingo, mission accomplished, a letter was waiting for him from Lejeune. "Assistant Secretary Roosevelt came back with glowing accounts of the splendid work being done by the Marine Corps in connection with the Gendarmerie," Lejeune wrote enthusiastically. "You certainly deserve the greatest credit for what you have done in making a soldier out of the ignorant Haitian."

But Butler had begun to brood about the virtue of leading American boys into battle, causing some to lose their lives and others to suffer permanent disablement, to protect American business interests in the Caribbean. He grew quietly cynical about some of the compliments paid to him.

In neighboring Santo Domingo revolutionists joined bandits in shaking down American plantation managers for money. Repulsed, they set cane fires and sought to prevent cane from being cut and ground. The American sugar interests there wanted Butler to come to their rescue once again.

"Members of the Sugar Association and myself," their spokesman, businessman Frank H. Vedder, wrote to Roosevelt, "desire to express to you our appreciation of . . . the improvement in conditions, the hard work being done by the marines in the field. . . . The dangers from bandit operations are by no means past or remote. Additional troops would be of great assistance in clearing up the situation."

To Butler's relief Roosevelt replied, "I appreciate, of course, that the complete elimination of bandit operations is at the present time exceedingly difficult, but I trust that the Acting Military Governor will be able to give all the protection necessary with the forces under his command."

Butler sought to convince the State Department that the Haitians would never cease to be anti-American until Washington allowed them to hold honest elections and choose their own President. Spies tipped off Dartiguenave, who grew chilly toward Butler for putting his job in jeopardy.

But Haiti received little attention now from the State Department, which was carefully studying developments in World War I. Reading about the war from his remote outpost, Butler regarded it with loathing as "madness . . . a European bloodbath." He fervently hoped that Wilson would have the good sense to keep American boys out of it.

When the President took America into the war, however, Butler instantly appealed to Lejeune for a combat assignment in France, where he felt that he would at least be serving his country instead of Wall Street. Lejeune replied that the State Department was so pleased with his work as an administrator in Haiti that it had refused to transfer him to the European war front. Unappeased, Butler moaned to Lejeune in June, 1917, "The service is becoming more and more detestable every day, and the knowledge that I am not allowed to fight for my country makes it even more unbearable."

He appealed to Roosevelt. "Secretary Roosevelt and I," replied John McIlhenny, head of the U.S. Civil Service Commission, "are of the same opinion that the work which you have in hand should not be interfered with or disturbed because it is the most potent factor in maintaining a peaceful occupation."

An entreaty to his father also failed to work. "Your father," wrote Representative W. L. Hensley, of the House Naval Affairs Committee, "has gone into all these matters with the Secretary of War concerning your ambitions. They feel you are doing a great work where you are, and for you to be transferred from there would turn things topsy-turvy."

Disconsolate, Butler threw himself into a new orgy of road-building. In forty-five days he built a new road from Port-au-Prince to Cape Haitien, across twenty-one miles of the roughest, densest tropical country he had ever seen. After he had driven the first car over it, Secretary of State Lansing cabled congratulations. McIlhenny wrote him, "I think your achievement in building a road from Port-au-Prince to Cape Haitien in such a time and at such a cost is a miracle."

"Someone has misled you," he replied impatiently, "concerning my value to this country, and to the aims of the U.S. down here, for I am simply a subordinate to the Chief of the American Occupation . . . and have no independent authority."

By now Butler was strongly suspicious that he was being held in Haiti by the War Department's lack of confidence in his fitness for a command in France. When he asked a friend in Washington to snoop and investigate for him, he was assured that his susicions were unfounded: The government was really having trouble finding a competent man to replace him.

He still didn't believe it. His instincts told him that his old enemies in the Navy Department were working against him. He had trodden on a good many other important toes as well during his two years in Haiti, and he had heard rumors spread by some naval officers that he had won all his medals and promotions because of his father's influence.

He did not hesitate to try to use that influence when Thomas Butler became chairman of the House Naval Affairs Committee in 1918. But his renewed pleas to be allowed to serve in the A.E.F. failed to move his father, and he remained bogged down disconsolately in Haiti. He grew increasingly unhappy with the government's management of the island's affairs.

Under wartime censorship Port-au-Prince's newspapers were suppressed, and their editors jailed, for suggesting that since Mr. Wilson was so concerned about the fate of poor little nations overrun by powerful military aggressors that he had gone to war in Europe for them, he might consider rescuing little Haiti from *its* invaders.

Some years later when Harding succeeded Wilson in the White House, Dartiguenave called upon him to remove all Marines from Haiti and liberate the Haitian people. To dramatize his case, Dartiguenave accused Butler of having dissolved the Haitian National Assembly by force of arms, without authority, conveniently ignoring the fact that he had begged Butler to do it and that he had written him upon his departure, "I regret to see you obliged to cease your services in this country, and I was well pleased with the broad and intelligent cooperation that you have constantly given to the Government."

Dartiguenave's memorial to Harding, published widely in the United States, "stirred up a hell of a commotion," as Butler put it. The Senate appointed an investigating committee with Senator Medill McCormick, of Illinois, as chairman. Butler was summoned as a witness. A lawyer for the American N.A.A.C.P. demanded to know on what authority he had presumed to dissolve the Haitian National Assembly.

"The President [Dartiguenave] himself dissolved the Congress," Butler replied. "I merely carried his decree of dissolution to the Assembly."

Haitian witnesses jeered at this assertion, but their faces fell when Butler produced the decree signed by Dartiguenave and his cabinet; it had been prudently saved among Butler's memorabilia. The upset Haitian politicians denounced it as a forgery, but were compelled to acknowledge it as authentic when it was compared with other documents signed by Dartiguenave. His case won, Butler saw no need to embarrass the State Department by also revealing that Secretary of State Robert Lansing had secretly ordered "any steps necessary" to stop the National Assembly from passing an anti-American constitution.

Soon afterward Secretary of the Navy Edwin Denby asked Butler to return to Haiti as High Commissioner with a "civilian financial adviser" who, Butler knew, would represent American big-business investors and dictate economic policy. He had had enough of letting Wall Street profiteers use the Marines as their private army. He would prefer not to go, he told Denby, and certainly not with any civilian financial adviser. In that case, Denby said coldly, he need not go at all.

In March, 1918, bursting with frustration over his inability to get into the action on France's battlefields, Butler decided to press the matter personally with Lejeune, who was now a general, during a medical leave to Washington for dentistry.

10

Lejeune finally succeeded in getting him detached from Haitian service, but to Butler's dismay, instead of being sent overseas, he was ordered to take over a swampy new Marine base at Quantico, Virginia, on the Potomac, thirty miles south of Washington. Here he had to train regiments of raw boots for the front and glumly watch them pull out for France without him.

He felt irked with his father for failing to use his influence to get him into combat. Thomas Butler had visited the front and had been greatly disturbed by the high casualties of American troops. Smedley wondered whether his father had refused to help him get overseas out of a dread of losing him in the European carnage.

He persisted in nagging Marine headquarters for an overseas command, but his refusal to be discreet even now antagonized his superior officers. Learning that a move was afoot to raise the rank of the Marine commandant to lieutenant general, he spoke out against it as a rank piece of opportunism. No similar promotions were being suggested, he pointed out acidly, for the leathernecks in the trenches of France.

His friends in the Corps moaned at this bull-in-a-china-shop gaffe, warning him that his indiscreet candor was hurting his career. He remained stubbornly convinced of his right to speak out vigorously against injustice in the Corps.

He finally found a way to get overseas when the 13th Marines came to Quantico for training. Josephus Daniels, Jr., son of the

Secretary of the Navy, was with the regiment. Meeting his father, Butler persuaded Daniels, Sr., that young Marines like his son needed the protection overseas of veteran Marine commanders like Smedley Butler. Despite the opposition of the desk admirals in Washington, Butler was finally ordered overseas with the regiment.

Bidding farewell to his family, Butler was happy in the conviction that he was heading for the front at last. For twenty years, he told his wife, he had been preparing for the big war that he had dreaded, yet had anticipated. At last he would be serving his country in its greatest hour of crisis. In his patriotic zeal his qualms about the commercial intrigues he had learned to suspect behind troop movements were swept away.

Anchoring at Brest on September 24, 1918, he and his men were assigned to a dreary Army debarkation center, Camp Pontanezen, consisting of seventeen hundred acres of mud flats occupied by 75,000 American soldiers, of whom 16,000 had the flu. Returning casualties had complained of scandalous conditions at Pontanezen, where they had been forced to await ships home lying in mud, hungry, chilled, and medically neglected.

Day after day he waited impatiently for his orders to move up to the fighting zone. After two weeks he was handed a telegram from A.E.F. Commander General John J. Pershing informing the thirty-seven-year-old Butler that he had been promoted to the rank of brigadier general, making him the youngest Marine ever to achieve that rank. And he was finally assigned his new command—in charge of Camp Pontanezen.

Butler read the telegram three times, unable to believe it. Then he let out a roar of fury. The bastards! *The unutterable bastards!* They couldn't do this to him. After twenty years as a fighting Marine, to be denied the opportunity to lead his men into battle and be forced to sit instead in a dirty mud hole a light-year away from the fighting!

To make matters worse, he discovered that one officer after another had been put in charge of the miserable concentration camp and pest trap that was now his responsibility, only to fail dismally in their attempts to clean it up. It was obvious to him that he had been handed a "lemon" of a command, ending his dreams of fighting in the Meuse-Argonne. Bitter, he added Pershing to his list of enemies in top echelons.

Pershing, actually, had been motivated only by the desperate need for a good administrator who could do something about the mess at Pontanezen, the linchpin for troops and equipment coming into France and for wounded and sick troops going home. Butler's record as an able administrator in Haiti and Quantico had marked him as the man for the job. So he was forced to watch glumly as the 13th Marines left for the front, leaving him behind in command of an all-Army outfit in Brest.

Shaking off his despond and self-pity, Butler went to work. Not long afterward writer Mary Roberts Rinehart arrived with orders from Secretary of War Newton Baker to investigate the terrible conditions at Pontanezen. Touring the camp talking to the troops, she was astonished to find morale high. One private told her enthusiastically, "I'd cross hell on a slat if Butler gave the word!" She wrote later:

> In charge of the camp was that dynamo of energy, courage and sheer ability, General Smedley Butler of the Marines. And Butler was no red tape man. In defiance of regulations he was issuing double rations of food, and serving hot soup all day long to those who needed it. He had issued, also, six blankets to each man, and as the gound under the tents was nothing but mud, he had raided the wharf at Brest of the duck-boards no longer needed for the trenches, carried the first one himself up that four-mile hill to the camp, and thus provided something in the way of protection for the men to sleep on.
>
> To have produced the *morale* I found under existing conditions was nothing short of a miracle of ability, and I said so. Even the flu, taking its daily toll of men in the hospital nearby, was practically non-existent in the camp. . . . I had never seen General Butler before, and I went prepared to send in a blistering report to Washington. . . . But the men were in fine condition, and cheerful.

Her report to Baker was so glowing that the Secretary of War promised to send Butler everything he needed.

Soon after the Armistice Butler threw the gears of camp opera-tion into reverse. In a single day 26,000 men were processed onto ships, 2,000 newcomers were processed into France, and 10,000 men fresh from the line were processed into camp. Every man back from the front was deloused, bathed, and freshly dressed and equipped within twenty-four hours. The camp was the outstanding marvel of American efficiency on French soil.

During an inspection visit by Pershing, the commander of the A.E.F. noticed that as Butler drove him around the camp, doughboy after doughboy failed to salute them. Irked, he snapped to Butler, "Don't you think they should be taught to salute?"

"Well, General," Butler said with a shrug, "if the Army had them from six months to six years and they haven't learned to salute, you can't expect a Marine to teach them in six days!"

He was always on the side of the powerless against the brass. One day while he was absent his superior, General Helmick, made a surprise inspection of Pontanezen. Finding wastefulness in one mess, Helmick savagely tongue-lashed the lieutenant in charge. When Butler learned about it, he phoned the Army Chief of Staff.

"If the general has any complaint with the camp," he stormed, "tell him to pick on me and not on a young lieutenant who is doing his level best!" When Helmick came to see him, Butler pounded on the desk and told his superior what he thought of him for "jumping on a boy."

After Butler's angry outburst had subsided, Helmick replied, "Now, Smedley, I'll talk. I've let you abuse me, your commander, for two reasons. First, because you've been of such tremendous value to my organization, and second, because I know I didn't do the right thing by that boy. I realize also that you've worked yourself into a state of nervous collapse to make the camp a success. I know you don't mean what you're saying. I never permit myself to be aroused by a tired man's utterances, when that tired man is a good man."

"General, by God," Butler said hoarsely, struck with admiration, "you are some commander!"

Helmick then went with Butler to the young lieutenant and apologized to him publicly in front of all the cooks and KP's.

Torn between court-martialing him for his frequent intransigence toward higher authority and decorating him for his accomplishments in an almost impossible job, the Army finally awarded him its Distinguished Service Medal. The Navy felt impelled to follow suit with its own Distinguished Service Medal. The French awarded him their Order of the Black Star. He wore these decorations proudly beside his World War I Victory Medal with French clasp.

But the reward he treasured most was the gratitude of hundreds of thousands of doughboys back from the misery of the trenches, grateful for his efforts to ease their hardships as they waited for evacuation home. He did a lot of hard thinking as he watched the wounded and maimed pass through Pontanezen, some with their nervous systems irreparably shattered.

"Gradually it began to dawn on me to wonder," he related later, "what on earth these American boys are doing getting wounded and killed and buried in France." This uneasy reflection began to plant seeds of doubt in his mind about the ethics of his chosen calling.

11

With America once more at peace and Congress slashing military funds drastically, the future of the Marine Corps looked bleak. Butler was indignant when Marine Corps headquarters failed to protest its reduction to a mere appendage of the Navy. In disgust he announced his decision to retire and wrote his father urging that John Lejeune be appointed the new commandant in 1920 to save the Corps.

Thomas Butler saw eye to eye with his son on the need to preserve the Marine Corps's independence and agreed that Lejeune, who had distinguished himself in the Battle of Meuse-Argonne, was the man to fight for it in Congress. So on January

30, 1920, Lejeune became the new commandant. He, in turn, coaxed Butler into staying on in command of Quantico to help in the struggle to save the Corps.

To dramatize the Corps's need of funds for modernization, Butler held summer maneuvers that restaged the Battle of the Wilderness between Grant and Lee. On the first day it was "fought" as it had happened; next day it was restaged with a significant difference—the use of modern equipment. The presence of President Warren G. Harding, a Civil War buff, helped win widespread news coverage. Butler's shrewd tactic was highly effective in getting a reluctant Congress to vote adequate funds for the Corps.

It was a forty-mile march from Quantico to the battleground. As usual wearing no insignia to identify him, Butler marched at the head of the column walking his horse, carrying full gear on his back in the hot July sun. When one soldier faltered, Butler told him gently, "Son, I'm more than twenty years older than you, but we're going to do this together." He said later, "I wanted to show them that they could force themselves to do things that would be necessary in war." And they all did.

His troops never learned that following one such battlefield exercise the forty-year-old commander experienced a minor heart attack, for which a doctor prescribed rest and digitalis. The word that spread through Quantico was that it was useless to try to fall out of a hike, because the Old Man would just pick up your pack, add it to his own, and hike right alongside you with it.

The humdrum garrison life of peacetime, with no alarums and excursions to divert him, took its toll of Butler's temper. "I was itching for a scrap—action—something with a snap to it," he admitted later.

But he was never irascible in any matter that pertained to ailing Marines who had served under him. In August, 1920, a private wrote him, "I have been a patient in St. Elizabeth's hospital for the Insane since Sept. 20, 1918. I am writing to ask if you will arrange to have me transferred to one of the institutions in Philadelphia, so that I can be close to the folks at home."

"I will look into the matter and let you know," Butler replied gently. "You can be assured that everything will be done for your comfort, for you are one of the prize soldiers of the Marine Corps, and we all like you very much."

He grew increasingly incensed at what he considered the ingratitude of the nation toward its veterans. Once the war crisis was over and Americans felt safe, he reflected, the shattered heroes of yesterday were ignored as the "bums" of today. He was particularly embittered by the indifference of big business toward the men in uniform who had so often been called upon to spill blood for corporate profits.

The profiteering of the Pennsylvania Railroad in the price they charged for transporting troops led him to write his father angrily, "I am at a loss to understand why the Pennsylvania people are so antagonistic to men in uniform. The railroad can haul civilians from Washington to Philadelphia and back every Sunday for $3.78 and want $14.00 to haul soldiers. . . . These Pennsylvania people are a lot of damned hogs and I hope that something will happen to them."

Butler raised Marine Corps morale by developing a great football team that became the talk of the sports world, and began building a sports stadium with volunteer Marine labor and with cement contributed by cement companies.

Proliferating veterans' groups vied with each other for the distinction of adding his name to their letterheads. He tactfully declined invitations to join, offering his view that all such groups "must be nonpolitical, and should never be heard on the floors of Congress." In June, 1923, he sent regrets to the Marine Corps Veterans Association explaining, "I have very decided views on associations, and I am not a member of any but the American Legion, and most inactive, at that—only joining it because General Lejeune requested me to do so." He considered the Legion too political and undemocratic, with leaders who used it as a mouthpiece for big-business interests.

Late in 1923 Butler's career took an unorthodox twist.

W. Freeland Kendrick, the new mayor of Philadelphia, urged him to take a leave from the Marines to become the city's Director of Public Safety. The job was that of a "supercop," in charge of the police and firemen, with the task of smashing the links between crime and politics in Philadelphia.

Under Prohibition the city had become one of the most corrupt municipalities in the country. Over eight thousand places sold bootleg liquor without fear of prosecution; gangsters ran wide-open gambling joints and brothels; robberies, holdups, and other crimes were soaring. All attempts to clean up the City of Brotherly Love had failed because of a profitable alliance among gangsters, speakeasy operators, and crooked ward bosses, who bribed and controlled the police.

Kendrick, a conservative Republican politician, had been elected mayor on a law-and-order campaign and was now under heavy pressure to keep his pledge. He was advised to bring in an outsider, preferably a military man, who could not be bought, bluffed, or bullied, to head the police. Brigadier General Smedley Butler, now a vigorous forty-two and a colorful war hero with an impressive list of credits in *Who's Who in the Services*, seemed a perfect choice to please the voters. He had even had police experience organizing the Haiti Gendarmerie.

But Butler declined the job. On November 21 he wrote Kendrick, "While this position would appeal to me very greatly if I believed there were the slightest chance of success, I am convinced that the present political conditions existing would . . . throw away the work of a lifetime in a perfectly hopeless undertaking."

He was relieved when the Navy ordered him to report for orders to the Scouting Fleet. But Kendrick and the Republican party of Pennsylvania now needed him desperately to still a storm of public criticism. So Kendrick, Congressman Bill Vare, and Pennsylvania's two senators went to the White House to plead with President Calvin Coolidge that Butler be given a year's leave of absence to clean up Philadelphia.

Only a man with Butler's reputation for total honesty, and the ability to discipline men while capturing their imagination and winning their loyalty, they told Coolidge, could reorganize the Philadelphia police force. The President finally agreed and sent word to Butler that the White House would like him to tackle the job in the interests of good government. His father warned him against it as a political quicksand, but Butler did not see how he could refuse a mandate from both the people of Philadelphia and the President.

His reluctant consent brought wondering letters from old comrades all over the world, many of whom imagined that he had resigned from the Corps. Butler assured them that it was only temporary. "This job is a terrible one and I will probably be cut to pieces," he wrote to Lieutenant Colonel H. L. Roosevelt in Paris. "On January 7 I will be sworn in as a Philadelphia cop, for better or worse."

12

Butler told a reporter for the Philadelphia *North American,* "Kendrick has his neck in a noose with me. If I fall or I am run out, he is going to go down also. If he reverses me just once I'll quit, and the resignation will be in the form of a telephone call telling him I am on my way back to Quantico, and that the keys to my office are on my desk. I do not care whether the state laws or city ordinances are right or wrong. From January 7 they are going to be enforced." He was not opposed to drinking in principle, he added. What was at stake was enforcement of the law, pure and simple, not the ethics of Prohibition.

Even before he took office, "Boss" Vare sent an emissary to him, Judge Edwin O. Lewis, to offer Vare's "suggestions" for key appointments in reorganizing the police department. None too politely, Butler made it clear what Lewis and Vare could do with their suggestions.

He rented a home in nearby Overbrook, but his wife and children seldom saw him there because he spent seven days a week on the job, working until after midnight.

Sworn in on January 7, 1924, he took the oath of office in his Marine uniform, but half an hour later changed it for one of his own design. Blue with gold trim, it had a cape taken from the

Marine mess jacket with a flaring red lining. It was dramatic and impressive, and meant to be.

He promptly summoned all police inspectors to his office.

"I want the lieutenants in your forty-two districts to clean up in forty-eight hours," he snapped, "or face immediate demotion. That is all." Then he visited each one of the districts until he had spoken to every man on the force. The new motto, he announced, was short and sweet: "Clean up or get out!"

In his first week on the job he raided and shut down 973 liquor and gambling joints, without even warning Mayor Kendrick. Philadelphians were electrified. The police winked at each other, convinced that Butler was a smart "grandstander" who would make a big splash for the headlines, then quiet down and take it easy. Vare would see to that.

Going night after night with only a few hours' sleep, he pressed his raids and inspections relentlessly. He demanded from his men a dedication to duty equal to his own, but many of them, cut off from former sources of graft, were hostile and resistant to the new broom sweeping too clean.

"Sherman was right about war," Butler sighed wearily, "but he should have tried leading the Philadelphia police!"

Nevertheless he began to show results. Worried Philadelphia bootleggers began unloading their stocks at cut prices. Many crooks and gamblers began streaming out of the city in search of more hospitable territory.

Encouraging excessive zeal among his forces, Butler took responsibility for police who went too far on raids by using axes freely to destroy furniture and fixtures, searching private homes and vehicles on suspicion, and closing premises that had a right to stay open to sell nonintoxicating beverages. Magistrates began refusing to issue search warrants to permit police to enter known speakeasies masquerading as private residences. Many cases were dismissed on grounds of insufficient or illegal evidence.

Butler realized that he would have to modify his tactics, and astonished Philadelphians by frankly confessing his mistakes to both the press and the police.

"Guard against anything that will embarrass Mayor Kendrick's administration," he now ordered police. "Keep away from the hippodrome stuff. I must admit that I have sinned in this latter respect more than any of you, and the only excuse I have to offer is that I was unduly excited and enthusiastic."

Such candor won the affection and respect of reporters, who found Butler colorful copy and loved to join him for midnight suppers on Chestnut Street. There was never any question he would not answer for them directly and honestly. But if they were for him, their publishers—with the exception of the Philadelphia *Record*—were not; their editorial pages sought to ridicule and discredit him relentlessly.

"They insisted on treating me like a queer animal from the circus," Butler related. "My chance remarks were twisted and distorted to paint me in the worst light. . . . About fifty of the minor officials and correspondents of the newspapers became my loyal friends, but they had no influence in shaping the editorial point of view."

By March angry Republican ward leaders were furious at Butler for disrupting their network of police control. They vigorously applauded City Treasurer Thomas J. Watson at a meeting when he shouted, "This country, as well as the Republican organization, would be a hell of a sight better off without Butler!" The Philadelphia City Council closed ranks against him.

"My foolish notion that the laws of our country applied to rich and poor alike accounted for the growing feeling of antipathy toward me," he recalled later, adding, "By the end of 1924 I had been cussed, discussed, boycotted, lied about, lied to, strung up, and reviled. Several times I was on the point of resigning. The only reason why I continued in my unpopular and uncomfortable position was to see what the hell was going to happen next!"

Try as he might, he was unable to break the power of the ward bosses. In April he was forced to admit that he had been double-crossed by about half of his police lieutenants, who had bowed to ward-boss pressure to permit shuttered saloons, gambling houses, and speakeasies to reopen.

Studying the structure, he found that every ward had one police station. The ward leader named the captain of the station, and the police thus belonged to the ward leader. In an attempt to destroy the power of the ward bosses, Butler now cut the stations down from forty-six to thirty-three.

Infuriated politicians, racketeers, and realtors, who hated him for having cost them the rents of fifteen hundred closed brothels as well as the income from other illegally operated properties, joined forces to demand that Kendrick fire him.

But nearly five thousand church congregations adopted resolutions in July demanding that the mayor give full support to the general. Added to this pressure were thousands of letters from women's clubs, civic groups, business organizations, and individuals. Kendrick, alarmed at being caught between the voters and the brokers of power, wavered back and forth.

A report that he was preparing to knuckle under to the political bosses brought another roar of protest from the citizenry. A mass meeting of four thousand Philadelphians resolved that Butler must be kept in office: "Since General Butler has been in command here, more has been accomplished for the suppression of vice and crime than in any period of like duration in this city!" They flooded Secretary of the Navy Curtis D. Wilbur with letters urging that Butler's leave of absence from the Marines be extended for another three years.

President Calvin Coolidge reluctantly agreed to extend the general's leave for one more year, but he pointed out to the citizens of Philadelphia that the Federal Government could not continue indefinitely to be responsible for solutions to local problems: "The practice of detailing officers of the United States military forces to serve in civil capacities in the different states on leaves of absence is of doubtful propriety and should be employed only in cases of emergency. . . . Local self-government cannot be furnished from the outside."

Reappointed, by the end of the year Butler had raided almost 4,000 speakeasies, shutting down 2,566, and had seized over a thousand stills, arresting 10,000 violators of the Volstead Act. But to his dismay, political pressure in the court system resulted in only 2,000 indictments by the grand jury, with only 300 convictions. Police magistrates, who were handpicked by the politicians, imposed only token fines on all but 4 percent of arrested speakeasy operators. Struggling to get honest law enforcement,

Butler complained to the press, was like submitting to Chinese water torture:

"Drops of water have been dripping on my head since I have been here. . . . Either I am unpopular, or the enforcement of the liquor laws is unpopular in this city. . . . When the people of Philadelphia or any other city stop playing the game of 'Enforce the law against others but not against me,' they will begin to win the fight against lawlessness."

He was bitter when he learned of a secret deal between the brewers of Philadelphia and the Republican State Campaign Committee. A royalty of two dollars for each barrel of illegal beer distributed was to be paid into the Republican campaign fund, provided the politicians put the White House under heavy pressure to recall Butler to duty with the Marines.

Toward the end of 1925, whether this deal was responsible or not, Coolidge refused to extend Butler's leave. The general was ordered to report after the first of the year to command the Marine post at San Diego. With his recall assured, Mayor Kendrick now shrewdly sought to make points with pro-Butler voters by declaring that he wished it were possible to keep the general as Director of Public Safety for the remainder of his own administration.

A "Keep Butler" movement sprang up all over Philadelphia. Forced to go along with it, Kendrick told one mass meeting, "To announce that General Butler is to leave his post here would be tantamount to inviting an army of criminals to Philadelphia." But the mayor lost no time in grooming his successor.

Meanwhile Butler had become increasingly irked by the fact that the pressure of powerful hotels and the Hotel Association had kept their ballroom social affairs, at which liquor was served to young teen-age girls from socially prominent Philadelphia families, from being raided for liquor violations.

Ordering a raid on a formal ball at the Ritz-Carlton Hotel, he seized evidence showing that bootleg liquor was being served. Confronting Kendrick, he demanded that the mayor institute padlock proceedings against the Ritz-Carlton.

"And I mean the *whole* hotel," he insisted. "Something must be done to teach these big fellows that they must obey the law as well as the little fellows!"

A howl of outrage was heard in the ranks of the Republican party's wealthiest adherents. Politicians were threatened with a wholesale withdrawal of campaign contributions unless Butler was now unceremoniously dumped. Greatly upset, Kendrick urged him to "lay off" the big hotels. To the mayor's horror, Butler firmly announced his intention to organize a special police squad in evening clothes to invade *all* Philadelphia hotels, and signal for raids whenever they found liquor-law violations.

His fighting spirit was now thoroughly aroused. Although he longed to get back to his beloved Marine Corps, it rankled him to leave a mission incomplete. If he left Philadelphia now, he would have enforced the law against small operators who bootlegged liquor to the poor, but not against the big operators who made it available to the rich. His egalitarian nature pressed him to balance the scales.

He also felt an obligation to the honest cops who had defied the ward bosses to support his fight against corruption. Once he was gone, he feared, they would be punished for their loyalty to him. He decided that he owed it to them to sacrifice his career in the Marine Corps to stay on and finish the job, especially since Kendrick had made it clear—or so Butler believed—that he needed and wanted him.

The morning papers carried the story that Butler was resigning from the Marine Corps to remain as Director of Public Safety. Appalled, the hotel owners of the city joined with local politicians in a demand that Kendrick fire Butler immediately. The mayor was reminded that the Hotel Association's cooperation with City Hall was absolutely essential for the success of a sesquicentennial celebration of American independence being planned for Philadelphia.

Worried and upset, Kendrick called Butler to his office and told him, "I don't want any resigned generals around me. You ought to go back to the Service where you belong. The President doesn't want you here."

13

Shocked at the mayor's spineless surrender, Butler stalked out, storming, "Oh, hell, I can't talk to such a weak fish!"

Kendrick then fired him by phone. In choice Marine language, Butler told Kendrick exactly what he thought of him. Clearing his desk, the general withdrew a blue-steel Army Colt .45 from it and inserted it in a holster engraved, "To General Smedley D. Butler from W. Freeland Kendrick."

"Give him this letter of resignation and the pistol," he told his aide. "He can publish the letter and he can do what he pleases with the gun. I'm going back to the troops!"

His letter of resignation declared, "Last week I decided that it was in keeping with my promise to the police of Philadelphia that if they stood up with me, I would do everything in my power to remain in Philadelphia. . . . I am being dismissed from public service because I am making the greatest sacrifice any Marine can make, and I should, without any other ties, be of more service to the City of Philadelphia than I was before." He had been fired, he charged, because "the gang that has ruled Philadelphia for many years" had been out to get him, and did.

The Philadelphia *Record,* which had consistently supported Butler during his two years as the city's supercop, declared, "He was honest; that was taken for granted or he would not have been appointed. But he was 100 percent honest. We think we are doing the mayor no injustice in expressing the belief that this was a little more than he had counted on."

Reviewing his experience in Philadelphia, Butler declared ironically, "The fact the mayor didn't know me led to my being chosen. The fact I didn't know the mayor led me to accept. I had a funny idea that law was applicable to everybody. I was a fool. I didn't get anywhere, except for getting a lot of money as the highest paid cop in America, $18,000. Had the kids educated, lost 35 pounds and my teeth, bought a car and ended up $300 in debt. . . . What Philadelphia really wanted was something to talk about, a real, live general. No other city had one as a cop. . . . They wanted to throw up a smoke screen and make people think Philadelphia had thrown off the yoke of crime."

Mary Roberts Rinehart, who visited Butler in Philadelphia to study his cleanup, wrote about it in her biography:

> He did a fine job. He replaced the old roundsman, fat and portly, with young and active men, and then he put into them something of the marine *esprit de corps*. He put the fear of God into the gamblers and dive keepers. He cut down the enormous graft which they had paid year after year. But they were only waiting. They could afford to wait. When Butler lost the front page they would come back. . . .
> I watched Butler and admired him; the same sheer ability, energy and knowledge of men which had succeeded at Brest were evident in all that he did. But it was an unbeatable game, that of the crooks, gamblers, bootleggers and dive keepers.

As soon as he was fired, the mayor of Syracuse, New York, sent him a wire urging him to head that city's new Committee of Public Safety. But now Commandant John Lejeune quickly insisted that he withdraw his resignation from the Corps.

"I told General Butler that I could not with equanimity contemplate his leaving the Marine Corps," his old friend told the press. "I have the highest regard for General Butler with whom I have served for twenty-seven years, and I don't want the Marine Corps to lose him." Butler was given a holiday leave with his family to his old home in West Chester for a "quiet, old-fashioned, jolly Christmas" before reporting to take over the San Diego Naval Operating Base.

On the eve of his departure Philadelphia *Record* reporter Paul Comly French and other newsmen who admired his honesty and courage gave him an informal midnight dinner. They presented him with a square silver token, explaining, "It's the only kind of money he'll accept—square!"

"Cleaning up Philadelphia's vice," he told them with a sigh, "is worse than any battle I was ever in."

One group of Philadelphia citizens raised funds for a bronze tablet to honor his services to the city. The inscription read: "He enforced the law impartially. He defended it courageously. He proved incorruptible." He thanked them but protested wearily, "If I have to keep earning that epitaph, it will wear me out!"

Visiting his father in Washington, he admitted that his health had been impaired by working eighteen hours a day and longer, and he was bitter at having been used.

"I was hired as a smoke screen," he charged. "The politicians were buying the reputation I had earned in twenty-six years' service as a Marine. I was to make a loud noise, put on a brass hat, stage parades, chase the bandits off the streets—and let vice and rum run their hidden course!"

He was outraged by the huge sums he saw being made illegally by everyone involved in violating the Volstead Act, while Marines who served their country were paid a paltry twenty dollars a month. In December, 1926, he wrote his father angrily, "I do not suppose thee or the other men who are responsible for this Government have ever stopped to think what these $20 a month men are doing towards the preservation of the dignity of this Government. Now where can this Government get such devoted service for a total cost per capita of $1,300 a year? Where can we hire men for $20 a month?"

His health still suffering, he began to think of retirement. But Lejeune urged him to stay in uniform: "In the years to come the Corps will need your enthusiasm, and I had in mind that you would receive the next promotion to the rank of Major General. My retirement according to age is not very far in the future, and there is always the possibility of one of the Major Generals causing a premature vacancy."

Brooding over the whole question of Prohibition and law enforcement, Butler began to suspect that perhaps he had been wrong in trying to enforce an unenforceable law that the majority of the American people did not seem to want and went out of their way to violate. The government was wrong, he finally decided, in trying to legislate morality.

In view of his fame as a stern enforcer of Prohibition, prudence suggested that he keep his changed views to himself. He was unpopular enough with the wets; to speak out now against the Volstead Act would only alienate millions of drys who considered him one of their knights in white armor. But popularity had never been as important to Smedley Butler as his compulsion to blurt out the truth in public and to kick sacred cows in the rump when they loitered in the path of justice.

On January 7, 1927, in Washington, D.C., he gave the reporters a story that flashed from coast to coast. The Volstead Act, he now declared, was "a fool dry act, impossible of enforcement." It was, furthermore, "class legislation," because the rich could avoid it and the poor could not.

The sensational denunciation of Prohibition by one of its leading Republican crusaders plunged the dry forces of the nation into consternation. Democrats, rejoicing, began laying plans to make repeal of the Volstead Act one of the key issues in the presidential campaign of 1928.

Butler's presence in Washington was occasioned by the outbreak of a fresh crisis in China. To his delight, Lejeune informed him that he would soon be headed overseas once more at the head of a combat brigade.

14

China was being torn by civil war between Chiang Kai-shek, commander in chief of the new Nationalist armies of the South, and northern warlords led by Chang Tso-lin. Chiang Kai-shek had organized an anti-British boycott and had threatened to clear China of all foreign imperialists. Warlord Chang Tso-lin, supported by the colonial powers, had declared himself dictator of North China.

As Chiang Kai-shek's forces fought their way north and battles broke out between his army and Chang Tso-lin's, panic swept foreign residents in the North. American missionaries and businessmen appealed to Washington for protection.

The forty-six-year-old decorated hero of the Boxer Campaign who had helped relieve the sieges of Tientsin and Peking was made commander of a new Marine expeditionary force—the 3d Marine Brigade. His orders were "to protect the lives and property of our Nationals in Tientsin; to offer temporary refuge in Tientsin for our Nationals; evacuation from the Interior and to make safe evacuation to the sea."

The War Department warned Butler to be extremely prudent in anything he did or said; the smallest error of judgment on his part might have disastrous consequences in the highly volatile situation. Not without good reason, Lejeune added some prudent parting advice: "Be careful to avoid talking to newspaper correspondents."

He arrived in Shanghai on March 25, 1927, to find tension running high. Chinese troops had attacked several consulates at Nanking, killing many foreigners, looting and burning the city. American businessmen and missionaries had escaped on gunboats to Shanghai, whose port was now swarming with ships. Never before in history had the war vessels of so many different nations anchored together in one harbor.

Barbed-wire entanglements had been erected, and the International Settlement was under martial law. All legations had ordered their nationals from the interior of China, from which there were daily reports of murders and outrages. A more violent version of the Boxer Rebellion seemed in the making, and the white settlements were gravely apprehensive.

Butler's 3d Marine Brigade disembarked at the Standard Oil dock in the Whangpoo River opposite Shanghai and set up tents in the Standard Oil compound. Shortly afterward Butler was taken aboard the flagship of Admiral C. S. Williams, who greeted him frostily.

"What do you think of the situation, and what do you think of our participation?"

"We don't have half enough men to perform our task here," Butler replied. "We need more men to do it properly."

The admiral snorted. "So you're one of these fellows who wants to build a big job for himself and get promoted."

Butler saw red. "I intend to retire in a year," he snapped, "and don't care whether I am promoted or not. You asked for my opinion and I gave it to you. Now if you don't care to take my advice, and some Americans are murdered in this town, and you sit quietly here with half of the Marines available in the United States doing nothing but guarding coal piles, you will be held responsible!"

The admiral glared at him, but not without an aspect of respect. He was soon one of Butler's chief admirers.

Careful to keep the American forces from getting involved in the fighting between the rival Chinese armies, Butler sought to maintain cordial relations with the Chinese people themselves. He had no stomach for any more Haiti-style interventions that would jockey him into the position of defending American business interests against native rebels, and he did not intend to risk a single Marine's life to get the job done he had been sent to China to do, unless it became absolutely necessary.

Military leaders of other nations sought to organize a punitive expedition against the Kuomintang for the Nanking uprising. To Butler's relief, Admiral Williams refused to have anything to do with the scheme, although it had the enthusiastic endorsement of the American minister at Shanghai.

On May 31 Butler wrote Lejeune, "Now for a little 'secret stuff.' The American Minister . . . is a nervous wreck. He sits up all night and talks in circles and would have had me in my grave had I stayed much longer. He feels discredited because our Government has not adopted his plan, which meant an invasion of China, followed by intervention and military Government, and is desirous of going home on leave to explain his side to the President with a hope of favorable action."

He later observed, "I held to the principle that the Chinese had to settle their own form of government and pick out their own rulers. Any attempt to solve the Chinese tangle would have been shadow boxing. All we could do was to see that mutinous Chinese troops didn't get out of hand and shoot Americans. It was up to me to prevent a repetition of the Boxer and Nanking difficulties."

When the danger to Shanghai seemed to ease while growing more critical in the North, Butler left two thousand Marines stationed in the city under Colonel Henry Davis, and led four thousand men up to Tientsin. Not too clear about the mission expected of him, he wrote his father asking for clarification. His father replied:

> I do not think that anyone knows our State policies concerning the situation in China. I do not believe there are any. . . . I have but one word of caution to give thee; do not hurt a Chinaman unless it is absolutely necessary in order to protect the life of Americans in China or other foreigners associated with them. Do not interfere in the Chinese quarrel. . . .
>
> I have not heard one person worthy of quoting who does not deplore the presence of Americans in China. . . . We are not in China to maintain order. In a single word, use thy open hand to protect our people but don't kill the Chinamen to protect their property. . . . The Congress will never permit the use of its military to permanently protect it.

Following this advice, he persistently reminded his men that they were there to keep the peace, not violate it. Any Marine who laid a hand on a ricksha coolie would be court-martialed, he warned, urging them to win goodwill for the Corps by friendly behavior. He himself cultivated the friendship of the Chinese Minister of Foreign Affairs and was invited to over twenty Chinese banquets. At one of them he met an American-educated Chinese woman named Mrs. Lu, who reminded him that he had helped evacuate her family by boat from Tientsin twenty-seven years earlier, when she had been three.

"I well remember carrying you," he said to her delight. "You considered me a hateful 'foreign devil' and shrieked lustily, struggling every inch of the way."

As fighting between the rival armies raged closer to Tientsin, the roar of guns echoed through the city. Butler kept the Marines on the alert as a defense force, as well as a rescue force ready to leave in minutes for any place in North China they were needed. To make sure that none of the warlords, whose allegiances were mercurial, entertained any notion of attacking his brigade, he invited them to review a dress parade.

Some warlords were not intimidated and demanded that Butler take his Marines out of China. Explaining firmly that they were not going home until American nationals no longer needed protection, he insisted that they recognize one square mile of the base at Tientsin as a sanctuary where Americans could move about safely without being shot at.

The warlords refused until he persuaded them by pointing out shrewdly that it was good insurance for them in their fight against Chiang Kai-shek's Nationalists: "What if you lose? Why, you can come into that square mile, too!"

When they protested against the flights of Marine planes over Chinese territory, Butler gave them pause for thought by reminding them, "You might want to escape in one some day." He also convinced them it would be imprudent to attack the American forces by taking them up in Marine planes for bombing practice.

He later declared that he had fulfilled United States foreign policy requirements by intimidating the most hostile of the Chinese warlords "with considerable ease." He shared the detestation of the Chinese people for the warlords and their troops, expressing his sympathy with the people in a letter to Lejeune:

> There is a movement out here which is gaining great headway and is being conducted by a society known as the "Red Spears." Their aims and policies are similar to those of the Boxers in 1900 and is causing considerable uneasiness on the part of our people. The "Red Spears" are farmers and their society is said to number twenty million members. They have been so terribly treated by the soldiers, who every fall regularly billet themselves on them, driving out the men and misusing the women.
>
> This the farmers have tired of and now murder every

soldier they can catch. I am on the side of the "Red Spears" and it may be this will be a good way to end this pathetic slaughtering of innocent people by a lot of brutal war-lords.

The troops of other nations in the International Settlement marched around their perimeter defenses to intimidate the warlords and discourage any thought of attack. After flexing his muscles to impress them similarly at first, Butler then discreetly sought to "keep in the background as much as possible, and not in any way behave like an army of occupation—more like a fire company, ready to spring out to the rescue of our people, behaving simply as rescue squads."

15

On November 5, 1927, his wife, having left the children in San Diego, arrived in Tientsin and joined him in a small hotel next to a godown where the Marines had been quartered during the Boxer fighting and where he had been carried when he was wounded in the leg.

China's civil war had quieted down for the moment. In a report from Shanghai Colonel Henry Davis wrote Butler:

I had dinner last night with General Chiang Kai-shek. How in the name of God he ever exercised the control over these people to the extent he did last summer is a mystery to me. Usually a man of strong character will demonstrate it in some way without ever speaking a word. This bird has nothing of that kind so far as I could see, and looked and acted like a love sick boob, his fiance, Miss May Soong [later Madame Chiang Kai-shek], also being present at the dinner. . . . Of all the stupid boobs I ever met he is it. I don't believe he ever was the brains behind the movement of last summer. . . . He looks like a stupid ricksha coolie and grunts like a pig when spoken to.

By the end of December Butler found himself in a financial bind and complained to his father of the struggle to get along on a brigadier general's pay of $530 a month, out of which he had to pay income tax and "maintain an establishment for Snooks [daughter Ethel] and Tom Dick in the United States, and send Tommy [Smedley, Jr.] thru college, to say nothing of supporting Bunny [wife Ethel] and myself here in China." He added, "I must entertain many, due to my official position, and I must pay for the little entertainment out of my own pocket."

His father consoled him with the reflection that although he might be better off financially if he were home with no challenge to his abilities, "thee would rot and the world would have been no better because thee happened to live in it."

Lejeune wrote him that at special ceremonies on December 7, with the Secretary of the Navy present, Lejeune had accepted the bronze tablet honoring Butler, presented by a committee of Philadelphia's grateful citizens, and it had been put up in the Navy Building in Washington. He also revealed that Thomas Butler was leading the fight in the House for a larger naval defense force, but the public was in a budget-cutting mood.

Butler wrote his father:

> Thy courage in advocating something which will cost money fills me with pride. Our people are all gluttons and their desire to hoard money is so great that they will probably turn on thee and beat thee to death. It would probably be a good thing for our nation if we were to get a good trimming sometime, and perhaps they would learn that there is more in this world than unnecessarily fat bank accounts. The amount of money wasted by five rich men in America in one year would be sufficient to build and maintain a navy capable of preserving our position as a world power.

The day before Christmas, 1927, the Standard Oil plant on the outskirts of Tientsin caught fire during a battle between the rival Chinese armies. Nine minutes after the alarm, Butler was leading a battalion of Marines to battle the blaze, utilizing fire-fighting experience he had gained as Director of Public Safety in Philadelphia. He arrived on the scene to find two huge warehouses blazing, with a warehouse filled with gasoline twenty feet away and six 3-million-gallon oil tanks close by. If they exploded, the death and devastation in Tientsin would be horrendous.

Putting in a call for another thousand Marines, he fought furiously to contain the fire. They built a sixteen-foot wall of earth, empty drums, doors, and anything else that wouldn't burn between the blazing warehouses and the stores of gas, and had the fire under control by nightfall. But at 3:00 A.M. the main drain of the plant blew up, showering the river with a stream of burning oil. They worked through Christmas Day building a bulkhead around the mouth of the drain, only to have ice floes carry off part of it. The river flamed again, threatening the foreign compound on the opposite shore.

They fought the conflagration for four days before Butler succeeded in bringing it under control.

On New Year's Eve he wrote his father, "It was a glorious fight and has done a great deal to weld this command together. . . . Everybody in Tientsin and Peking is highly pleased with the magnificent showing of our men."

Standard Oil estimated their loss at a million dollars but thanked Butler for having saved them four million more. At the height of the blaze the admiring official in charge of the company's Tientsin holdings had vowed to donate twenty thousand dollars toward a recreation hall for the Marines. Once the fire had been brought under control, however, Butler heard no more of the promise. He was disgusted with the company but on principle did not remind them. When he told Smedley, Jr., about it, his outraged son swore never to use a tank of Esso gas in his car for the rest of his life, and kept *his* word.

Butler began having dark thoughts once more about the use of Marines to defend big-business profits overseas. Was the government's professed concern for the protection of Americans in China during the civil war the real reason for the presence of the Marines? Or was it to defend the properties of Standard Oil and other big American corporations?

Serving under him in China was David M. Shoup, later to win a Congressional Medal of Honor at Tarawa and become a commandant of the Marine Corps as well as a celebrated critic of the Vietnam war. "Butler was one helluva soldier—no doubt about his military capabilities," Shoup recalled later in admiration. "I really felt I wanted to emulate him in every way. Everything I saw in Tientsin indicated that he was a helluva showman, too, but a good warrior in the service of his country."

The author questioned General Shoup about the Marines' mission in China in 1927–1928. "I would say it was pretty hard to say *who* we were supporting there," he replied. "It was just our presence there that was the thing. I heard no solid reason for why we were being sent; we were just told we were going to fight the Chinese. We didn't know what the mission was. But we landed at the Standard Oil docks and lived in Standard Oil compounds and were ready to protect Standard Oil's investment. I wondered at the time if our government would put all these Marines in a position of danger, where they might sacrifice their lives in defense of Standard Oil. Later I discovered that of course it would, and did. It was only some years later that I learned that General Butler had been thinking the same way. I thought I had been alone in suspecting it."

16

All through 1928 Butler nevertheless carried out his orders scrupulously and prevented a shot from being fired in anger. In March he wrote his father that he was wary of involvement with any other power represented in China because of his suspicion of their selfish interests:

> The Japanese are most anxious to control all of North China, particularly Manchuria, and will sacrifice anything and back anyone who will assure to them this control. . . . The British are perfectly willing . . . if the Japanese will allow them to have the Yangtze Valley and, unless I am

greatly mistaken, these English "cousins" of ours will be absolutely guided by their own selfish political and commercial interests. . . . It behooves us to keep absolutely aloof from everyone and to do nothing which is not directly in line with the saving of lives.

Letters from home told him that his father had become very ill. Deeply worried, he wrote Thomas Butler in April:

> I do so hope . . . thee will not run thy legs off for this fool Navy. The American people never do know what they want and it is up to a few men like thee to guide them and persuade them to do the right thing but, after all . . . thy children think more of thy health than all the ships afloat. . . . We are so wholly controlled by selfish capital . . . abetted by foolish, short-sighted but no doubt well-meaning pacifists. We can never hope to be prepared for an emergency and sooner or later will suffer.

That was the last communication between them. His father died on May 26, 1928. When the news reached him in Tientsin, Butler wept. He was so stunned by the loss of the father who had been as much confidant and friend as parent that six weeks later he wrote his mother, grieving:

> Father always took pride in the fact that I was ever to be found at the front, and now, though it is simply killing me, I must go on and on trying to do the Nation's work. Ah, I don't care any more but must pretend I do—just hate it all, but Father drove himself to death for the Navy and I must do the same, I suppose. . . . I am all confused and dazed. Does thee know I am unable positively to remember the last time I saw Father? . . . Father has left us all such a beautiful reputation for kindly firmness that I am constantly overwhelmed with the responsibility of living up to it. . . . Be sure to write me fully any message that Father may have left for me, and if in his suffering he didn't leave any—make up one. It will be all the same—I must have something to go on.

As usual when he was depressed, he threw himself into an

orgy of activity. Storms having washed away a bridge on the Tientsin-Peking main road in September, he ordered the Marines to build a temporary structure out of scrap lumber to keep the highway open. The delighted villagers urged him to allow the bridge to remain; instead he magnified Chinese-American goodwill by building a more permanent bridge for them. Chinese officials named it after him and made him an honorary Chinese citizen. He then offered to rebuild the whole road from Peking to Tientsin with Marine equipment, to make it suitable for motor use, if they would supply soldier labor. They happily provided fifteen hundred Chinese troops for the job, which he personally supervised. The Chinese peasants were grateful for the road and bridges that helped them get their fresh produce to market.

When the road was officially opened, the governor of the province held a celebration at which Butler was the guest of honor. Ancient Chinese custom decreed that when the citizens of a town or district unanimously voted a man to be a great public benefactor, he could be awarded an Umbrella of Ten Thousand Blessings—a magnificent canopy of red satin with small silk streamers proclaiming his greatness. No foreigner in Tientsin or Peking had ever rated one. But now the people of Tientsin presented a Blessings Umbrella to Smedley Butler.

Soon afterward he drove into Boxertown just as a detached column from Chiang Kai-shek's army advanced into the opposite end of the town to loot it. His car kicked up so much racket that it sounded like machine-gun fire. The Nationalists, thinking he had an army behind him, fled. Despite Butler's protests that he had done nothing at all to help them, the people of Boxertown hailed him as a deliverer.

When he received a second Blessings Umbrella with its silk streamers inscribed in Chinese, one banner read, "Your kindness is always in the minds of people." The other: "General Butler loves China as he loves America."

The second award moved him deeply, because Boxertown was the very same town from which Boxers, twenty-eight years earlier, had poured fire on his company, killing three Marines and wounding nine. After he made a speech recalling this event, he learned that five old men in the crowd that had just presented him with Boxertown's greatest honor had been among the Boxers who had shot at him in 1900.

He was equally popular with his men, frequently working beside them when there was physical labor to be done. Junior officers were so caught up by his gung-ho leadership, General Shoup recalled, that they, too, worked voluntarily beside the enlisted men. "Never before or since," one of them said later in awe, "have I ever known a general who could actually inspire officers to want to do physical labor."

In the fall of 1928 Butler followed developments by radio in the presidential race between Herbert Hoover and Al Smith, deeply interested in the campaign issues that touched two facets of his personal experience—Prohibition and Latin American relations. He wrote Lejeune in October, "There seems no doubt that Hoover will be elected President—I guess, however, the country will survive."

Orders for the Marines to begin pulling out of China came from President Coolidge in December. As he left China in January, 1929, Butler's affection and admiration for the Chinese people was so great that he wrote Lejeune, "It may be that when I am retired I will live among them." Their enthusiasm for him was equally unrestrained. A friend with the Asiatic Fleet wrote him, "The sendoff which the newspapers at Tientsin gave to you and Mrs. Butler was a great and just tribute to the cordial relations which you had so successfully established, not only with the Americans and the Chinese, but with everybody you came in contact with during your stay in North China."

Butler was awarded the Yangtze Service Medal and in July, 1929, promoted to major general—at forty-eight the youngest Marine officer ever to have reached this rank. The Navy Department declared, "Probably no finer example of successful arbitration by American officers has been demonstrated in recent years than the peace-making achievements that crowned General Butler's efforts in China in 1927 and 1928."

17

Back home, Butler winced when Lejeune asked him to take command of the Parris Island, South Carolina, base. Weary after his China stint, he felt a need to renew his ties with kith and kin in his hometown of West Chester. He talked of retiring.

"I had better begin to think what is best for me and my family," he told Lejeune. "I have given over thirty years of my best to the Marine Corps."

He was given a long leave home, where he became aware of a rising tide of American sentiment matching his own growing distrust of the reasons for which armed forces were sent overseas. It had begun with a belated disillusionment over World War I, sparked by such books as *All Quiet on the Western Front* and *Merchants of Death*. In 1925 a National Committee on the Cause and Cure of War had been founded, and a rapidly developing pacifist movement had compelled the government to enter disarmament negotiations. By August, 1928, the antiwar movement was worldwide.

Assigned once more to command the base at Quantico, Butler made it a Marine showplace and developed Marine football, baseball, and basketball teams with such high esprit de corps that they played the best college teams of the East and often beat them. His fatherly interest in his men led him to help them with personal problems, get them out of trouble, and encourage them to write home. The admiration of Marines' families was expressed in a typical letter to him from Philadelphia: "My brother in the Marines just came back from Nicaragua and he ask to be transferd to Phila. his Mother was Ill you comeplied with his wishes. His Mother was opertad for Tumbers but it was a baby boy and to day it was Christend Smedley D. Butler Ruth."

Military and patriotic organizations persistently sought to lure him into joining. He wired the Sons of the American Revolution, "My ancestors were all Quakers and I regret to say took no part, as far as I know, in the American Revolutionary War, so I am not entitled to be a Son of the American Revolution." Actually, recently discovered evidence indicates that his great-great-grandfather, William Butler, although a Quaker, probably served in the Revolution, along with three brothers.

He did, however, finally yield to the pleas of American Legion official James J. Deighan that he attend the national convention in Scranton as a guest of honor. "The success of the 11th National Convention . . . last week was in large part due," Deighan wrote him gratefully afterward, "to the fact that you were our guest. . . . The Legionnaires are all for you."

News came that John Lejeune was resigning as commandant to head the Virginia Military Academy and would be replaced by Butler's other old friend, Buck Neville, now a major general. Thirty years had gone by since they had been an inseparable trio in the feverish days of the Cuban campaign. Butler began to feel the weight of time and too many campaigns. The endless demands on him made retirement and rest seem alluring.

Asked once too often for a speech, he replied in October, 1929, "I am not a crusader or a propagandist, nor have I message for anybody, so there is no object in my appearing anywhere, except for money." He began to charge stiff lecture fees to cut down demands for him to travel everywhere to address luncheons and meetings as guest of honor.

Perusing the morning papers on October 2, he noted a statement by Charles E. Mitchell, of the National City Bank: "I know of nothing fundamentally wrong with the stock market or with the underlying business and credit situation."

The following day there was a minor panic on the New York Stock Exchange, and a day later the market collapsed. On October 29 the bottom fell out in the blackest day in stock-market history, and within two weeks over thirty billion dollars in stock values were wiped out.

The Great Depression had begun, and with it a swift rush of events that would involve Smedley Butler in a fantastic plot to overthrow the American Government.

At first the American people imagined that the stock-market crash was something that merely affected Wall Street. In a message to Congress President Hoover reassured them that there was nothing to worry about; business confidence had been reestablished. Bootleggers, gang wars, and crime continued to be the major preoccupation of the public.

Despite Butler's reluctance, more and more organizations insisted upon hearing the general who never pulled his punches speak out on the law-and-order problem. There was a ground swell in Pennsylvania to nominate Philadelphia's former crimebuster for governor on the Republican ticket. A friend wrote from Washington, "I note that some of the politicos may draft you as Dictator for Washington."

In December, 1929, Butler was glad when a demand arose for a Senate investigation of the use of Marines to intervene in Latin American affairs. He upset the Hoover Administration by shooting from the hip in an extemporaneous speech he made in Pittsburgh, revealing that the State Department had rigged the Nicaraguan elections of 1912 by ordering him to use strong-arm methods during the Marine intervention.

"The opposition candidates in Nicaragua were declared bandits when it became necessary to elect our man to office," he explained. And he said of Diaz, "The fellow we had there nobody liked, but he was a useful fellow to us, so we had to keep him in. How to keep him in was a problem." Then he described how the election had been rigged, under orders, for that purpose. "When a Marine is told to do something," he said, "he does it."

Butler's disclosures, picked up by the press, created a sensation in Washington. Alarm bells rang in the State Department; the last thing the administration wanted was an investigation concerning Marines then stationed in Nicaragua. Officials angrily attacked Butler for "loose talk."

Secretary of State Henry L. Stimson wrote a furious memo to Secretary of the Navy Charles Francis Adams:

> . . . If the remarks are authentic, I consider them a highly improper and false statement as to American policy, and that I should call it to your attention for appropriate action.

> There is nothing that can do this Government more dis-
> service than such a misstatement of our policy in a Latin
> American country, and I am astounded that such an expres-
> sion—if he is correctly quoted—should emanate from a com-
> missioned officer of the United States.

Navy Secretary Adams, a wealthy, polo-playing yachtsman, sent for Butler and delivered a blistering reprimand, declaring that he was doing so at the direct personal order of the President of the United States. Butler saw red.

"This is the first time in my service of thirty-two years," he snapped back, "that I've ever been hauled on the carpet and treated like an unruly schoolboy. I haven't always approved of the actions of the administration, but I've always faithfully carried out my instructions. If I'm not behaving well it is because I'm not accustomed to reprimands, and you can't expect me to turn my cheek meekly for official slaps!"

"I think this will be all," Adams said icily. "I don't ever want to see you here again!"

"You never will if I can help it!" Butler rasped, storming out of his office livid with anger.

Just two days after his attack on the government's gunboat diplomacy, which provoked a great public commotion, Undersecretary of State J. Reuben Clark privately submitted to Secretary of State Stimson the draft of a pledge that the United States would never again claim the right to intervene in the affairs of any Latin American country as an "international policeman." The Clark Memorandum, which later became official policy—for a while at least—repudiated the (Theodore) Roosevelt Corollary to the Monroe Doctrine that Smedley Butler had unmasked as raw gunboat diplomacy.

18

Defying Adams, Butler continued to express his convictions freely and publicly about current problems on which he felt qualified to speak out. He was delighted in May, 1930, when Congress, over President Hoover's veto, passed a Spanish-American War pension bill for veterans. With the unemployment rate climbing steadily to almost five million that year, he urged passage of a bonus bill for all veterans. The government had a solemn obligation to citizens who had risked their lives to protect it, Butler insisted, to see to it that they, their wives, and their children were not allowed to languish in hunger, poverty, and despair.

Two deaths that year saddened him. His brother Horace was killed in a car accident in Texas, and his old friend Buck Neville died suddenly after briefly replacing Lejeune as commandant.

Now Butler was the senior-ranking major general in the Marine Corps, the logical choice as next commandant. An official inspection report had also praised Quantico as the finest post in the United States. But on the same day that it appeared, Marine Corps headquarters sent Butler a curt letter suggesting that he make fewer speeches, because his Quantico post was in poor shape as a result of his frequent absences.

In July, 1930, Secretary Adams paid a visit to Quantico, undoubtedly to lay the groundwork for an official excuse to reject Butler's fitness to be appointed commandant. Butler was equally determined to demonstrate that the rebuke he had received about the "poor shape" of his post was totally unwarranted. Escorting Adams everywhere over the barracks and parade grounds, he proved that Quantico was a model of efficiency. The dress-uniform review of his crack regiments was flawless, and the Marine air squadron performed brilliant maneuvers.

The secretary acidly observed that Quantico was the most

expensive place in the nation for training men. Controlling his temper, Butler pointed out the sports stadium built at almost no cost to the taxpayers.

"That's one of your damned follies!" Adams muttered. He was clearly attempting to provoke the volatile Butler into flaring up, and Butler knew it. Clenching his jaw, the general remained outwardly calm but could not resist telling a sharply barbed joke about "an old buzzard" who couldn't be pleased by anything.

Several weeks later a Navy selection board met to choose a new commandant. One staff admiral declared that he'd be damned before he'd see Butler made commandant; in no time at all the damned fellow would be trying to run the whole Navy. Others agreed. Adams happily discarded Butler's name and proposed instead Brigadier General Ben H. Fuller who, despite being junior in rank, was approved by the board.

The news was the last straw for Butler, who now determined to retire within a year to devote himself to advocating the defense of the United States as he believed it ought to be defended. Resolutely opposed to military intervention overseas on behalf of Wall Street interests, he planned to arouse the American people into preventing any more. At the same time he had doubts about the wisdom of entering world disarmament agreements, as leading pacifists proposed. Could the United States afford to disarm and trust the word of military dictators like Italy's Mussolini, with Hitler's swiftly growing Nazi party in Germany already laying the groundwork for a new war by renouncing the Versailles Treaty?

In a speech before the influential Contemporary Club of Philadelphia on January 19, 1931, he declared, "I agree with Dr. Hull of Swarthmore; if we could all lay down our arms, there couldn't be any war. But there are mad-dog nations who won't get the word, who will refuse to sign the agreement, or, if they sign it, refuse to abide by it."

Seeking to impress his listeners with the kind of men dictators were, he added, "A friend of mine said he had a ride in a new automobile with Mussolini, a car with an armored nose that could knock over fences and slip under barbed wire. He said that they drove through the country and towns at seventy miles per hour. They ran over a child and my friend screamed. Mussolini said he shouldn't do that, that it was only one life and the affairs of the state could not be stopped by one life."

His listeners gasped audibly. Arms akimbo, his head thrust forward angrily, Butler demanded in a scornful voice, "How can you talk disarmament with a man like *that*?"

He had been told that the audience was a private one and that he could speak in confidence, but he soon learned that there was no such thing as confidential speech for a man so often in the public eye. Among his listeners, unknown to him, was an Italian diplomat from Washington who had been invited to attend.

The outraged diplomat at once reported Butler's remarks to Italian Ambassador de Martino. The embassy sent a frantic cable to Rome, then filed an official protest with the State Department. The morning papers broke the story, and it made sensational headlines. A high-ranking American officer, wearing the Marine uniform on active duty, had publicly insulted the head of a friendly power.

Secretary of State Henry L. Stimson felt compelled to deliver a formal apology to Mussolini: "The sincere regrets of this government are extended to Mr. Mussolini and to the Italian people for the discourteous and unwarranted utterances by a commissioned officer of this government on active duty."

The Washington military-diplomatic bureaucracy now decided that this time Butler had gone too far. Formal charges against him were hastily drawn and presented to President Hoover, who promptly signed them. On the morning of January 29 Marine Commandant Ben Fuller phoned Butler at Quantico.

"General Butler, you are hereby placed under arrest to await trial by general court-martial. You will turn over your command to your next senior, General Berkeley, and you will be restricted to the limits of your post. The Secretary of the Navy wishes you to know that this action is taken by the direct personal order of the President of the United States."

The charges were "conduct to the prejudice of good order and discipline" and "conduct unbecoming an officer and a gentleman." These accusations were known in the armed forces as

Mother Hubbard charges because they "covered everything."
Most Marine officers were convinced that the powers-that-be had
decided to "throw the book" at Old Gimlet Eye and drum him
out of the Corps dishonorably, in revenge for his well-known
fighting man's scorn of Washington's desk warriors.

Butler notified Brigadier General Randolph C. Berkeley, his
junior officer at Quantico and a good friend, that he was
under arrest—the first general officer to be placed under arrest
since the Civil War. Butler's two-star command flag was lowered
on the Quantico flagstaff, and he offered his sword to Berkeley,
who indignantly refused to accept it.

Berkeley was outraged that Smedley Butler, who wore eighteen
decorations and was one of only four military men in American
history who had ever been awarded two Medals of Honor, should
be put under arrest by a telephone call. He was even more
indignant that Butler had been confined to the post, hindering his
ability to arrange for his own defense at the court-martial.

Defying the wrath of Adams, Berkeley himself went to Washington to get Butler's old comrade-in-arms Henry Leonard, who
had lost an arm fighting beside him in the Boxer Rebellion and
who now had a law practice in the Capital, to act as Butler's
counsel. Leonard rushed off to Quantico immediately.

A prisoner on his own post, Butler was wryly amused by an
invitation to be guest of honor at a sportsmen's dinner. His aide-
de-camp, L. C. Whitaker, replied dryly for him: "As General
Butler is under arrest, he will be unable to attend."

19

News of his arrest brought an outpouring of sympathy and support for him not only among his far-flung and influential staunch
friends but also among millions of Americans who despised
Mussolini and everything the dictator stood for. Admiring Butler

for speaking out against fascism, they were appalled that he was being court-martialed for being a patriot who believed in democracy, the Constitution, and the Bill of Rights, and distrusted dictators who denied such civil liberties to their own people.

Butler also had the support of millions of veterans who knew him as a magnificent fighting man and hero, as well as a general who was on the side of the enlisted man against the brass; and of hundreds of thousands of admirers who still remembered the courageous fight he had waged against the crooked politicians and racketeers of Philadelphia.

Many Americans, moreover, were fed up with the Hoover Administration for sitting on its hands with the Depression rapidly worsening, and esteemed a public leader who at least had the courage of his convictions and spoke them bluntly. Italian-American anti-Fascists also rallied to Butler's support by bitter protests against Stimson's apology to Mussolini.

The administration grew alarmed as a rolling tidal wave of angry criticism of Butler's arrest swept across the country.

"Unless we are mistaken," declared a Washington *Daily News* editorial, "the American people are likely to consider these Cabinet officials guilty of a strange timidity toward Mussolini on one hand and of an unwarranted harshness toward a splendid American soldier on the other."

Public opinion on the side of Butler made itself felt so quickly and emphatically that the administration found it necessary to ameliorate the conditions of his arrest. His restriction to the post was lifted, allowing him to travel where he needed to in order to arrange for his defense.

He wired New York Governor Franklin D. Roosevelt, who had presented him with one of his Medals of Honor as Undersecretary of the Navy, "Am in great trouble. Can you assist me in securing services of John W. Davis as counsel?" Davis, a leading Wall Street corporation lawyer, had been the unsuccessful Democratic candidate for President in 1924. Roosevelt persuaded Davis to agree to argue Butler's case at the trial.

A visit to Butler's aunt, lawyer Isabel Darlington, also enlisted Roland S. Morris, a former ambassador to Japan, as Henry Leonard's counsel in preparing the case.

Thousands of sympathetic messages poured into Quantico. Butler was deeply touched by two letters especially: Both Governor Roosevelt and former Secretary of the Navy Josephus Daniels volunteered to testify in his behalf at the court-martial. That news stunned Adams and Hoover.

The trial date was set for February 16. Butler was impatient to have it sooner, anxious to get all the facts before the public, but Leonard and Morris argued that the torrent of favorable publicity was helping his case. They proved correct. Protests against the court-martial were pouring into the White House by the sackful. The trial threatened to become a cause célèbre, with implications for the whole system of military justice, especially after a Marine colonel denounced American court-martials as basically unjust.

The impending trial was also throwing a spanner into Secretary of State Stimson's plans for forging an international naval arms limitation agreement. Crucial to that agreement were preliminary negotiations between Italy and France, which feared Italian and German fascism. Resisting Stimson's pressure to sign an arms limitation agreement with Mussolini, the French cited as justification popular American support of Butler's view that Mussolini could not be trusted and widespread protest over his arrest for saying so.

Mussolini himself, alarmed by the bad press he was getting in the United States, with a few notorious exceptions, sent word to Stimson that he considered the whole incident an "unfortunate error" and believed it would be best for all concerned if the whole plan to court-martial Butler could be quietly dropped.

Stimson, who now realized that he had a tiger by the tail, passed the word to the crestfallen Adams. The Secretary of the Navy now had to beat a hasty retreat with as much dignity as he could muster out of his humiliating predicament. He sent Leonard a letter announcing his decision to "settle" the matter by calling off the court-martial and simply detaching Butler from his command with a reprimand, placing him on the inactive list with the limbo status of "awaiting orders."

In polite language Leonard told Adams to go to hell. A few hours later, after checking with his principals, the Secretary of

the Navy then offered to let the whole thing drop by just detaching Butler from the command and issuing a reprimand.
Again Leonard turned him down flatly. Adams frantically tried
a third proposal. The administration would settle, he now
pleaded, for an official letter of apology. There would be no
court-martial and no removal of Butler from Quantico.

Roaring a third refusal, Leonard demanded that Adams stop
dawdling and proceed to trial. By now the administration, in a
state of near panic, meekly asked Leonard just what terms for
settling the matter would be acceptable to General Butler.

Leonard, jubilant at this abject surrender, conferred with
Morris and Butler. Angry at his persecutors, Butler wanted to
insist upon the court-martial, but as he confided to a relative on
February 12, "Mother and Bunny [his wife] were both breaking
under the strain," and he decided that it wasn't worth their
anguish to fight the establishment to a finish. "I feel we could
have licked them badly," he added, "but now I have a club over
their heads, as they were warned that we would tell if they tried
any more persecutions."

Since he had already won a clear moral victory, he decided
he could afford to let the government save a little face. He agreed
to write a letter reiterating his explanation that the Mussolini
speech had been made at a private club meeting and expressing
regret that anything he had said "caused embarrassment to the
Government." He would accept an official gentle "reprimand,"
which was, however, not to be written by Adams but by Leonard
himself for Adams to sign. In return for these concessions the
government would announce that it was dropping its court-
martial and was immediately restoring the general to his command with full rank and privileges, without prejudice of any
kind.

The administration hastily accepted Butler's terms, and the
suitable papers were drawn. On February 9 the court-martial was
canceled, and a mild reprimand credited Butler's explanation
that his speech had been intended to be "confined to the limits
of four walls," as well as acknowledging his "long record of
brilliant service." One newspaper headlined the story: "YOU'RE A
VERY BAD BOY"— SAYS ADAMS TO BUTLER.

The general's admirers grinned in delight. He was released from arrest and restored to duty, his command flag once more fluttering over Quantico. It was a signal and remarkable victory for a lone Marine officer to win over the President of the United States and the Secretaries of State and the Navy.

"I was glad to see Smedley Butler get out of his case as he did," Will Rogers wrote in his column on March 15, 1931. "You know that fellow just belongs in a war all the time. He don't belong in Peace time. He is what I would call a natural born warrior. He will fight anybody, any time. But he just can't distinguish Peace from war. He carries every medal we ever gave out. He has two Congressional Medals of Honor, the only man that ever got a double header.* You give him another war and he will get him another one. . . . I do admire him."

The press was reluctant to let the story die. The wire services carried journalist Cornelius Vanderbilt's revelation that he had been the one who had told Butler the true story about Mussolini. He corrected a few details. After running down the child, Vanderbilt said, Mussolini had observed the journalist looking back in horror and had patted his knee reassuringly, saying, "Never look back, Mr. Vanderbilt—always look ahead in life." Italian officials now sought to deny that Vanderbilt had ever ridden in a car with Mussolini.

Butler was appalled, but not too surprised, to read that Ralph T. O'Neill, national commander of the American Legion, had presented to Italian Ambassador de Martino a resolution in praise of Mussolini, passed by the National Executive Committee. There were powerful and influential wealthy elements in the Legion leadership who admired Mussolini's shackling of Italian labor unions under the guise of fighting Reds.

Now that he had defeated the attempt of his enemies to court-martial him, Butler revealed to his friends that he intended to go ahead with his original plan to retire at the end of the year. On March 1 he informed the press, barking, "Get this clear—I are not *resigning!*"

---

* Rogers's mistake was a common error. In addition to Smedley Butler, three other Americans have each won two Congressional Medals of Honor.

20

Butler now found himself in greater demand than ever as a public speaker. The Alber Lecture Bureau of Cleveland pleaded with him to take a leave of absence and satisfy the groups all over the country clamoring to hear him. He was offered half of all admission fees charged, with a minimum guarantee of $250, plus $25 a day expenses and railroad fare.

At the same time Philadelphia's Mayor Mackey asked him if he would assist in raising funds for the city's Committee for Unemployment Relief. Applying for a two months' leave of absence to make a speaking tour, he turned over half his fees of about six thousand dollars to the unemployed and also to the Salvation Army, which he respected as being genuinely responsive to the needs of both the poor and the doughboys in trenches.

He explained the impulse for his decision by a letter he had received while he was under arrest during the Mussolini affair. "General," a veteran had written him, "the stamp on this letter cost me the two of my last four cents, but I wanted you to know that I am for you."

"I almost cried," Butler admitted. "I feel that if that poor fellow could give me half of what he had, I can give him half of what I've got." He was also strongly influenced in his sympathy for the luckless by his aunt, Isabel Darlington, who headed the Chester County Poor Board and fought county authorities vigorously to increase welfare funds.

Publishers begged him for a book. "I am making far more money out of making speeches than I ever could out of writing a book," he replied practically, "so unless Bobbs-Merrill are going to outbid the public . . . I would be cutting off my nose to spite my face by writing instead of talking." But he finally con-

sented to dictate his war memoirs to adventure writer Lowell
Thomas, who published them as a book, under the title *Old
Gimlet Eye.*

Aware that his imminent retirement meant a sharp drop in
income and an increase in expenses, with little or nothing saved,
he sought to organize his time as profitably as possible. He accepted radio offers to relate his experiences in the Marines.

If Butler did not consciously seek publicity, there was little
doubt that the headlines sought him out. His rapport with the
press was explained by one newsman's observation that he was
"colorful copy and a helluva guy." He often said himself, "There
are three types of people who understand me—Marines, police-
men, and newspapermen." His chief interest in stories about him
in the press was less vanity than a determination to disseminate
views he held strongly.

With the first ominous rumblings of war beginning to be heard
in both Europe and Asia, he was determined to steel the American people against letting themselves be dragged into any more
foreign wars. He would tell them the whole truth about the use
that had been made of the Marines by the government in the
name of protecting democracy and "American interests" abroad.

On August 21, 1931, invited to address an American Legion
convention in Connecticut, he made the first no-holds-barred
antiwar speech of his career. It stunned all who heard it or read
it in the few papers that dared report it in part:

> I spent 33 years . . . being a high-class muscle man for
> Big Business, for Wall Street and the bankers. In short, I
> was a racketeer for capitalism. . . .
>
> I helped purify Nicaragua for the international banking
> house of Brown Brothers in 1909–1912. I helped make
> Mexico and especially Tampico safe for American oil inter-
> ests in 1916. I brought light to the Dominican Republic
> for American sugar interests in 1916. I helped make Haiti
> and Cuba a decent place for the National City [Bank] boys
> to collect revenue in. I helped in the rape of half a dozen
> Central American republics for the benefit of Wall Street. . . .
>
> In China in 1927 I helped see to it that Standard Oil

went its way unmolested. . . . I had . . . a swell racket. I was rewarded with honors, medals, promotions. . . . I might have given Al Capone a few hints. The best he could do was to operate a racket in three cities. The Marines operated on three continents. . . .

We don't want any more wars, but a man is a damn fool to think there won't be any more of them. I am a peace-loving Quaker, but when war breaks out every damn man in my family goes. If we're ready, nobody will tackle us. Give us a club and we will face them all. . . .

There is no use talking about abolishing war; that's damn foolishness. Take the guns away from men and they will fight just the same. . . . In the Spanish-American War we didn't have any bullets to shoot, and if we had not had a war with a nation that was already licked and looking for an excuse to quit, we would have had hell licked out of us. . . .

No pacifists or Communists are going to govern this country. If they try it there will be seven million men like you rise up and strangle them. Pacifists? Hell, I'm a pacifist, but I always have a club behind my back!

Earlier that same day, before Hoover had had a chance to read the speech, reporters asked the President if he would seek to delay the general's retirement.

"I assume that if General Butler wishes to retire, the authorities will approve," Hoover answered cautiously. "The general is a very distinguished and gallant officer and I have no doubt that if the country has need, it always can secure his services." Next day, when Butler's attack on big business was reported, attempts to get any statement from the White House met with icy silence.

And on that day, providing a punctuation mark to Butler's doubts that the Kellogg-Briand Pact protected any nation from aggression, Japan invaded Manchuria and reduced the pact to a worthless scrap of paper.

On October 1, 1931, friends of Smedley Butler from all stations in life, and from all periods of his career, gathered at Quantico as his two-star command flag was hauled down once more, this time with full honors. At the age of fifty, after spending all of his life but the first fifteen years in a Marine uniform, under fire over 120 times, he retired from the Corps and was once more a civilian.

In his farewell speech to his beloved leathernecks his voice was more than customarily hoarse, and tears misted his fierce glare. "It has been a privilege to scrap for you just as you have scrapped for me," he told them. "When I leave I mean to give every one of you a map showing you exactly where I live. I want you to come around and see me, especially if you ever get into trouble, and I will help you if I can. I can give you a square meal and a place to sleep even if I cannot guarantee you a political job."

He meant every word, gave out the maps, and kept his promise for as long as he lived.

21

Demands flooded in now for Butler's services as a lecturer. He had embarrassed governments, large and small, including his own, by his relentless candor, but his courage and honesty had won the admiration of millions of Americans. His speeches became more vitriolic than ever, scorching the hides of the powerful and the highly placed.

He met eager requests for articles by magazines and newspaper syndicates with the help of his friend E. Z. Dimitman, who was now night city editor of the Philadelphia *Inquirer*. Dimitman would flesh out his views on war and peace, which Butler then edited and revised to his own satisfaction.

There never seemed to be enough money. Although he received some lecture fees up to $500, the average fee came to $250 and in many cases turned out to be far less. Most of what he managed to earn went into putting Tom Dick through Swarthmore and Smedley, Jr., through California Tech and M.I.T., and paying off the house he and Ethel had bought in Newtown Square, Pennsylvania.

It was an old square farmhouse that had been gutted by fire except for its walls. Butler had rebuilt it with glass-enclosed porches and a huge, high hallway in which he erected his two treasured Chinese Blessings Umbrellas, opened like canopies at each end of the hall. He had thought to remodel the house for $35,000, but it had turned out to cost far more, and he was forced to sell most of the land to pay off the mortgage.

As a civilian Butler was close-fisted with money, gently but firmly resisting the endless letters he received begging for hand-outs, because he had no money to spare. His thrifty wife kept an old, ragged, shabby fur coat in the closet, over thirty years after he had brought it home for her from the Boxer Rebellion. She never wore it, but could not bring herself to throw it away. He himself upset many military organizations by canceling his membership and journal subscriptions without offering any ex-planation. He was too proud to admit the real reason; he simply had to prune expenses.

Out of uniform, he took pride in his appearance and dressed well but conservatively. Unable to break the traditions of thirty-three years of dress parade, he polished his shoes daily and buffed the buttons on his white, custom-made summer suits. His thought patterns, too, continued to dwell primarily on military concerns.

One of his objectives was to stir up a demand that the Marine Corps be removed from under the thumb of politically appointed desk admirals of the Navy and set up as a separate branch of the armed forces under their own leaders. He gave his reasons in an article called "To Hell with the Admirals! Why I Retired at Fifty," which appeared in *Liberty Magazine* on December 5, 1931:

> The clique of desk-admirals who seem to hold sway in the Navy Department in Washington demand an Annapolis man as head of the Marine Corps. They desire to have the Corps an insignificant part of the naval service, a unit di-rectly under their collective thumb. It dismays and appalls them to learn of the heroic deeds of Marines on foreign

duty. They feel it detracts from the prestige of the navy. . . .

This group of admirals did everything possible to keep me from being named commandant. . . . And now those officers of the Marine Corps who have been particularly loyal and friendly to me . . . are being transferred all about the country and abroad. . . . As I go I am tempted to say to that shipless clique: "To hell with the admirals!"

Outraged, Admiral Pratt issued a statement denouncing his broadside. The tablet that had been erected in his honor in the Navy Building was removed. Later located and rescued by a Butler Memorial Commission, it was installed in Philadelphia's City Hall after his death.

Another article Butler wrote for *Liberty* stirred the wrath of the Honduras Government by exposing the collaboration of Honduran and other Central American dictators with American banking and commercial interests. The controlled Honduran press accused him of misrepresenting the situation and showered him with epithets. From Tegucigalpa a *New York Times* correspondent wired, "It is realized that he is now retired, and not subject to the restraint which can be imposed on an officer in active service."

More and more of Butler's attention was directed to the steadily worsening Depression and what it was doing to the country. He was outraged when hunger marchers who had gone to Washington on December 7 were denied admission to the White House to petition for jobs.

During 1932 stocks fell 90 percent, farm products 60 percent, industrial production 50 percent. By the end of the year fifteen million Americans were in the ranks of the unemployed. Homeowners and farmers were being dispossessed for nonpayment of taxes and debts. Outraged neighbors in many communities were setting up roadblocks with guns to bar outside bidders at foreclosure auctions so that the property could be bought for a song and returned to its owners. Alarmed bankers saw this development as a Communist threat.

Butler's antagonism toward big business intensified. On February 14, 1932, the United Press quoted him as saying, "I've about come to the conclusion that some American corporations abroad are, in a measure, responsible for trouble with the natives simply because of the way they treat them. . . . I've seen hundreds of boys from the cities and farms of the United States die in Central American countries just to protect the investments of our large corporations." How could Washington criticize Japan for its takeover in Manchuria, he demanded, when we ourselves had been just as imperialistic?

In the spring Pennsylvania Governor Gifford Pinchot urged Butler to throw his hat into the political ring and oppose James J. Davis, former Secretary of Labor under Hoover, for the Republican nomination for senator. His admirers were already demanding that Butler run for governor.

"I am not going to run for the Senate or governorship," he growled to newspaper friends, "and then have the politicians laugh at me." But Pinchot's entreaties were too strong and persistent, and Butler reluctantly agreed.

Stumping the state, he appealed to Republican voters with a platform promising jobs for the unemployed and home property loans for debtors. Campaigning for a bonus bill, he placed all his decorations and uniforms in a vault, publicly vowing never to wear them again until soldiers got their bonus. Although he was personally popular, two issues he campaigned for in 1932—Prohibition and the soldiers' bonus—were not.

Despite receiving half a million votes, he was defeated. Paul Comly French of the Philadelphia *Record* revealed that Governor Pinchot had set Butler up for defeat to eliminate him as a political threat, making a secret deal to support Davis. The Pinchot political machine had been used against Butler in key election districts.

Reporter Jesse Laventhol, later city editor of the Philadelphia *Record*, who had been Butler's press secretary during the campiagn, told the author, "Butler's sponsors failed him . . . , trading off votes for Davis in return for electing certain state senators to give the governor control of that body."

So Smedley Butler never went to Congress like his father.

22

In the early summer of 1932 over twenty thousand veterans and their families joined in a Bonus Army march to Washington, camping on the edge of the Capital to demand payment of a two-billion-dollar cash bonus to all veterans. The House, under pressure, quickly passed the Patman Bonus Bill on June 17, but the Republican Senate rejected it, 62 to 18.

Butler was indignant at the failure of Congress to honor America's pledge to its fighting men and was thoroughly disgusted with Hoover's failure to do anything about the plight of the nation except issue optimistic reports that prosperity was "just around the corner."

On June 30, while the Democratic convention was in session, he announced that he might, for the first time in his life, vote Democratic "if the right man is nominated for President." It was no secret that he saw the right man as New York's governor, Franklin D. Roosevelt, who had already broadcast an impressive speech on the need of the American Government to discover its "forgotten man."

When Roosevelt won the nomination, pledging a New Deal along with the repeal of Prohibition, Butler wired him, "We salute your nomination as one of the greatest blessings granted any nation in an hour of desperate need." He offered to help F.D.R.'s campaign any way he could, and Roosevelt asked him to get in touch with Democratic campaign manager James A. Farley, or Roosevelt's chief secretary, Louis Howe. Butler soon began stumping for F.D.R. In a speech before the General Society of Mechanics and Tradesmen in New York on July 7 he warned that the government had to be rescued from "the clutches of the greedy and dishonest":

Today, with all our wealth, a deathly gloom hangs over us. Today we appear to be divided. There has developed, through the past few years, a new Tory class, a group that believes that the nation, its resources and its man-power, was provided by the Almighty for its own special use and profit. . . . On the other side is the great mass of the American people who still believe in the Declaration of Independence and in the Constitution of the United States.

This Tory group, through its wealth, its power and its influence, has obtained a firm grip on our government, to the detriment of our people and the well-being of our nation. We will prove to the world that we meant what we said a century and a half ago—that this government was instituted not only to secure to our people the rights of life, liberty and the pursuit of happiness, but the right to eat and to all our willing millions the right to work.

A lecture bureau urged him to undertake a national speaking tour of 100,000 miles through the United States. He agreed, not only to earn the money involved but also because he saw the trip as a way to get to know his fellow Americans better. He knew more about the Cacos of Haiti than the residents of Michigan Boulevard, more about the thinking of Nicaraguans and Chinese than of Manhattanites and Californians. As "a stranger to my native land and to my fellow citizens," he felt a strong compulsion to "see America last" and learn about them, too. So he began visiting over one hundred cities in forty-eight states, "keeping my eyes and ears open all the time."

Years of delivering training talks to his troops and pep talks before and during battle had made him an articulate extemporaneous speaker. Without a note to refer to he held audiences spellbound, and each time he delivered a talk it was different. A fast thinker on his feet, he spoke in the colorful idiom of everyday language, which he used with the impact of a shower of arrows.

He was only partially successful in his attempts to civilianize his colorful barracks argot. One Milwaukee newspaper, describing a speech he made at a First Methodist Episcopal church in September, 1932, ran a story headlined: BUTLER TALKS IN CHURCH,

USES NICE LANGUAGE. "Only one 'hell' and two 'damns' spiced his remarks throughout the evening."

What he heard and saw on his tour convinced him that Americans were hungry for a change in the administration, especially for a turn away from foreign affairs to home problems. But he found no indication that Main Street America either wanted revolutionary change or thought it likely, despite alarm over a Red menace in the conservative press.

"I held personal conversations with more than two thousand persons in all walks of life," he said on October 2, 1932, after his tour, "and they gave me a new and true insight into the people of America. I learned that the average American is convinced that no change in the form of our government is necessary or advisable."

The attempt by conservatives to smear "anyone who utters a progressive thought" as a Red, he pointed out, was helping a "handful of agitators in their vain efforts to foment disorder and discontent with our form of government." He branded Republican warnings that a Democratic victory would turn America socialist an absurd myth.

When a new political group called the Roosevelt Republican Organization was formed in Philadelphia, Butler was asked to take a leading role in it. Louis Howe assured him that Roosevelt would be most grateful for any help he could give the governor in that capacity.

A week before Election Day Butler made a slashing attack on Hoover in a speech to an enthusiastic rally of Queens, New York, veterans, describing himself as "a member of the Hoover-for-Ex-President League because Hoover used gas and bayonets on unarmed human beings."

"Nobody has any business occupying the White House who doesn't love his own people," he declared, adding, "I was raised Republican, but I was born American. I have no ring through my nose, and I vote for whom I please."

He insisted that the bonus must be paid: "The bonus is an amount of money that the American people owe the soldier, but anybody demanding it is charged with lack of patriotism. During the war nobody charged the officers of the Bethlehem Steel

Corporation or any of the other corporations who received enormous bonuses with 'raiding the Treasury.'"

American big business, he accused, had been responsible for United States entry into World War I and was now "getting ready to start another one in the East."

On November 8 Butler's choice for President won, and the House of Representatives went Democratic by a margin of three to one. A chorus of newspaper fury and frustration reflected the dismay of banking and industrial interests over Roosevelt's election.

Less than three weeks before the President-elect's inauguration, an unsuccessful attempt was made to assassinate him at Miami. Could the assassin's bullet possibly have been negotiated for, Butler speculated, by a big-business cabal that hated Roosevelt and dreaded a New Deal?

23

Many veterans' posts now started a movement to have Butler appointed administrator of the U.S. Veterans Bureau in January, 1933, and sent resolutions to Roosevelt to this effect.

Soon after the N.R.A. began, General Hugh Johnson asked Butler to work with him in administering the program. Butler thanked him but refused, explaining, "I don't want to be tied up with anything I don't know about."

Meanwhile he watched with fascination the swift unfolding of developments in the New Deal from the time Roosevelt declared at his inauguration on March 4, 1933, "Let me assert my firm belief that the only thing we have to fear is fear itself."

Next day the new President proclaimed a national bank holiday and embargoed the exportation of gold. The famous "Hundred Days Congress," in a special session called by the President, swiftly enacted into law the principal policies of the

New Deal. As the American people stirred with new hope that at last the government was beginning to fight the nightmare Depression, Butler noted with satisfaction that the bankers and industrialists of the nation were horrified.

Meanwhile between July and December he had been pursued and wooed by Jerry MacGuire, the bond salesman for Grayson M.-P. Murphy and Company, who had sought to enlist him in the schemes of the financial group he represented. It was with some relief that he was temporarily freed from these persistent attentions on December 1, when MacGuire went abroad on an unexplained mission for his backers.

Early in December, 1933, Butler began touring the country for the V.F.W. and made headlines by speaking out with characteristic bluntness to attack the leadership of the American Legion. He told a large gathering of veterans in New Orleans that the V.F.W. commander "would not sell out his men as the officers in charge of the American Legion have."

Sharing the platform with Senator Huey Long, he urged Long to concentrate on fighting for the veterans' bonus and forget less important matters. "What the hell do you know about the gold standard?" he challenged Long. "Don't pay any attention to what the newspapers say. Stand by your friends and to hell with the rest of them!"

Taking Long's political demagoguery at face value, he believed him to be sincere in his advocacy of a redistribution of national wealth and praised him as a man "with nerve enough to maintain a fight against Wall Street." He urged the veterans to "make Wall Street pay, to take Wall Street by the throat and shake it up." If they wanted to get the bonus that had been promised them, they would have "to organize . . . to get together . . . to do as the veterans of other wars have done."

It was a fighting speech in the classic populist vein, and it sparked national controversy. The *Cincinnati Times Star*, a newspaper controlled by American Legion officials, angrily accused Butler of advocating a "soldier dictatorship."

Interviewed afterward in Atlanta about his attack on the Legion, he stuck by his guns and added fuel to the fire by stating grimly, "I've never known one leader of the American Legion who has never sold them out!"

As for the *Star's* accusation that he wanted a military dictatorship, he replied with a speech denouncing crackpot rightist movements that advocated such a course for America. His suspicions about Clark and Maguire were obviously very much on his mind when he made it.

"To many it may seem strange for a military man to denounce dictatorship," he declared. "Generally it is the military men who are advocates of this stern measure. . . . But we do not need a dictator and we would not have one anyway, because our temperament and traditions forbid it."

He made it clear that he was stumping the country only on behalf of the ordinary "forgotten soldier," just as F.D.R. had crusaded for the "forgotten man."

He told reporters, "I went on the retired list after thirty-three years of making wars, to rock and rock. So many former soldiers came to me with their pathetic stories that I bounced out of retirement. All we soldiers are asking is that the nation give us the same break that is being given the manufacturers, the bankers, the industrialists. . . . Jimmie [Van Zandt] and I are going around the country trying to educate the soldiers out of the sucker class."

If American Legion officialdom was furious at Butler's charges, the rank and file were not. Typical of the barrage of fan mail cheering him on was a letter from a Los Angeles Legionnaire: "Every word you say is true, and I, as an ex-soldier and one of the rank and file, respectfully request that you assume the active leadership of the ex-servicemen. These five million men and their families need you for a leader and will stick through thick and thin. The leadership of the American Legion voice actually the opposite of the true wishes of the membership. . . . Sir, the ex-serviceman of the United States is at your command."

But Butler's first bombshell was mild compared to his next broadside against the establishment, made in his Atlanta speech to the V.F.W. the next day. *The New York Times* featured it under the headline GEN. BUTLER LAYS WAR TO BANKERS.

War was "largely a matter of money," he told the veterans who had gathered to hear him. "Bankers lend money to foreign countries and when they cannot repay the President sends Marines to get it. I know—I've been in eleven of these expeditions." The world was not yet through with war, he warned, but "we can help get rid of it when we conscript capital along with men."

He pointed out that soldiers who went through the horrors of war were not the same when they came back, adding vehemently, "We ought to make those responsible pay through the nose." That was why the V.F.W. was calling for immediate payment of the soldiers' bonus, in addition to compensation asked for disabled veterans and pensions for veterans' widows and orphans.

Ex-servicemen were made the butt of an Economy Act passed by Congress, Butler charged, because "the principle of taking care of soldiers is nothing at all but an old-age pension to which the nation eventually will come, and the bankers don't want it." He added caustically, "If Charles Dawes got ninety million dollars for a sick bank, soldiers ought to get it for sick comrades." Pointing out that veterans could muster twenty million votes among themselves and their families, he urged them to use this pressure at the polls to force decent care of the disabled.

If the "Democrats take care of you," he advised, "keep them in. If not—put 'em out!" He warned veterans not to believe "the propaganda capital circulates" in the press, which he condemned as largely capitalist-controlled. "The paper that takes the part of the soldier," he charged, "loses advertising."

His concern for disabled veterans was not mere rhetoric. He met many of them in the eighteen veterans' hospitals he visited during his tour of the country. His walks through the wards to talk with them filled him with an angry grief. In his days of combat he had seen many men killed and wounded. But the crushing impact of seeing fifty thousand young men gathered together in "living graveyards," forgotten by their country and the people for whom they had sacrificed arms, legs, faces, and minds, moved him to rage against the old men in power who had doomed them to lives of empty despair.

"Seventeen years ago they were the pick of the nation," he wrote grimly. ". . . In the government hospital at Marion, Ohio, 1,800 wrecks are in pens. Five hundred are in a barrack, under nurses, with wires all around the buildings and enclosing the porches. All have been mentally destroyed. They don't even look like human beings." He added in cold rage, "A careful study of their expressions is highly recommended as an aid to the understanding of the art of war."

On February 19, 1934, all the disabled veterans in the Veterans Administration hospital at Albuquerque signed a petition to Butler, urging him to testify in Congress to demand passage of the Bonus Bill and restoration of adequate compensation to disabled veterans. He replied, "I am doing everything humanly possible to help the veterans," and urged them to swamp Congress with letters and postcards.

George K. Brobeck, legislative representative for the V.F.W., wrote Butler:

> Every member of our National Staff is deeply appreciative of your fine cooperation in our battle for the disabled men. I can think of no greater service that America's military leaders might dedicate themselves to than the one you have carried on so unceasingly, and I wish to repeat what Admiral R. E. Coontz said to me the other day. . . . "You always know where Butler is and whether you like it or not, he is always on the level."

24

Army posts he visited often hailed the ex-Marine with a military band, partly a tribute to his fame as commandant of the Army camp at Pontanezen, but even more for his championship of the Bonus Army and veterans' hospitals. Wherever he spoke to veterans' meetings and rallies, enthusiastic ex-soldiers invariably outnumbered ex-Marines in his audience.

In his speeches for the V.F.W. he continued to plead their cause, along with assailing war-makers and demanding payment of the veterans' bonus. In March he was urged to attend the Indiana convention of the V.F.W. at Marion, which had the largest veterans' hospital in the United States.

John R. James, its chairman, asked him to come and "say something to these poor boys here to cheer them up in their lonesome surroundings. We need you here at this time more than any other person in the country. The Veterans all love you and look to you to guide them and tell them what to do. . . . I am unable to mention your name in a meeting without getting a round of applause."

He was gratified to read on April 12, 1934, that the Senate had voted an inquiry into the manufacture of and traffic in arms. Senator Gerald P. Nye, of North Dakota, as chairman of the Senate Munitions Investigating Committee. began holding public hearings stressing the heavy profits made by American financiers and armament-makers during World War I.

The Nye Committee produced shock waves by exposing the pressures exerted by the armament industry on the government to take America into that war. Oswald Garrison Villard, editor-publisher of *The Nation*, wrote, "I never dreamed that I should live to see the time when public opinion in the United States would be practically united in recognizing that we were lied to and deceived into going to war . . . and when Congress would actually put a stop to those processes by which Wilson, House, Lansing and J. P. Morgan and Company brought us into the war." The Nye investigation, continuing until 1936, strengthened isolationist sentiment in the United States and inspired a series of neutrality acts during 1935–1937.

Following the hearings closely, Butler was tremendously impressed and influenced by their disclosures. They also confirmed his suspicions that big business—Standard Oil, United Fruit, the sugar trust, the big banks—had been behind most of the military interventions he had been ordered to lead. In a broadcast over Philadelphia radio station WCAU he described his experiences in "the raping of little nations to collect money for big industries" that had large foreign investments.

Authentication for this view came thirty-eight years later when Milan B. Skacel, President of the Chamber of Commerce of Latin America in the United States, acknowledged on October 16, 1971, "Most of us freely admit that some of the past business practices of U.S. firms in Latin America were unconscionable."

Testifying before the Nye Committee, Eugene G. Grace, president of Bethlehem Steel, admitted that his corporation had received almost three million dollars in bonuses during World War I. He nervously expressed concern that such a revelation might "leave a bad taste" in the mouths of veterans who had served their country for a dollar a day, but nevertheless labeled their bonus movement an "unfortunate" enterprise.

"Bethlehem Steel made ten times as much money during the war as before," Butler roared over WCAU, "and this band of pirates calls the soldiers Treasury raiders!"

He urged reporter friends to get transcripts of the Nye hearings and read them, insisting, "You fellows ought to know this stuff." One wanted to know what had prompted him, even before the Nye disclosures, to "pull the whiskers off" the face of commercialism behind the pomp and patriotic glory of war.

"As a youngster, I loved the excitement of battle," he replied. "It's lots of fun, you know, and it's nice to strut around in front of your wife—or somebody else's wife—and display your medals, and your uniform. But there's another side to it, and that's why I have decided to devote the rest of my life to 'pulling off the whiskers.'"

During his V.F.W. lecture tour he met an old war comrade, G. D. Morgan, who was now adjutant of the V.F.W. post in Hazlehurst, Mississippi, and confided in him about the scheming of MacGuire, Doyle, and Clark. On May 14, 1934, Morgan wrote him, "My Dear Smed: I wish you would send me the Statistics as near as possible that you have on those two Ex-Service men and the Banker. We are getting in the middle of a hot Congressional Campaign and one Senator has been very adverse to our cause, so we want to shoot the works."

That month the Farmer-Labor party of Colorado urged Butler

to become the party's candidate for President in 1936, stating, "We know of no other man in the U.S. that is as well informed on the situation with the nerve to carry out, make possible these reforms, and that has the confidence of the masses. The people need you badly."

25

In August, when Jerry MacGuire returned from Europe, the bond salesman had insisted upon another meeting with Butler on a matter "of the utmost importance." And at their discussion in the empty restaurant of Philadelphia's Bellevue Hotel, MacGuire had sought to get him to agree to lead a Fascist coup to capture the White House.

While smoking out the plot as far as he could and then getting reporter Paul Comly French to investigate it for corroborative evidence in preparation to exposing it, Butler continued his crusade against war and on behalf of justice for the veterans. Once more he found himself running into censorship trouble.

Radio station WAVE, carrying his speech on October 3 to the V.F.W. national convention, cut him off the air for "objectionable language" used before "a mixed audience." The convention unanimously adopted a resolution condemning WAVE for "unceremoniously curtailing the address of General Butler, an honored and beloved member of this organization."

Louis G. Burd, Adjutant of the Butte, Montana, post, wrote him:

> . . . This assertion is just some more of the same old hooey to mislead the public. In our opinion you were cut off simply because you are one man before the public who has the courage to . . . give the public the true facts that they hunger to hear, and in a language of which there is no misunderstanding. . . . Be assured, General, that this effort

to prevent the searchlight from being turned onto the malefactors of great wealth and veterans' enemies will prove futile [to stop] your untiring fight for justice for the veterans and the common people.

On Armistice Day Butler was vigorously applauded for a speech to a New York Jewish congregation appealing to all religious groups to "stop the war racket." He created a sensation in the press by flatly declaring that he would never again carry a rifle on foreign soil. He proposed two constitutional amendments. The first would make it impossible for war to be declared except by the exclusive vote of those physically able to fight. The second would prevent United States warships from going beyond a two-hundred-mile limit, and airplanes from going more than five hundred miles from the American coastline.

On the same night from Richmond, Virginia, American Legion Commander Frank N. Belgrano, Jr., a banker, indirectly replied in an angry speech attacking "radical tendencies":

"Some, it would seem, have forgotten that our country requires of us high and willing duty today as it did when we went forth to fight an enemy in the open. We are facing a new and more dangerous foe today. It has seeped quietly into our country and whispered into the ears of our workers and our people everywhere that our ideals of government are out of date. We of the Legion are mobilized to meet that enemy and we are calling upon loyal Americans everywhere to join us in ridding our country of this menace."

To Butler that sounded suspiciously like the reams of propaganda the American Liberty League was now sending out, along with lecturers, to denounce the "socialism" of the Roosevelt Administration and call for a return to the doctrines of a laissez-faire economy.

The League's campaign failed to make any impact in the congressional elections of 1934, however, and F.D.R. won an enormous Democratic majority in both houses of Congress.

Meanwhile gossip was spreading around Washington that the American Legion was going to provide the nucleus of a Fascist army that would seize the Capital. John L. Spivak, a crack reporter whose specialty was exposing American Fascists and of whom Lincoln Steffens once said, "He is the best of us," heard about it from an eminent Washington correspondent with excellent sources of information and decided to investigate it.

The rumors also reached the McCormack-Dickstein Committee of the House of Representatives. This was the first House Un-American Activities Committee, at that time equally oriented against Fascist and Communist activities. Under Representative John W. McCormack, later Speaker of the House, it spent considerable time and energy unmasking Fascist agents in America. Not until 1939, when a new version of HUAC was reconstituted under the chairmanship of Martin Dies, did this committee become infamous for its relentless persecution directed almost exclusively against liberals and leftists of every persuasion, while ignoring subversion on the right.

One of the McCormack-Dickstein Committee's investigators contacted Butler to ask if there was any truth in the rumors that he could shed light on. Now that he had Paul Comly French's testimony to corroborate his own, Butler decided that there was little more to be gained by playing MacGuire along; between French and himself, the plotters' secret plans had been ferreted out to a significant extent.

Come hell or high water, press ridicule or denunciations terming him a madman, he was now determined to testify before the committee and spread the plot for a Fascist takeover of the United States all over the front pages. He would destroy it before it had a chance to crush democracy in the country he loved and had served all his life.

But would he be believed, even with the support of French's testimony? What if he wasn't? Worse, what if he had waited too long to unravel the whole sordid story, and it was already too late to stop the conspirators?

Major General Smedley Darlington Butler (*Marine Corps photo*)

Smedley at seven, with doting aunts Rose Darlington (left) and Mrs. Bertha Pierce Mott, at the Butler family home near West Chester, Pennsylvania

Smedley (right) at nine with younger brother, Samuel

Marines at Portsmouth, New Hampshire, 1898, following their return from Spanish-American War (*Marine Corps photo*)

hero at nineteen, Cap-
n Butler sports a mous-
he when invalided
me from the Boxer
mpaign in China.

With wife, Ethel, 1905

Major Butler and his battalion salute General George Goethals, builder of the Panama Canal, at Camp Elliott in the Canal Zone, 1909.

Building the Panama Canal, 1910

Vera Cruz campaign, Mexico, 1914; Butler at right; close friends Lieutenant Colonel W. C. Neville (center) and Colonel John A. Lejeune (next to Butler), both later Marine Commandants (*Marine Corps photo*)

Representative Thomas Butler visits his son at Panama, 1911.

With wife and children, Haiti, 1915

A lieutenant colonel in the Marine Corps, Butler also becomes Commandant of the Haitian Gendarmerie, with rank of major general, December, 1915 to May, 1918. (*Marine Corps photo*)

General John Pershing decorates Major General Butler with Army Distinguished Service Medal in 1919. He was also awarded Navy Distinguished Service Medal and French Order of the Black Star, while already holding two Medals of Honor.

One of the duckboard streets built by General Butler
in the mud of Camp Pontanezen at Brest, France, 1918

Secretary of the Navy Edwin
Denby and Butler at Quan-
tico, May, 1922 (*Marine
Corps photo*)

Butler (left) on the march
to Battle of Wilderness maneuvers, 1924. Only the two
stars on his collar distinguish
him from rank-and-file leathernecks. (*Marine Corps
photo*)

As Philadelphia's Director of Public Safety, on loan from the Marines, 1924–1925, General Butler discusses police problems with Superintendent of Police William B. Mills.

As Director of Public Safety, Butler greets Al Smith, Governor of New York.

Called upon as consultant for the film "Tell It to the Marines," made in San Diego in 1926, General Butler supervises authenticity of a scene with Lon Chaney, Eleanor Boardman, and William Haines.

Butler on Marine tractor with a Chinese general and province governor, at Peichang, China, cooperating to build the Tientsin-Peking motor road in October, 1928

Driving the last four spikes into "Butler Bridge," built by the Marines at Peichang, in October, 1928, to replace a bridge on the Tientsin-Peking road washed out by storms

Representatives of grateful Chinese of the Peking and Tientsin Districts award General Butler their highest honor, an Umbrella of Ten Thousand Blessings, in 1928, signifying appreciation of the people under the shelter of a good leader. Inscriptions in Chinese read: "You have saved a part of Tientsin from trouble. Your kindness is always in the mind of the people. You love Chinese as well as your own people." (*Marine Corps photo*)

THE RETURN OF THE NATIVE
(with everything but the hot stove)

WELCOME HOME!

While General Butler served in China in 1927–1928, grateful Philadelphians presented a plaque in his honor to the Navy Department, commemorating his services as Director of Public Safety. Left of the tablet his mother; to her left Marine Commandant Lejeune. Far right, ex-Governor Gifford Pinchot, of Pennsylvania; to his left Representative Thomas Butler, the general's father. The plaque now stands in Philadelphia's City Hall. (*Underwood & Underwood photo*)

Cartoonist Charles Bell depicts the return from China in 1929 of General Butler loaded down with the awards presented to him by the grateful Chinese.

As Commandant of Quantico in January, 1929, General Butler returns to cheer on the famous football team of the Marines, which he developed. (*Marine Corps photo*)

With son Thomas Richard Butler, February, 1929, at the family home in West Chester, Pennsylvania

Phoenix Gazette, Wednesday, February 4, 1931

NOT DOING SO WELL WITH HIS "BUTLING"

I MUST HAVE SPILLED THE BEANS!

MUSSOLINI

SMEDLEY BUTLER

PHILADELPHIA SPEECH

An Arizona newspaper cartoonist looks at the controversy caused by General Butler in his speech attacking Mussolini in January, 1931, bringing about attempts to court-martial him.

Last days at Quantico, getting ready for civilian life in 1931. His car is a La Salle.

Retired at his new home in Newtown Square, Pennsylvania, Butler puts away his uniform, cap, and sword and prepares for a lecture tour of the country, campaigning to keep America out of war. (*International News Photos, Inc.*)

THE POT AND THE KETTLE

In the February 16, 1935, edition of the *Philadelphia Record*, cartoonist Jerry Doyle depicts the embarrassment of wealthy Americans seeking to convince the McCormack–Dickstein Committee that soapboxing Reds are a menace to America, with Butler proving that they are the real threat to democracy by arming and financing Fascist plots.

George Seldes, veteran foreign correspondent, author, and editor of anti-Fascist news weekly *In Fact,* helped expose the American Liberty League as a fountainhead of pro-Fascist movements and plots in America.

John L. Spivak, former foreign correspondent for International News Service, who uncovered suppressed testimony of the McCormack–Dickstein hearings on the plot to seize the White House (*Drawing by Ben Solowey*)

Former Speaker of the House John McCormack, who headed the McCormack-Dickstein Committee that heard testimony of the plot and verified General Butler's charges

Time out from crusading for peace; a visit to son-in-law Lieutenant John Wehle (left) and grandchildren, August, 1937

Launching of the U.S.S. *Butler,* a destroyer named after him, in February, 1942

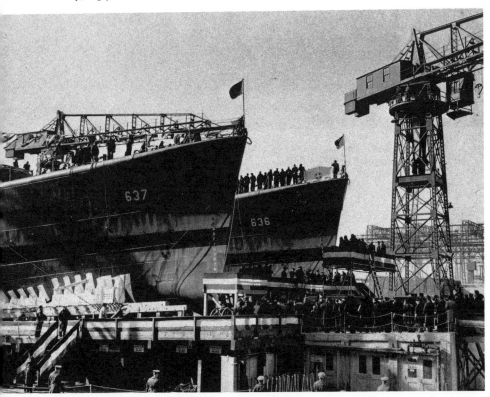

Ethel Butler presents her late husband's sword to the Marine Corps museum in Washington in 1953.

PART THREE

The
Conspiracy
Explodes

1

The McCormack-Dickstein Committee agreed to listen to Butler's story in a secret executive session in New York City on November 20, 1934. The two cochairman of the committee were Representative John McCormack, of Massachusets, and New York Representative Samuel Dickstein, who later became a New York State Supreme Court justice. Butler's testimony, developed in two hours of questions and answers, was recorded in full.

Simultaneously Paul Comly French broke the story in the Stern papers, the Philadelphia *Record* and the New York *Post*. Under the headline "$3,000,000 Bid for Fascist Army Bared," he wrote:

> Major General Smedley D. Butler revealed today that he has been asked by a group of wealthy New York brokers to lead a Fascist movement to set up a dictatorship in the United States.
>
> General Butler, ranking major general of the Marine Corps up to his retirement three years ago, told his story today at a secret session of the Congressional Committee on Un-American Activities.

McCormack opened the hearing by first noting that General Butler had been in the Marine Corps thirty-three years and four months and had received the Congressional Medal of Honor twice, establishing his integrity and credibility as a witness. Then he invited the general to "just go ahead and tell in your own way all that you know about an attempted Fascist movement in this country."

"May I preface my remarks," Butler began, "by saying, sir,

that I have one interest in all of this, and that is to try to do my best to see that a democracy is maintained in this country?"

"Nobody who has either read about or known about General Butler," replied McCormack promptly, "would have anything but that understanding."

Butler then gave detailed testimony about everything that had happened in connection with the plot, from the first visit of Mac-Guire and Doyle on July 1, 1933.

Some of his testimony was not released in the official record of the hearings, for reasons that will be discussed later, but was nevertheless ferreted out, copied, and made public by reporter John L. Spivak. This censored testimony is indicated by the symbol † to distinguish it from the official testimony eventually released by the McCormack-Dickstein Committee. The same was true of testimony given by reporter Paul Comly French, who followed Butler as a witness, and the same symbol (†) indicates the censored portions.*

Butler first described the attempts made by MacGuire and Doyle to persuade him to go to the American Legion convention and make a speech they had prepared for him.

> BUTLER: . . . they were very desirous of unseating the royal family in control of the American Legion, at the convention to be held in Chicago, and very anxious to have me take part in it. They said that they were not in sympathy with the . . . present administration's treatment of the soldiers. . . . They said, "We represent the plain soldiers. . . . We want you to come there and stampede the convention in a speech and help us in our fight to dislodge the royal family."

He told of MacGuire's revelation that he was the chairman

---

* The reader who wishes to examine the official testimony is referred to the government report, *Investigation of Nazi Propaganda Activities and Investigation of Certain Other Propaganda Activities: Public Hearings Before the Special Committee on Un-American Activities, House of Representatives, Seventy-third Congress, Second Session, at Washington, D.C., December 29, 1934. Hearings No. 73-D.C.-6, Part 1.* Extracts of the censored testimony are revealed in the books *A Man in His Time*, by John L. Spivak, and *1000 Americans*, by George Seldes.

of the Legion's "distinguished guest committee," on the staff of National Commander Louis Johnson, and that at MacGuire's suggestion Johnson had put Butler's name down as one of the distinguished guests to be invited to the convention.

> † BUTLER: [MacGuire said] that Johnson had been taken this list, presented by MacGuire, of distinguished guests, to the White House for approval; that Louis Howe, one of the secretaries of the President, had crossed my name off and said that I was not to be invited—that the President would not have it.

This tale had struck Butler as peculiar, since the President had been grateful for the general's assistance in winning Republican votes for him away from Hoover, and their relations had always been cordial and warm.

> BUTLER: I thought I smelled a rat, right away—that they were trying to get me mad—to get my goat. I said nothing. . . .
> CHAIRMAN: When you say you smelled a rat, you mean you had an idea that they were not telling the truth?
> BUTLER: I could not reconcile . . . their desire to serve the ordinary man in the ranks, with their other aims. They did not seem to be the same. It looked to me as if they were trying to embarrass the administration in some way. . . . I was just fishing to see what they had in mind. So many queer people come to my house all the time and I like to feel them all out.

MacGuire had told him, Butler revealed, that invitation or no invitation, he and his supporters had figured out a way for Butler to address the Legion convention.

> BUTLER: I said, "How is that, without being invited?"
> They said, "Well, you are to come as a delegate from Hawaii."
> I said, "I do not live in Hawaii."
> "Well, it does not make any difference. There is to be no delegate from one of the American Legion posts there in

Honolulu, and we have arranged to have you appointed by cable, by radio, to represent them at the convention. . . .

I said, "Yes; but I will not go in the back door."

They said, "That will not be the back door. You must come."

I said, "No; I will not do this."

"Well," they said, "are you in sympathy with unhorsing the royal family?"

I said, "Yes; because they have been selling out the common soldier in this Legion for years. These fellows have been getting political plums and jobs and cheating the enlisted man in the Army, and I am for putting them out. But I cannot do it by going in through the back door."

"Well," they said, "we are going to get them out. We will arrange this."

Butler described the second visit of MacGuire and Doyle a month later, at which time MacGuire had unfolded a new plan they had developed to get Butler to the speaker's platform at the Chicago convention of the Legion.

BUTLER: . . . I was to get two or three hundred legionnaires from around that part of the country and bring them on a special train to Chicago with me. . . . they would sit around in the audience, be planted here and there. . . . I was to appear in the gallery. These planted fellows were to begin to cheer and start a stampede and yell for a speech. Then I was to go to the platform and make a speech. I said, "Make a speech about what?"

"Oh," they said, "we have one here."

. . . They pulled out this speech. They said, "We will leave it here with you to read over, and you see if you can get these fellows to come."

I said, "Listen. These friends of mine that I know around here, even if they wanted to go, could not afford to go. It would cost them a hundred to a hundred and fifty dollars to go out there and stay for five days and come back."

They said, "Well, we will pay that."

I said, "How can you pay it? You are disabled soldiers. How do you get the money to do that?"

"Oh, we have friends. We will get the money."

Then I began to smell a rat for fair. . . .

To test the seriousness of their purpose and the extent of their backing, he had challenged their claim to have access to the funds they claimed to have.

> BUTLER: . . . they hauled out a bank deposit book and showed me, I think it was $42,000 in deposits on that occasion, and on another occasion it was $64,000. . . .
> CHAIRMAN: Do you know on what bank that was?
> BUTLER: I do not. They just flipped the pages over. Now, I have had some experience as a policeman in Philadelphia. I wanted to get to the bottom of this thing and not scare them off, because I felt then that they had something real. They had so much money and a limousine. Wounded soldiers do not have limousines or that kind of money. They said, "We will pay the bill. Look around and see if you cannot get two or three hundred men and we will bring them out there and we will have accommodations for them."

Butler described MacGuire's third visit, without Doyle, during which the bond salesman had inquired as to his progress in rounding up soldiers to take to the convention. Pointing out to MacGuire that the speech given him urged a return by the United States to the gold standard, Butler had demanded to know what that had to do with the ostensible reasons for which he was being asked to go to Chicago.

> BUTLER: . . . MacGuire had said, "We want to see the soldiers' bonus paid in gold. We do not want the soldier to have rubber money or paper money. We want the gold. That is the reason for this speech."

Butler had then sought to get MacGuire to reveal the source of the funds on deposit in his name.

> BUTLER: He said that it was given to him by nine men, that the biggest contributor had given $9,000 and that the donations ran all the way from $2,500 to $9,000.
> I said, "What is the object?"
> He said the object was to take care of the rank and file of the soldiers, to get them their bonus and get them properly cared for.

Well, I knew that people who had $9,000 to give away were not in favor of the bonus. That looked fishy right away.

He gave me the names of two men; Colonel Murphy, Grayson M.-P. Murphy, for whom he worked, was one. He said, "I work for him. I am in his office."

I said to him, "How did you happen to be associated with that kind of people if you are for the ordinary soldier and his bonus and his proper care? You know damn well that these bankers are not going to swallow that. There is something in this, Jerry MacGuire, besides what you have told me. I can see that."

He said, "Well, I am a business man. I have got a wife and family to keep, and they took good care of them, and if you would take my advice you would be a business man, too."

I said, "What has Murphy got to do with this?"

"Well," he said, "don't you know who he is?"

I said, "Just indirectly. He is a broker in New York. But I do not know any of his connections."

"Well," he said, "he is the man who underwrote the formation of the American Legion for $125,000. He underwrote it, paid for the field work of organizing it, and had not gotten all of it back yet."

"That is the reason he makes the kings, is it? He has still got a club over their heads."

"He is on our side, though. He wants to see the soldiers cared for."

Butler revealed that he had then expressed sharply critical sentiments about the Legion. He later discovered that these remarks had been expunged from the record.

† BUTLER: "Is he [Murphy] responsible, too, for making the Legion a strikebreaking outfit?"

"No, no. He does not control anything in the Legion now."

I said: "You know very well that it is nothing but a strikebreaking outfit used by capital for that purpose and that is the reason we have all those big clubhouses and that is the reason I pulled out from it. They have been using these dumb soldiers to break strikes."

He said: "Murphy hasn't anything to do with that. He is a very fine fellow."

I said, "I do not doubt that, but there is some reason for his putting $125,000 into this."

2

In September, 1933, when he had gone to Newark for a convention of the 29th Division, Butler testified, MacGuire had unexpectedly showed up at his hotel to remind him that the time for the American Legion convention was rapidly approaching and to ask whether he was finally ready to take a contingent of veterans to Chicago.

BUTLER: I said, "No; I am not going to Chicago."

"Why not?"

I said, "You people are bluffing. You have not got any money," whereupon he took out a big wallet, out of his hip pocket, and a great, big mass of thousand dollar bills and threw them out on the bed.

I said, "What's all this?"

He says, "This is for you, for expenses. You will need some money to pay them."

"How much money have you got there?"

He said, $18,000."

"Where did you get those thousand dollar bills?"

"Oh," he said, "last night some contributions were made. I just have not had a chance to deposit them, so I brought them along with me."

I said, "Don't you try to give me any thousand dollar bill. Remember, I was a cop once. Every one of the numbers on these bills has been taken. I know you people and what you are trying to do. You are just trying to get me by the neck. If I try to cash one of those thousand dollar bills, you would have me by the neck."

"Oh," he said, "we can change them into smaller denominations."

I said, "You put that money away before somebody walks in here and sees that money around, because I do not want to be tied up with it at all. I told you distinctly I am not going to take these men to Chicago."

"Well, are you going yourself?"

I said, "Oh, I do not know. But I know one thing. Somebody is using you. You are a wounded man. You are a bluejacket. You have got a silver plate in your head. I looked you up. . . . You are being used by somebody, and I want to know the fellows who are using you. I am not going to talk to you any more. You are only an agent. I want some of the principals."

He said, "Well, I will send one of them over to see you."

I said, "Who?" He said, "I will send Mr. Clark."

"Who is Mr. Clark?"

"Well, he is one of our people. He put up some money."

"Who is he?"

"Well, his name is R. S. Clark. He is a banker. He used to be in the Army."

"How old a man is he?" He told me.

"Would it be possible that he was a second lieutenant in the Ninth Infantry in China during the Boxer campaign?"

He said, "That is the fellow."

He was known as the "millionaire lieutenant" and was sort of batty, sort of queer, did all sorts of extravagant things. He used to go exploring around China and wrote a book on it, on explorations. He was never taken seriously by anybody. But he had a lot of money. An aunt and an uncle died and left him $10,000,000.

Having established contact with one of the plot's principals, Butler testified, he had been visited by Clark within the week and invited to travel in a private car to the Chicago convention with the millionaire, who revealed that he would arrange an opportunity for Butler to deliver the gold-standard speech.

BUTLER: He said, "You have got the speech?" I said, "Yes. These fellows, Doyle and MacGuire, gave me the speech." I said, "They wrote a hell of a good speech, too." He said,

"Did those fellows say that they wrote that speech?" I said, "Yes; they did. They told me that that was their business, writing speeches." He laughed and said, "That speech cost a lot of money."

In testimony afterward censored, Butler revealed that the speech had apparently been written for the millionaire by the chief attorney for J. P. Morgan and Company, who had been the 1924 Democratic candidate for President.

> † Butler: Now either from what he said then or from what MacGuire had said, I got the impression that the speech had been written by John W. Davis—one or the other of them told me that.

Clark had been amused, Butler testified, that MacGuire and Doyle had claimed the authorship. Butler had pointed out that a speech urging a return to the gold standard did not seem to be relevant to the reasons he was being asked to go to the convention. Clark had reiterated MacGuire's explanation that he wanted to see the soldiers' bonus paid in gold-backed currency, not in inflated paper money.

> Butler: "Yes," I said, "but it looks as if it were a big-business speech. There is something funny about that speech, Mr. Clark." . . .
>
> Clark said ". . . I have got $30,000,000. I do not want to lose it. I am willing to spend half of the $30,000,000 to save the other half. If you go out and make this speech in Chicago, I am certain that they will adopt the resolution and that will be one step toward the return to gold, to have the soldiers stand up for it. We can get the soldiers to go out in great bodies to stand up for it."
>
> This was the first beginning of the idea, you see, of having a soldiers' organization, getting them to go out in favor of the gold standard. Clark's thought was, "I do not want to lose my money."

In a censored portion of the testimony, Butler explained why Clark thought that Roosevelt would permit himself to be pressured by such tactics.

† BUTLER: He said, "You know the President is weak. He will come right along with us. He was born in this class. He was raised in this class, and he will come back. He will run true to form. In the end he will come around. But we have got to be prepared to sustain him when he does."

This blatant snobbery and fatuous assumption about the President had been too much for Butler, and he had snapped a refusal to go to Chicago.

BUTLER: He said, "Why not?"
I said, "I do not want to be mixed up in this thing at all. I tell you very frankly, Mr. Clark, I have got one interest and that is the maintenance of a democracy. That is the only thing. I took an oath to sustain the democracy, and that is what I am going to do and nothing else. I am not going to get these soldiers marching around and stirred up over the gold standard. What the hell does a soldier know about the gold standard? You are just working them, using them, just as they have been used right along, and I am going to be one of those to see that they do not use them any more except to maintain a democracy. And then I will go out with them any time to do that."

At this point, Butler testified, Clark had offered him an outright bribe to win his cooperation.

BUTLER: He said, "Why do you want to be stubborn? Why do you want to be different from other people? We can take care of you. You have got a mortgage on this house," waving his hand, pointing to the house. "That can all be taken care of. It is perfectly legal, perfectly proper."
"Yes," I said, "but I just do not want to do it, that's all." Finally I said, "Do you know what you are trying to do? You are trying to bribe me in my own house. You are very polite about it and I can hardly call it that, but it looks kind of funny to me, making that kind of proposition. You come out into the hall, I want to show you something."
We went out there. I have all the flags and banners and medals of honor, and things of that kind. . . . They have been given me by the Chinese and the Nicaraguans and the

Haitians—by the poor people. I said to him, "You come out here. Look at that and see what you are trying to do. You are trying to buy me away from my own kind. When you have made up your mind that I will not go with you, then you come on and tell me."

After being left in the hall to inspect the trophies and think about their significance, Butler testified, Clark had joined him in the office at the back of the house. The millionaire had then asked permission to make a long-distance call.

> BUTLER: He called up Chicago and got hold of MacGuire at the Palmer House and he said to MacGuire, "General Butler is not coming to the convention. He has given me his reasons and they are excellent ones, and I apologize to him for my connection with it. I am not coming either. You can put this thing across. You have got $45,000. You can send those telegrams. You will have to do it in that way. The general is not coming. I can see why. I am going to Canada to rest. If you want me, you know where you can find me. You have got enough money to go through with it."
>
> . . . The convention came off and the gold standard was endorsed by the convention. I read about it with a great deal of interest. There was some talk about a flood of telegrams that came in and influenced them and I was so much amused, because it all happened right in my room.
>
> Then MacGuire stopped to see me on his way back from the convention. This time he came in a hired limousine . . . and told me that they had been successful in putting over their move. I said, "Yes, but you did not endorse the soldier's bonus."
>
> He said, "Well, we have got to get sound currency before it is worth while to endorse the bonus."

Not long afterward, Butler testified, MacGuire had called again to ask him to go to Boston for a soldier's dinner that was being given in the general's honor.

> BUTLER: He said, "We will have a private car for you on the end of the train. You will make a speech at this dinner and it will be worth a thousand dollars to you."

I said, "I never got a thousand dollars for making a speech."

He said, "You will get it this time."

"Who is going to pay for this dinner and this ride up in the private car?"

"Oh, we will pay for it out of our funds."

"I am not going to Boston. If the soldiers of Massachusetts want to give a dinner and want me to come, I will come. But there is no thousand dollars in it."

So he said, "Well, then, we will think of something else."

He had next seen MacGuire, Butler testified, while in New York to make an election speech on behalf of a former Marine running for local office in a municipal campaign. MacGuire had then sought to draw Butler out on his subsequent plans.

> BUTLER: He said, "You are going on a trip for the Veterans of Foreign Wars. You are going around recruiting them, aren't you?" I said, "Yes; I am going to start as soon as this campaign is over."
>
> CHAIRMAN: When was this campaign?
>
> BUTLER: This was in November, 1933. All of this happened between July and November, everything I told you. . . . He said, "You are going out to speak for the veterans." I said, "Yes. . . . You know, I believe that sooner or later there is going to be a test of our democracy, a test of this democratic form of government. The soldiers are the only people in this country who have ever taken an oath to sustain it. I believe that I can appeal to them by the millions to stand up for a democracy, because they have more stake in a democracy than any other class of our citizens, because they have fought for it. I am going out to the Veterans of Foreign Wars. They are my kind, overseas people, old regulars, and see if I cannot get a half a million of those fellows and preach this to them, that we have got to stand up against war. I have got an object in doing it. I believe that sooner or later we are going to have a showdown, because I have had so many invitations to head societies and to join societies, all of them with a camouflaged patriotic intent. They are rackets, all of them."

MacGuire had then exposed the forward edge of a new plan to use the general, startling Butler by a proposal to join him in his travels around the country.

> BUTLER: He said, "Well, that is what we are for. . . . I want to go around with you . . . and talk to the soldiers in the background and see if we cannot get them to join a great big superorganization to maintain the democracy.
>
> I said, "I do not know about you going along, Jerry. Of course, I cannot keep you off of the train. But there is something funny about all this that you are doing and I am not going to be responsible for it and I do not want any more to do with it. You are a wounded soldier and I am not going to hurt you, but you must lay off this business with me, because there is too much money in it."
>
> "Well, I am a business man," he said. . . . "I do not see why you will not be a business man, too."
>
> I said, "If fiddling with this form of government is business, I am out of it; if that is your business."
>
> "Oh," he said, "I would not disturb this form of government."
>
> I said, "You have got some reason for getting at these soldiers other than to maintain a democracy."

Although Butler did not testify to having been offered, and turning down, $750 for every speech he made to veterans' groups during his tour in which he inserted a short reference favoring the gold standard, a special tribute was paid to him on this score by a secret report he did not know of that reached the White House.

It had been written by Val O'Farrell, a former New York City detective who had become one of the city's leading criminal and civil investigators. On December 11, 1933, O'Farrell had written to presidential secretary Louis Howe:

> My dear Colonel:
>   . . . Before he [Butler] left for Atlanta, he was approached by a representative of the bankers gold group system, and offered the sum of seven hundred and fifty dol-

lars for each speech if he would insert some short reference in favor of continuing the bankers gold standard. This would have meant an additional ten thousand dollars to General Butler, but he told the representative of the gold group that even if he were offered a hundred thousand dollars to do this, his answer would be "no."

Notwithstanding the fact that I do not know General Butler, who has been occasionally subject to harsh criticism for the things he has done or failed to do, I felt it my duty to report this incident to you as it shows him to be a man of exceptional character.

You can probably obtain the name of the representative of this gold group from General Butler, or if you are interested, I may be able to get it for you.

3

Butler found himself fascinated by MacGuire, suspecting that the bond salesman might be playing some kind of shrewd con game with Clark, using his contact with Butler as a lever with which to pry money out of the alarmed millionaire.

> BUTLER: I began to get the idea that he was using Clark—to pull money out of Clark by frightening him about his $30,000,000—and then he was coming to me; and then he would go back and tell Clark, "I have been to see Butler, and he will go along if you will get me $5,000 more." In other words, I could see him working both ends against the middle and making a sucker out of Clark. However, if Clark wanted to get rid of his money, it was none of my business. . . .
>
> Now, he [MacGuire] is a very cagey individual. He always approaches everything from afar. He is really a very nice, plausible fellow. But I gather, after this association with him, that due to this wound in his head, he is a little inconsistent, a little flighty. He is being used, too, but I do

not think Clark is using him. My impression is that Murphy uses him; and he uses Clark, because Clark has the money.

During MacGuire's trip to Europe, Butler testified, the bond salesman had sent him a postcard from Nice in February, 1934, and a short note later from Berlin, both of the "having wonderful time" variety. Then after MacGuire's return, upon his urging to see Butler on a matter of the utmost importance, they had met in the empty restaurant of Philadelphia's Bellevue Hotel, on August 22, 1934.

> BUTLER: He told me all about his trip to Europe. . . . He said, "I went abroad to study the part that the veteran plays in the various set-ups of the governments that they have abroad. I went to Italy for two or three months and studied the position that the veterans of Italy occupy in the Fascist set-up of government, and I discovered that they are the background of Mussolini. They keep them on the pay rolls in various ways and keep them contented and happy; and they are his real backbone, the force on which he may depend, in case of trouble, to sustain him. But that set-up would not suit us at all. The soldiers of America would not like that. I then went to Germany to see what Hitler was doing, and his whole strength lies in organizations of soldiers, too. But that would not do. I looked into the Russian business. I found that the use of the soldiers over there would never appeal to our men. Then I went to France, and I found just exactly the organization we are going to have. It is an organization of supersoldiers." He gave me the French name for it, but I do not recall what it is. I never could have pronounced it, anyhow. But I do know that it is a superorganization of members of all the other soldiers' organizations of France, composed of noncommissioned officers and officers. He told me that they had about 500,000, and that each one was a leader of ten others, so that it gave them 5,000,000 votes. And he said, "Now, that is our idea here in America—to get up an organization of that kind."

Investigators for the McCormack-Dickstein Committee were able to uncover a report on this French "superorganization," the Croix de Feu, that MacGuire had written about to Robert S.

Clark and Clark's attorney, Albert Grant Christmas, from France on March 6, 1934:

> I had a very interesting talk last evening with a man who is quite well up on affairs here and he seems to be of the opinion that the Croix de Feu will be very patriotic during this crisis and will take the [wage] cuts or be the moving spirit in the veterans to accept the cuts. Therefore they will, in all probability, be in opposition to the Socialists and functionaries. The general spirit among the functionaries seems to be that the correct way to regain recovery is to spend more money and increase wages, rather than to put more people out of work and cut salaries.
>
> The Croix de Feu is getting a great number of new recruits, and I recently attended a meeting of this organization and was quite impressed with the type of men belonging. These fellows are interested only in the salvation of France, and I feel sure that the country could not be in better hands because they are not politicians, they are a cross-section of the best people of the country from all walks of life, people who gave their "all" between 1914 and 1918 that France might be saved, and I feel sure that if a crucial test ever comes to the Republic that these men will be the bulwark upon which France will be saved.

During their meeting in Philadelphia, Butler testified, MacGuire had revealed the plans of his group to develop an American Croix de Feu.

> BUTLER: I said, "What do you want to do with it when you get it up?"
>
> "Well," he said, "we want to support the President."
>
> I said, "The President does not need the support of that kind of an organization. Since when did you become a supporter of the President? The last time I talked to you you were against him."
>
> He said, "Well, he is going to go along with us now."
>
> "Is he?"
>
> "Yes."
>
> "Well, what are you going to do with these men, suppose you get these 500,000 men in America? . . ."

"Well," he said, "they will be the support of the President."

I said, "The President has got the whole American people. Why does he want them?"

He said, "Don't you understand the set-up has got to be changed a bit? . . . He has got to have more money. There is not any more money to give him. Eighty percent of the money now is in Government bonds, and he cannot keep this racket up much longer. . . . He has either got to get more money out of us or he has got to change the method of financing the Government, and we are going to see to it that he does not change that method. He will not change it."

I said, "The idea of this great group of soldiers, then, is to sort of frighten him, is it?"

"No, no, no; not to frighten him. This is to sustain him when others assault him."

I said, "Well, I do not know about that. How would the President explain it?"

He said: "He will not necessarily have to explain it, because we are going to help him out. Now, did it ever occur to you that the President is overworked? We might have an Assistant President, somebody to take the blame; and if things do not work out, he can drop him."

He went on to say that it did not take any constitutional change to authorize another Cabinet official, somebody to take over the details of the office—take them off the President's shoulders. He mentioned that the position would be a secretary of general affairs—a sort of a supersecretary.

CHAIRMAN: A secretary of general affairs?

BUTLER: That is the term used by him—or a secretary of general welfare—I cannot recall which. I came out of the interview with that name in my head. I got that idea from talking to both of them, you see [MacGuire and Clark]. They had both talked about the same kind of relief that ought to be given the President, and he [MacGuire] said: "You know, the American people will swallow that. We have got the newspapers. We will start a campaign that the President's health is failing. Everybody can tell that by looking at him, and the dumb American people will fall for it in a second."

And I could see it. They had that sympathy racket, that

they were going to have somebody take the patronage off of his shoulders and take all the worries and details off of his shoulders, and then he will be like the President of France. . . .

Now, I cannot recall which one of these fellows told me about the rule of succession, about the Secretary of State becoming President when the Vice President is eliminated. There was something said in one of the conversations that I had, that the President's health was bad, and he might resign, and that [Vice President] Garner did not want it, anyhow, and then this supersecretary would take the place of the Secretary of State and in the order of succession would become President. That was the idea.

In corroborative testimony Paul Comly French described what MacGuire had told him about the conspirators' plans.

FRENCH: During the course of the conversation he continually discussed the need of a man on a white horse, as he called it, a dictator who would come galloping in on his white horse. He said that was the only way; either through the threat of armed force or the delegation of power, and the use of a group of organized veterans, to save the capitalistic system.

He warmed up considerably after we got under way and he said, "We might go along with Roosevelt and then do with him what Mussolini did with the King of Italy."

It fits in with what he told the general, that we would have a Secretary of General Affairs, and if Roosevelt played ball, swell; and if he did not, they would push him out.

He expressed the belief that at least half of the American Legion and the Veterans of Foreign Wars would follow the general if he would announce such a plan.

In censored testimony Butler revealed that MacGuire had implicated General Hugh Johnson, head of the N.R.A., as Roosevelt's own choice to become an assistant President.

† BUTLER: He said, "That is what he [Roosevelt] was building up Hugh Johnson for. Hugh Johnson talked too damn

much and got him into a hole, and he is going to fire him in the next three or four weeks."

I said, "How do you know all this?"

"Oh," he said, "we are in with him all the time. We know what is going to happen."

After having revealed the plans of the plotters, Butler testified, MacGuire had then bluntly asked the general to be the Man on a White Horse they were looking for.

> BUTLER: He said, ". . . Now, about this superorganization —would you be interested in heading it?"
>
> I said, "I am interested in it, but I do not know about heading it. I am very greatly interested in it, because you know, Jerry, my interest is, my one hobby is, maintaining a democracy. If you get these 500,000 soldiers advocating anything smelling of Fascism, I am going to get 500,000 more and lick hell out of you, and we will have a real war right at home. You know that."
>
> "Oh, no. We do not want that. We want to ease up on the President." . . .
>
> "Yes; and then you will put somebody in there you can run; is that the idea? The President will go around and christen babies and dedicate bridges, and kiss children. Mr. Roosevelt will never agree to that himself."
>
> "Oh, yes; he will. He will agree to that."
>
> I said, "I do not believe he will." I said, "Don't you know that this will cost money, what you are talking about?
>
> He says, "Yes; we have got $3,000,000 to start with, on the line, and we can get $300,000,000, if we need it."
>
> "Who is going to put all this money up?"
>
> "Well," he said, "you heard Clark tell you he was willing to put up $15,000,000 to save the other $15,000,000."

Butler had then probed for particulars of the cabal's plans for organizing their projected military superorganization.

> BUTLER: "How are you going to care for all these men?"
>
> He said, "Well, the Government will not give them pensions, or anything of that kind, but we will give it to them.

We will give privates $10 a month and destitute captains
$35. We will get them, all right."

"It will cost you a lot of money to do that."

He said, "We will only have to do that for a year, and
then everything will be all right again."

. . . He said that they had this money to spend on it,
and he wanted to know again if I would head it, and I said,
"No, I am interested in it, but will not head it."

Seeking to persuade him to change his mind, Butler testified,
MacGuire had sought to impress him with the importance of the
interests who were involved in the plot.

> BUTLER: He said, "When I was in Paris, my headquar-
> ters were Morgan & Hodges. We had a meeting over there.
> I might as well tell you that our group is for you, for the
> head of this organization. Morgan & Hodges are against
> you. The Morgan interests say that you cannot be trusted,
> that you will be too radical, and so forth, that you are too
> much on the side of the little fellow; you cannot be trusted.
> They do not want you. But our group tells them that you
> are the only fellow in America who can get the soldiers
> together. They say, 'Yes, but he will get them together and
> go in the wrong way.' That is what they say if you take
> charge of them."

According to MacGuire, Butler testified, the Morgan interests preferred other noted military figures as head of the projected veterans' army. Discussion of these choices was also
eliminated from the published version of the hearings.

> † BUTLER: [MacGuire said,] "They are for Douglas Mac-
> Arthur as the head of it. Douglas MacArthur's term expires
> in November, and if he is not reappointed it is to be pre-
> sumed that he will be disappointed and sore and they are
> for getting him to head it."
>
> I said, "I do not think that you will get the soldiers to
> follow him, Jerry. . . . He is in bad odor, because he put
> on a uniform with medals to march down the street in
> Washington, I know the soldiers."

"Well, then, we will get Hanford MacNider. They want either MacArthur or MacNider. . . ."

I said, "MacNider won't do either. He will not get the soldiers to follow him, because he has been opposed to the bonus."

"Yes, but we will have him in change [charge?]."

And it is interesting to note that three weeks later after this conversation MacNider changed and turned around for the bonus. It is interesting to note that.

He [MacGuire] said, "There is going to be a big quarrel over the reappointment of MacArthur . . . you watch the President reappoint him. He is going to go right and if he does not reappoint him, he is going to go left."

I have been watching with a great deal of interest this quarrel over his reappointment to see how it comes out. He [MacGuire] said, "You know as well as I do that Mac-Arthur is Stotesbury's son in law in Philadelphia—[Stotesbury being] Morgan's representative in Philadelphia. You just see how it goes and if I am not telling the truth."

I noticed that MacNider turned around for the bonus, and that there is a row over the reappointment of MacArthur.

4

Convinced by now of the seriousness of the plot, and its magnitude, Butler had endeavored to learn how far along the conspirators were in the creation of the new superorganization that would control the proposed veterans' army. MacGuire gave him some tips on recognizing its appearance.

BUTLER: Now, there is one point . . . which I think is the most important of all. I said, "What are you going to call this organization?"

He said, "Well, I do not know."

I said, "Is there anything stirring about it yet?"

"Yes," he says; "you watch; in two or three weeks you will see it come out in the paper. There will be big fellows in it. This is to be the background of it. These are to be the villagers in the opera. The papers will come out with it." He did not give me the name of it, but he said that it would all be made public; a society to maintain the Constitution, and so forth. They had a lot of talk this time about maintaining the Constitution. I said, "I do not see that the Constitution is in any danger."

Butler's next observation, possibly the most significant in all his testimony, was missing from the published version of his testimony. It was the link between the conspiracy and the powerful interests Butler had good reason to believe were the "big fellows" in the background.

† BUTLER: . . . and in about two weeks the American Liberty League appeared, which was just about what he described it to be.

The American Liberty League, which had brokerage head Grayson M.-P. Murphy as its treasurer and Robert S. Clark as one of its financiers, also had John W. Davis, alleged writer of the gold-standard speech for Clark, as a member of the National Executive Committee. Its contributors included representatives of the Morgan, Du Pont, Rockefeller, Pew, and Mellon interests. Directors of the League included Al Smith and John J. Raskob. The League later formed affiliations with pro-Fascist, antilabor, and anti-Semitic organizations.

It astonished Butler that former New York Governor Al Smith, who had lost the 1928 presidential race to Hoover as the Democratic candidate, could be involved in a Fascist plot backed by wealthy men. But the "happy warrior" who had grown up on New York's East Side had traded his brown derby for a black one. He was now a business associate of the powerful Du Pont family, who had cultivated him through Du Pont official John J. Raskob, former chairman of the Democratic party. Under their influence Smith had grown more and more politically conservative following his defeat.

Butler's query about Smith, and MacGuire's reply, were both deleted from the official testimony of the hearings.

> † BUTLER: I said, "What is the idea of Al Smith in this?"
>
> "Well," he said, "Al Smith is getting ready to assault the Administration in his magazine. It will appear in a month or so. He is going to take a shot at the money question. He has definitely broken with the President."
>
> I was interested to note that about a month later he did, and the *New Outlook* took the shot that he told me a month before they were going to take. Let me say that this fellow [MacGuire] has been able to tell me a month or six weeks ahead of time everything that happened. That made him interesting. I wanted to see if he was going to come out right. . . .

In testimony that was also censored, Paul Comly French revealed that MacGuire had implicated the Du Ponts to him, indicating the role they would play in equipping the superarmy being planned by the plotters.

> † FRENCH: We discussed the question of arms and equipment, and he suggested that they could be obtained from the Remington Arms Co., on credit through the Du Ponts.
>
> I do not think at that time he mentioned the connections of Du Ponts with the American Liberty League . . . but he skirted all around the idea that that was the back door; one of the Du Ponts is on the board of directors of the American Liberty League and they own a controlling interest in the Remington Arms Co. . . . He said the General would not have any trouble enlisting 500,000 men.

In a story it ran on November 21, 1934, *The New York Times* noted, "According to General Butler . . . he was to assemble his 500,000 men in Washington, possibly a year from now, with the expectation that such a show of force would enable it to take over the government peacefully in a few days."

During his last talk with MacGuire, Butler had once more pressured him to explain the persistent bond salesman's personal stake in the conspiracy.

BUTLER: I asked him again, "Why are you in this thing?"
He said, "I am a business man. I have got a wife and
children."

In other words, he had had a nice trip to Europe with
his family, for nine months, and he said that that cost plenty,
too. . . .

So he left me, saying, "I am going down to Miami and
I will get in touch with you after the convention is over,
and we are going to make a fight down there for the gold
standard, and we are going to organize."

After he had been urged over forty times to accept the leadership of the Fascist coup d'etat being planned, while he gathered
as much information about it as he could, Butler had then sought
to gather corroborative evidence through reporter Paul Comly
French.

BUTLER: . . . in talking to Paul French here—I had not said
anything about this other thing, it did not make any difference about fiddling with the gold standard resolution, but
this [the Fascist plot] looked to me as though it might be
getting near that they were going to stir some of these soldiers up to hurt our Government. I did not know anything
about this committee [the American Liberty League], so I
told Paul to let his newspaper see what they could find out
about the background of these fellows.

Although Butler recalled having induced French to check into
the case, former Philadelphia *Record* city editor Tom O'Neil
gave the author his recollection that Butler had approached him
and told him the whole story. O'Neil recalled that he had agreed
to assign French to investigate. Probably Butler first approached
French, who had referred him to the city editor.

Butler gave the McCormack-Dickstein Committee his view
that the plot might have been hatched out of a racket that Mac-
Guire had been working as a moneymaking scheme.

BUTLER: I felt that it was just a racket, that these fellows
were working one another and getting money out of the
rich, selling them gold bricks. I have been in 752 different

towns in the United States in three years and one month, and I made 1,022 speeches. I have seen absolutely no sign of anything showing a trend for a change of our form of Government. So it has never appealed to me at all. But as long as there was a lot of money stirring around—and I had noticed some of them with money to whom I have talked were dissatisfied and talking about having dictators—I thought that perhaps they might be tempted to put up money.

Butler testified that his last encounter with MacGuire had been with reference to French's attempt to talk to him.

> CHAIRMAN: Did you have any further talks with him?
> BUTLER: No. The only other time I saw or heard from him was when I wanted Paul to uncover him. He talked to me and he telephoned Paul, saying he wanted to see him. He called me up and asked if Paul was a reputable person, and I said he was. That is the last thing I heard from him.
> CHAIRMAN: The last talk you had with MacGuire was in the Bellevue in August of this year?
> BUTLER: August 22; yes. The date can be identified.

He concluded his testimony by urging the committee to question several persons about the plot in addition to MacGuire—notably Murphy, Doyle, and Legion Commander Frank N. Belgrano. This request was also stricken from the official record.

Butler was aware that Chairman McCormack was himself a Legionnaire and that the revelations of the plot implicating Legion officials might be painful to him. But Butler also knew that McCormack was a determined foe of Nazi propaganda and a staunch supporter of New Deal measures. Butler counted on his indignation over the conspiracy to bring about a full-scale investigation by the Department of Justice.

5

After Butler had completed his testimony, Paul Comly French took the witness chair to report on his own investigation of the plot, in which a candid two-hour conversation with MacGuire at the latter's office figured prominently.

Describing these talks on the premises of Grayson M.-P. Murphy and Company, French verified every allegation about the plot the general had attributed to MacGuire. In addition French reported the more open statements MacGuire had made to him about the nature of the conspiracy and how it would work. More frank with French, apparently, than he had dared to be with the general, MacGuire made little attempt to disguise the Fascist nature of the proposed putsch with euphemistic phrases about "supporting the President."

> FRENCH: We need a Fascist government in this country, he insisted, to save the Nation from the Communists who want to tear it down and wreck all that we have built in America. The only men who have the patriotism to do it are the soldiers and Smedley Butler is the ideal leader. He could organize a million men overnight.
>
> During the conversation he told me he had been in Italy and Germany during the summer of 1934 and the spring of 1934 and had made an intensive study of the background of the Nazi and Fascist movements and how the veterans had played a part in them. He said he had obtained enough information on the Fascist and Nazi movements and of the part played by the veterans, to properly set up one in this country.
>
> He emphasized throughout his conversation with me that the whole thing was tremendously patriotic, that it was saving the Nation from Communists, and that the men they deal with have that crackbrained idea that the Communists

are going to take it apart. He said the only safeguard would be the soldiers. At first he suggested that the General organize this outfit himself and ask a dollar a year dues from everybody. We discussed that, and then he came around to the point of getting outside financial funds, and he said that it would not be any trouble to raise a million dollars.

French's use of the phrase "crackbrained idea" to describe the notion by financiers and captains of industry that the country needed to be saved from communism was obviously his own, and not MacGuire's, expression.

Censored in French's testimony was his revelation of the sources to which MacGuire had said that he could turn for the funds to finance the veterans' army.

† FRENCH: He said he could go to John W. Davis [attorney for J. P. Morgan and Company] or Perkins of the National City Bank, and any number of persons to get it.

Of course, that may or may not mean anything. That is, his reference to John W. Davis and Perkins of the National City Bank.

French testified that MacGuire had sought to impress him by indicating high-level support for the conspiracy from important movers and shakers of the American Legion.

FRENCH: He then pushed a letter across the desk and said that it was from Louis Johnson, a former national commander of the American Legion.

CHAIRMAN: Did he show you the letter?

FRENCH: I did not read it. He just passed it over so I could see it, but he did not show it to me. He said that he had discussed the matter with him along the lines of what we were now discussing, and I took it to mean that he had talked of this Fascist proposition with Johnson, and Johnson was in sympathy with it.

During the conversation he also mentioned Henry Stevens, of Warsaw, N.C., a former national commander of the American Legion, and said that he was interested in the program. Several times he brought in the names of various former national commanders of the American Legion, to give me the impression that, whether justly or unjustly, a group in the American Legion were actively interested in this proposition.

CHAIRMAN: In other words, he mentioned a lot of prominent names; and whether they are interested or not, you do not know, except that he seemed to try to convey to you that they were, to impress on you the significance of this movement?

FRENCH: That is precisely the impression I gained from him.

As MacGuire had grown increasingly comfortable with him, French testified, the plotter had grown candid and enthusiastic about the Fascist rewards that would follow seizure of the White House. French's use of the word "brilliant" in the following portion of testimony was obviously sarcastic.

FRENCH: He had a very brilliant solution of the unemployment situation. He said that Roosevelt had muffed it terrifically, but that he had the plan. He had seen it in Europe. It was a plan that Hitler had used in putting all of the unemployed in labor camps or barracks—enforced labor. That would solve it overnight, and he said that when they got into power, that is what they would do; that that was the ideal plan.

He had another suggestion to register all persons all over the country, like they do in Europe. He said that would stop a lot of these Communist agitators who were running around the country.

He said that a crash was inevitable and was due to come when bonds reached 5 percent. He said that the soldiers must prepare to save the Nation.

If Roosevelt went along with the dictatorship as the King had done in Italy, MacGuire had suggested, Butler could have the proposed labor camps put under his own control.

† FRENCH: . . . he suggested that Roosevelt would be in sympathy with us and proposed the idea that Butler would be named as the head of the C.C.C. [Civilian Conservation

Corps] camps by the President as a means of building up
the organization. . . .

French then testified that MacGuire had told him the plotters
could obtain arms and equipment from the Remington Arms
Company, on credit through the Du Ponts. His testimony also
implicated the American Liberty League.

> † FRENCH: I do not think at that time he mentioned the
> connection of Du Ponts with the American Liberty League,
> but he skirted all around it. That is, I do not think he men-
> tioned the Liberty League, but he skirted all around the
> idea that that was the back door; one of the Du Ponts is
> on the board of directors of the American Liberty League
> and they own a controlling interest in the Remington Arms
> Co. . . . He said the General would not have any trouble
> enlisting 500,000 men.

It was because MacGuire saw the general as the indispensable
man of the putsch, French testified, that he persisted in his efforts
to win Butler's adherence to the scheme.

> FRENCH: When I left him he said that he planned to get
> in touch with the general and again try to persuade him to
> accept the leadership of this organization; that he was going
> to Miami in a couple of weeks for the national convention
> to do a little work.
> CHAIRMAN: To beat the bonus?
> FRENCH: Yes.
> CHAIRMAN: I thought he was for the bonus.
> FRENCH: He was at first.
> BUTLER (*interposing*): He wants it paid in gold. Clark
> told me that he had been for the bonus or that he would be
> for the bonus if we could get the gold standard restored.
> FRENCH: Then he said he would be in Miami. I told him
> that the general was going out on a rather lengthy speaking
> tour and did not know how to get to him. He said that he
> would either see him before he went to Miami or, if he
> could not, after he came back from Miami. But he did not
> see him and in a couple of days the general went out West.

Then I went back to see MacGuire on the 27th of September and talked to him for only a few minutes this time. In the meantime I had tried to get in touch with him once when I was in New York, but he was then in Miami and could not. At this time he said that he was extremely sorry that he could not get to Newtown Square [Butler's hometown], but hoped to do so soon; that things were moving nicely. Everything is coming our way, is the way he expressed it.

6

That same afternoon the committee grilled Jerry MacGuire, who had also been summoned to testify at the executive session. MacGuire, who earned only $150 a week as a bond salesman, contradicted himself on the amount of money he had received from sponsors and what he had done with it. He denied Butler's allegation that he had thrown eighteen thousand-dollar bills on the bed at the Newark hotel during the 29th Division convention to bribe Butler into going to the Legion convention in Chicago.

But he could not explain what he had done with at least thirty thousand in letters of credit, funds advanced to him by either Clark or Clark's attorney, Albert Grant Christmas, and which MacGuire had had with him at the Legion convention in Chicago the following October, at which he had been both a delegate and a member of the "distinguished guest committee."

The McCormack-Dickstein Committee found five significant facts that lent validity to Butler's testimony. Clark, who wanted the Legion to pass a gold-standard resolution, had given MacGuire those funds. In the long-distance call Clark had allegedly made to Chicago while Butler was listening, he had instructed MacGuire, "You can put this thing across alone. You've got $45,000. You can send those telegrams." MacGuire could not explain how he had spent those funds. But telegrams had, indeed, flooded the convention, and the Legion had passed the resolution.

Corroboration of Butler's testimony about MacGuire's mission in Europe was borne out by the committee's finding that he had spent large sums of money on that trip to study Fascist movements in Italy, Germany, and France. The committee found, too, that he and Clark had handled large sums of money for various organizations, that he had been active in organizations mentioned by Butler, and that he had acted as cashier for one organization. His accounts of some of these financial transactions failed to satisfy the committee, and he was curtly instructed to reappear the following day for further questioning.

Interviewed by reporters afterward, MacGuire declared that he was a personal friend of General Butler's and had last seen him six months earlier when he had gone to Philadelphia to sell some bonds. They had talked about an adequate military force for the nation, MacGuire insisted, and about world affairs in general, but he denied ever discussing a Fascist army or movement. A little desperately MacGuire suggested that "General Butler must be seeking publicity," and called the general's testimony "a pacifist stunt." His attorney, Norman L. Marks, called it "a joke and a publicity stunt for General Butler."

7

Smedley Butler's reputation as an honest patriot made what he had testified to under oath impossible for the press to ignore. On November 21, 1934, in the center of its front page, *The New York Times* carried a two-column headline:

Gen. Butler Bares 'Fascist Plot'
To Seize Government by Force

Says Bond Salesman, as Representative of Wall St. Group, Asked
Him to Lead Army of 500,000 in March on Capital—Those
Named Make Angry Denials—Dickstein Gets Charge

Reading the *Times's* account of the secret hearings, Butler was struck by a unique arrangement of the facts in the story. Instead of beginning with a full account of his charges, there was only a brief paragraph restating the facts in the headline. This was followed by a whole string of denials, or ridicule of the charges, by prominent people implicated. Extensive space was given to their attempts to brand Butler a liar or lunatic. Only at the tail of the story, buried inside the paper, did the *Times* wind up its account with a few brief paragraphs mentioning some of his allegations.

Many papers that picked up the story dropped the tail carrying even those cursory details of the plot. Newspaper publishers had little reason to be fond of the firebrand general who, in his speech to veterans in Atlanta almost a year earlier, had warned them not to believe the capitalist-controlled press, which, Butler charged, suppressed facts unfavorable to America's powerful corporations.

The New York Times did note, however, that Butler had told friends in Philadelphia that General Hugh S. Johnson, former N.R.A. administrator, had been among those slated for the role of dictator if Butler turned it down and that J. P. Morgan and Company and Grayson M.-P. Murphy and Company were both involved in the plot.

"It's a joke—a publicity stunt," Jerry MacGuire was quoted as insisting. "I know nothing about it. The matter is made up out of whole cloth. I deny the story completely."

General Johnson growled, "He had better be pretty damn careful. Nobody said a word to me about anything of this kind, and if they did I'd throw them out the window. I know nothing about it."

Thomas W. Lamont, partner in J. P. Morgan and Company, gave his comment: "Perfect moonshine! Too unutterably ridiculous to comment upon!" J. P. Morgan himself, just back from Europe, had nothing to say.

"A fantasy!" scoffed Colonel Grayson M.-P. Murphy. "I can't imagine how anyone could produce it or any sane person believe it. It is absolutely false so far as it relates to me and my firm, and I don't believe there is a word of truth in it with respect to Mr. MacGuire."

Colonel Murphy specifically denied to reporters that he had financed any Fascist plot and called the statement that he had made out a check for General Butler's Chicago expenses "an absolute lie." He declared that he did not know General Butler and had never heard of the reputed Fascist movement until the charges had been published. He insisted that in 1932 he had voted for President Roosevelt, the target of the alleged plot.

Asked about these denials, Butler snorted to a *New York Times* reporter, "Hell, you're not surprised they deny it, are you? What they have to say they'll say before the committee." He wanted them under oath, as he had been.

In Washington General Douglas MacArthur, Chief of Staff, was unavailable for comment because of a real or a diplomatic "heavy cold." His aides, however, expressed amazement and amusement that MacArthur had been named by Butler as an alternate choice of the plotters for dictator if Butler persisted in refusing the offer.

"All the principals in the case," George Seldes noted in his book *Facts and Fascism*, "were American Legion officials and financial backers."

Secretary of War George H. Dern, Secretary of the Navy Claude A. Swanson, and a large number of senators and congressmen urged the McCormack-Dickstein Committee to get to the bottom of the conspiracy.

"We are going to make a searching investigation of the evidence submitted by General Butler," McCormack announced. "Our original information came from several different sources. General Butler was not the first source of our information. . . . We have been in possession of certain information for about five weeks and have been investigating it. We will call all the men mentioned in the story, although Mr. Clark is reported to be in Europe."

"From present indications," declared Dickstein, "Butler has the evidence. He's not going to make any serious charges unless he has something to back them up. We'll have the men here with bigger names than his." He added that Butler had substantiated most of the statements attributed to him and had denied none. Both McCormack and Dickstein emphasized that the general had repulsed all proposals from the Fascist group.

Dickstein indicated that about sixteen persons mentioned to the committee by Butler would be subpoenaed and that an open hearing might be held within a week.

8

Returning from Washington, Butler was besieged by reporters at his home in Newtown Square.

"My name has been used all around the country by organizations," he told them. "They'd get some vets and say, 'See, we have Butler with us.' They were using me. The investigators who have been running this thing down found my name popping up everywhere, so they wanted to know what I knew about it—and I'm not the only man in this thing."

Next day Dr. W. D. Brooks, of Jackson, Michigan, wired the President:

> Very obviously Wall St. plans to take over the U.S. Govt. if Hoover re-elected. Very obviously Butler is telling the truth. I have been looking for just this attempt at a Wall St. coup if your policies looked like succeeding. Wall St. is the enemy of our govt. and Butler is giving it to you straight— don't doubt that for a minute.

The writer was unable to ascertain the identity of Dr. Brooks, but apparently his opinion carried some weight at the White House, because Louis Howe referred his wire to Attorney General Homer S. Cummings "for acknowledgment and consideration." A demand for prosecution of the conspirators came from many V.F.W. posts all over the country, which passed resolutions praising Butler for exposing the plotters.

Typical was the resolution of Philadelphia Post 37 on November 22, 1934:

> Whereas Major General Smedley D. Butler has again exhibited his patriotism, sterling integrity and incorruptible character by exposing a sinister clique of adventurers who would undermine and destroy our form of government, and whereas such treasonable activities by men of money and of influence are more dangerous to our institutions than radical groups in our midst, therefore be it resolved . . . that it commend General Butler for his patriotic spirit and hereby expresses its deep gratitude for his great service to our country. And be it further resolved that the Clair Post hereby respectfully requests the Attorney General of the United States to take proper legal action against all guilty parties involved.

If the press seemed overeager to emphasize denials of Butler's charges, the people of grass-roots America were far readier to believe the man who had exposed the plot. Letters of encouragement poured in from all over the country. One Nebraska woman wrote him:

> It is heartening to find a man who has the courage to fight that Octopus, Wall St. More power to you. There are millions of honest people in the United States who applaud you and would follow you heart & soul. Read of MacNider's name being linked with the case. Heard him speak before a woman's club in Omaha. Sized him up as being that kind of tripe. Here's hoping you expose these traitors to a showdown. Yours for justice. . . .

Jerry MacGuire returned as a witness for a second day of secret grilling by the McCormack-Dickstein Committee. Again he denied Butler's charges that he had approached the general on behalf of a plot to establish a Fascist dictatorship.

He testified that he had received thirty thousand dollars from Robert Sterling Clark to be deposited in the Hanover Trust Company to the credit of "The Committee for a Sound Dollar and Sound Currency, Inc." He and his backers had only wanted to interest Butler in *that* committee, MacGuire insisted, because as an important and popular public figure the general could command attention for their movement. They wanted to give him the opportunity to "make a little money" in the process.

Although Clark, his attorney A. G. Christmas, Walter E. Frew, and others were behind the Committee for a Sound Dollar and Sound Currency, their names had been carefully omitted from its records. MacGuire testified that as far as he knew, Clark had never had any interest in a Fascist organization. But the Mc-Cormack-Dickstein Committee located letters from MacGuire written from Europe to Clark and Christmas that proved otherwise.

To many questions thrown at him MacGuire answered evasively, "It is too far back," or "I cannot recall." At the conclusion of his testimony Dickstein told reporters that MacGuire was "hanging himself" by contradictions in his story and by forced admissions made during his testimony. When this opinion was quoted in a few evening newspapers, Dickstein observed that he had meant it to be "off the record."

Norman L. Marks, the attorney who had accompanied Mac-Guire at the secret hearings, told reporters that MacGuire had denied ever having had any connection with any Fascist organization of any sort; that he had ever been the "cashier" for any Fascist group; or that he had gone to Europe to study the Fascist movement. MacGuire's European trip, Marks alleged, had been solely for purposes of private business.

McCormack declared that all information about the testimony would be withheld because it had been given in closed executive session. But the fact that the committee regarded the testimony as important, he added, was shown by the decision to recall MacGuire for further questioning. Despite Dickstein's earlier statement that sixteen people named by Butler would be subpoenaed, McCormack said that the committee had not yet decided whether to call additional witnesses. Noting that the most important witness, apart from MacGuire, was Robert S. Clark, "a wealthy New Yorker with offices in the Stock Exchange Building," who was abroad, McCormack indicated that if the facts warranted, a public hearing would be held. Leaders of important organizations like the American Legion and the V.F.W. would then be invited to appear before the committee.

The Associated Press reported from Indianapolis that banker Frank N. Belgrano, Jr., national commander of the Legion, had denied that the Legion was involved "in the slightest degree" in any plot to supply an army for a "march on Washington." Highly placed Legion officials in Washington also characterized as "horsefeathers" a rumor that a group of "big-business men" had promised the Legion payment of adjusted service certificates, in return for a pledge to support the Fascist movement.

Louis Johnson, former Legion national commander, declared in Fairmont, West Virginia, that he could not recall having written the letter to Jerry MacGuire, promising to see him about the Fascist army plan, that MacGuire had shown briefly to Paul Comly French. If he had written such a letter, Johnson insisted, it would show that he and the Legion were unalterably opposed to any dictatorship.

On November 22 the Associated Press struck a low blow at Butler by getting Mayor Fiorello LaGuardia, of New York, to express an opinion of the conspiracy based on what he had read about it in the press. The AP ran this "news item" under the headline "COCKTAIL PUTSCH," MAYOR SAYS:

> Mayor LaGuardia of New York laughingly described today the charges of General Smedley D. Butler that New York brokers suggested he lead an army of 500,000 exservice men on Washington as "a cocktail putsch." The Mayor indicated he believed that some one at a party had suggested the idea to the ex-marine as a joke.

Reading the press treatment of the scanty disclosures that had leaked out of the closed hearing, Butler was not surprised by the attempts to minimize and ridicule his exposure of the conspiracy. He had expected to be pilloried for his audacity in pinning a traitors' label on powerful American interests. He hoped, however, that the press would eventually be compelled to print the whole story of the plot as it had unfolded to him, when he testified at a public hearing along with French's corroboration.

The committee would surely have to subpoena all the people who were implicated, in one way or another, to testify at that open meeting under oath.

9

Fresh support for Butler's exposé came from Van Zandt, who revealed to the press that he, too, had been approached by "agents of Wall Street" to lead a Fascist dictatorship in the United States under the guise of a "Veterans Organization."

He revealed that Butler had informed him about the plotters' solicitation of the general two months earlier and had warned him that he, too, would be contacted by them at the V.F.W. convention in Louisville, Kentucky. Van Zandt said he had asked Butler the purpose of the organization and the general had replied that it sought to return the American dollar to the gold standard and, in MacGuire's words, "to get rid of this fellow in the White House."

In addition to Butler and himself, Van Zandt told reporters, MacArthur, Colonel Theodore Roosevelt, Jr., and former Legion Commander Hanford MacNider had recently been sounded out on their interest in leading the proposed Fascist veterans organization. He also charged that MacGuire had spent months in Europe studying Fascist organizations as models for an American one.

Theodore Roosevelt, Jr., decried as "ridiculous" the idea that he could be used to wrest the powers of the Presidency away from his fourth cousin, Franklin D. Roosevelt.

McCormack declared that the committee was continuing to give serious consideration to General Butler's charges and might call Van Zandt to testify on the proposals made to him and others he had named. MacGuire would be called before the committee again in executive session, he announced, for scrutiny of his bank accounts and records. But McCormack indicated that he intended to keep the scope of the investigation circumscribed by legal considerations.

"We don't intend to drag in names that come to us through rumors," he told reporters. "If investigation discloses there is sufficient reason to subpoena witnesses, we will do so. Simply because someone mentions the name of Mr. Lamont or General Johnson is not sufficient to ask them to appear before the committee."

Meanwhile the focus of the committee's interest was shifted when it turned its attention to investigating charges that some left-wing unions had used a three-million-dollar fund to "foment and carry on strikes." *The New York Times* ran headlines reading "Reds Fund Activity in Fur Industry" and "Red Union Funds Traced at Hearing." Buried in third-rank subheads, and in the body of the story, was further information about the Fascist plot.

A news dispatch from Paris reported that Robert Sterling Clark was sending a lawyer to New York to answer charges made by Butler and "clear the matter up." Clark declared himself bewildered by the mention of his name and said he would send the lawyer "if the whole affair isn't relegated to the funny papers by Sunday."

"MacGuire went to Europe for me, but his visit had nothing to do with politics," he insisted. "He visited France, Italy and Germany and was in Paris in February of this year. He spent four months on the Continent. His trip was made for the purposes of investigating the financial situation, the possibilities of monetary stabilization and commercial trends."

When reporters showed him Van Zandt's accusation that Mac-Guire had returned to the United States with copious data for setting up an American Fascist regime, he exclaimed, "My God, what is back of all this? I saw all of MacGuire's reports. I cannot imagine him doing anything else on the side."

Although he was on vacation in Paris, Clark declared, he was ready to return to testify if the committee summoned him.

10

MacGuire showed up a third time for interrogation by the committee, this time with the bankbooks, canceled checks, and other financial records he was ordered to produce. Before entering the committee room accompanied by his counsel, he asked permission to read to the committee a cablegram he had received from Albert Grant Christmas, Clark's lawyer, in Paris:

> Read this wire when you testify. Reports of the Butler testimony in Paris outrageous. If reports are correct, my opinion is that a most serious libel has been committed. I am returning at once to testify as to our anti-inflation activities.

MacGuire now testified that on September 24, 1933, on the date Butler had said he was approached by MacGuire in the Newark hotel and offered eighteen thousand-dollar bills, MacGuire had been in Chicago. He claimed to have registered at the Palmer House on September 21, remaining in Chicago until October 8, so that he could not have met Butler in Newark on the twenty-fourth.

But committee investigators found that he had indeed called upon Butler that day and had had available at least sixteen thousand dollars, largely in thousand-dollar bills. Unless Mac-Guire had shown them to him, Butler could not possibly have known about them, lending strong verification to the general's charge that they had been tossed on his bed as a bribe.

MacGuire produced the bank accounts of the Committee for a Sound Dollar and Sound Currency, Inc., of which he was an official, and whose purpose he described as "opposing monetary inflation in the United States." He and his lawyer now insisted that the only discussions MacGuire had had with Butler concerned financial backing for a contracting concern.

MacGuire reluctantly admitted receiving $75,000 from Clark for an "unexplained purpose," the McCormack-Dickstein Committee report later noted, while working on a drawing account of $432 a month. This $75,000 was in addition to $30,000 he had also received from Walter E. Frew, of the Corn Exchange Bank, for the Committee for a Sound Dollar and Sound Currency, Inc. "Whether there was more, and how much more," said the report, "the [McCormack-Dickstein] Committee does not yet know."

MacGuire admitted spending almost $8,000 on the trip to Europe, ostensibly to buy bonds, but the investigators noted the trip had resulted in detailed reports to MacGuire's backers on various Fascist organizations abroad.

Although he still denied having tossed the eighteen thousand-dollar bills on Butler's bed in the Newark hotel, the committee found bank records showing he had bought letters of credit six days later from Central Hanover Bank, paying for them with thirteen thousand-dollar bills.

The testimony of MacGuire under oath flatly contradicted everything Butler had testified to. The McCormack-Dickstein Committee was left with no other option than to conclude either that Butler was lying, in which case the whole plot was a fabrication or fantasy, or that MacGuire was lying, in which case Butler's charges were true, and the dangerous conspiracy of which he warned was a reality.

> McCormack: Did you leave a speech with him—a speech that he was to make to the convention if he went out there?
> MacGuire: No, sir.
> McCormack: Was anything said about weakening the influence of the administration with the soldiers?
> MacGuire: No, sir; I do not believe the administration was mentioned, as far as President Roosevelt or anybody down there are concerned. . . .
> McCormack: Was there some talk about his going out as an individual Legionnaire and having two or three hundred Legionnaires go out to Chicago, too?
> MacGuire: No, sir. . . .

McCormack: At any time did you take out a bank book and show him deposits in it?

MacGuire: No, sir. . . .

McCormack: Did he at any time ask you where you got the money?

MacGuire: I never had any money, and he never asked me if I had any. . . .

McCormack: Did you know that Mr. Clark had a personal talk with General Butler?

MacGuire: It seems to me that he mentioned it to me, but I am not sure. . . .

McCormack: Did you know that Mr. Clark talked with him about going to the convention?

MacGuire: No, sir; I do not. . . .

McCormack: Did Mr. Clark call you up in Chicago at any time?

MacGuire: Mr. Clark? No, sir. . . .

McCormack: Did he ever call you up in Chicago from General Butler's home?

MacGuire: No, sir; to my recollection he did not. . . .

McCormack: Did you tell him [Butler] at that time that you went abroad to study the part that the veterans played abroad in the set-up of the governments of the countries abroad?

MacGuire: No, sir. . . .

McCormack: Did you talk with him about the forming of an organization of that kind here?

MacGuire: No, sir. . . .

McCormack: You previously testified that you only had one transaction in the swapping of checks with Christmas [Clark's attorney] of $20,000 and until later, when you paid him back the balance?

MacGuire: No; I believe that was paid back to Christmas in cash.

McCormack: What have you got to show that?

MacGuire: I haven't got anything to show it.

McCormack: Did you receive a receipt from Christmas?

MacGuire: No, sir; not necessarily; as far as that goes, he is an old friend of mine. . . .

At this point McCormack produced subpoenaed bank records showing that MacGuire had cashed letters of credit in the amount of $30,300, prior to the Legion convention in Chicago. MacGuire claimed that this money was meant to allow him to buy bonds in case he came across a good buy.

> McCormack: What did you do with that $30,300 in Chicago?
>
> MacGuire: I kept that money in cash and put it in a safe deposit box with the First National Bank. . . .
>
> McCormack: What became of that money?
>
> MacGuire: That money was brought back and returned to Mr. Christmas.
>
> McCormack: In cash?
>
> MacGuire: Yes.
>
> McCormack: When did you return this $30,300 to Mr. Christmas?
>
> MacGuire: I do not remember the date. . . .
>
> McCormack: Did you get a receipt for it?
>
> MacGuire: No, I did not get a receipt for it. . . .
>
> McCormack: Let me ask you this: why should you have cashed the letters of credit in Chicago and put that money in a safe deposit box?
>
> MacGuire: Because I felt that if I had a chance to buy the bonds I could buy them right off for cash.
>
> McCormack: Wouldn't letters of credit be accepted just as cash?
>
> MacGuire: They probably would.
>
> McCormack: Wouldn't they be safer than cash on your person?
>
> MacGuire: They probably would, yes; but there is no objection to getting the cash, is there? . . .
>
> McCormack: Did you buy any bonds?
>
> MacGuire: No, sir.
>
> McCormack: What bonds did you want to buy? . . .
>
> MacGuire: I think Chicago Sanitary District 4's.
>
> McCormack: Whom did you talk to about buying the Chicago Sanitary District 4's?
>
> MacGuire: I did not talk to anybody.
>
> McCormack: Whom did you speak to about it?
>
> MacGuire: I didn't speak to anybody. . . .

McCormack next turned to subpoenaed reports that MacGuire had sent back from Europe and cited the one he had sent back praising the Croix de Feu as a model veterans organization. He also read out another report MacGuire had submitted to his backers on the Fascist party of Holland.

> McCORMACK: And in this report you also said: "I was informed that there is a Fascist Party springing up in Holland under the leadership of a man named Mussait who is an engineer by profession, and who has approximately 50,000 followers at the present time, ranging in age from 18 to 25 years. It is said that this man is in close touch with Berlin and is modeling his entire program along the lines followed by Hitler in Germany. . . ." So you studied this Fascist Party when you were in Holland, did you?
>
> MacGUIRE: No, sir; I did not. It was a matter of public information in the press and was reported so in the letter. . . .

The committee examined tellers from the Central Hanover Bank and Trust Company and other banks on financial transactions that had taken place between MacGuire and Clark, on the account of Albert Christmas, Clark's attorney.

Evidence was found that the day before MacGuire had allegedly seen Butler in Newark, he had drawn six thousand dollars in thousand-dollar bills from a "special account" in the Manufacturers Trust Company and had also been given ten thousand dollars in thousand-dollar bills by Christmas in Clark's presence. The committee was convinced that MacGuire had been the "cashier" for the planned veterans organization.

The committee also found evidence that disproved MacGuire's alibi that he had been in Chicago on September 24, as well as his contention that he had not seen Butler on that day at the Newark hotel. And it was established beyond dispute that he had written detailed letters to Clark and Christmas reporting on the Black Shirts of Italy, the Brown Shirts of Germany, and the Croix de Feu of France.

McCormack announced grimly that he would subpoena Clark as soon as he returned from Europe. "As the evidence stands," he declared, "it calls for an explanation that the committee has been unable to obtain from Mr. MacGuire."

On November 26, 1934, referring to MacGuire's testimony,

Representative Dickstein declared, "You can't get away from it —somebody is trying to shield somebody on something that looks rotten, and honest people don't do that."

11

When the committee called no further witnesses from among those named in the testimony, gossip swept Washington that the uncalled witnesses were simply too powerful to be subpoenaed.

Investigating, reporter John Spivak learned that the only one known to have been called to testify was California banker Frank N. Belgrano, commander of the American Legion. Checking into why he had not testified, Spivak found that he had been informed he could return home without having to answer a single question. The reporter could not verify a rumor that Belgrano had met with President Roosevelt at the White House, after which he had been taken off the committee's hook.

When Spivak tried to learn more about this from the committee itself, Dickstein revealed that he didn't know why Belgrano had been sent home without being questioned, and McCormack declined to answer any questions on the subject.

Apparently in response to Spivak and other newsmen pressing for an explanation of what the committee was doing about Butler's charges, McCormack announced on November 25 that the committee would make a statement the next day detailing the testimony it had received. He declared that it would reveal "several important inconsistencies" between the testimony of MacGuire and statements attributed to him in the press. McCormack also went out of his way to emphasize vigorously that General Butler could not be accused of "publicity seeking" in making public his exposure of the plot.

Next day, November 26, the committee's preliminary findings were released in an eight-thousand-word statement signed by

McCormack and Dickstein. It began: "This committee has had no evidence before it that would in the slightest degree warrant calling before it such men as John W. Davis, General Hugh Johnson, General James G. Harbord, Thomas W. Lamont, Admiral William S. Sims or Hanford MacNider. The committee will not take cognizance of names brought into the testimony which constitutes mere hearsay. This committee is not concerned with premature newspaper accounts, when given and published prior to the taking of testimony. . . ."

In 1971 McCormack told the author that he had always tried to operate by the rules of courtroom law, eliminating hearsay evidence he considered legally inadmissible. Dickstein had given the same explanation of the committee's modus operandi in 1934, whereupon Spivak had pointed out, "But your published reports are full of hearsay testimony." Dickstein had merely blinked and said, "They are?"

The committee statement withheld passing judgment on the testimony it had heard as premature, but the two chairmen indicated that they intended to pursue their inquiry further by calling Clark and Christmas to testify on their return from Europe, to question them about the thousand-dollar bills.

The New York Times reported:

COMMITTEE CALM
OVER BUTLER 'PLOT'

Has No Evidence to Warrant
Calling Johnson and Others
Named, It Declares

The so-called plot of Wall Street interests to have Major Gen. Smedley D. Butler head a Fascist movement to take over the national government and restore the gold dollar failed yesterday to emerge in any alarming proportions from the statement by the Congressional Committee on Un-American Activities on the evidence before it. . . .

But the committee was far from being as "calm" about the matter as the *Times* story insisted. On that same day Dickstein wrote to President Roosevelt, "The committee on C.U.A.A. has issued the enclosed short report on Gen. Butler's charges, which we have made public, as the pressure brought to bear on the committee made this course absolutely imperative. . . . I should very much like to have a conversation with you at your convenience."

The day after the *Times* ran its "Committee Calm" version of the preliminary McCormack-Dickstein statement, a refutation of this interpretation by Dickstein compelled the paper to print a revised article of the retraction. Now a new headline no longer carried the word "plot" in scoffing quotes:

BUTLER PLOT INQUIRY
NOT TO BE DROPPED

Dickstein Says Committee Will
Get to the Bottom of Story—
Awaits Clark's Return

The Congressional Committee on Un-American Activities still intends to get to the bottom of the story of a Wall Street plot to put Major Gen. Smedley D. Butler at the head of a Fascist army here, Representative Samuel Dickstein, vice chairman, said yesterday. The committee's statement of the evidence, he explained, was intended only to satisfy the great public interest in the plot.

Mr. Dickstein said that the committee was pleased that this preliminary report was received "neither as a whitewash of notable persons nor as sensationalism because of the startling nature of the possibilities, but simply as an indication of the purpose of the committee to proceed carefully in such an important matter."

Dickstein emphasized that the committee was far from satisfied with the story told by MacGuire, whose memory had failed to produce any satisfactory account of the funds that he had handled for Clark and Christmas. Furthermore, although Clark and Christmas had cabled from abroad that they were willing to return to testify, Dickstein said that they had not done so and that the committee would like to question them both. As soon as their presence was assured, a special executive session of the committee would be called to hear them.

On November 30 President Roosevelt replied to Dickstein, thanking him for sending him the preliminary report on the testimony and declaring, "I am interested in having it. I take it that the committee will proceed further."

12

On December 3, 1934, *Time* magazine ran a first-page story that attempted to ridicule Butler under the headlines "Plot Without Plotters." The story opened with a pseudoaccount of Butler on a white horse assembling 500,000 veterans at a C.C.C. camp at Elkridge, Maryland, and crying, "Men, Washington is but 30 miles away! Will you follow me?" The men all shout, "We will!" Then Butler's army marches south to Washington on Highway 1 while an ammunition train supplied by Remington Arms Company and E. I. du Pont de Nemours and Company brings up the rear.

Also in the column on horseback behind Butler, according to *Time*'s burlesqued version of the plot, are "that grim, old-time cavalryman, General Hugh Samuel Johnson" and MacArthur; behind them, three past national commanders of the American Legion—MacNider, Johnson, and Henry Stevens. They are followed in a shiny limousine by J. P. Morgan and his partner, Thomas W. Lamont.

Then, in *Time*'s parody, Butler ("his spurs clinked loudly") strides into Roosevelt's study and barks, "Mr. President, I have 500,000 men outside who want peace but want something more. I wish you to remove Cordell Hull as Secretary of State." Roosevelt promptly telephones for Hull's resignation.

"And now, Mr. President, I ask you to fill the vacancy which has just occurred in your Cabinet by appointing me Secretary of State." Roosevelt signs the commission for Butler, who then tells him, "Let it be understood that henceforth I will act as the nation's executive. You may continue to live here at the White House and draw your salary but you will do and say only what I tell you. If not, you and Vice-President Garner will be dealt with as I think best. In that event, as Secretary of State, I shall succeed to the Presidency, as provided by law." The President nods assent, and the United States becomes a Fascist state. *Time* then commented:

> Such was the nightmarish page of future United States history pictured last week in Manhattan by General Butler himself to the special House Committee investigating un-American Activities. No military officer of the United States since the late tempestuous George Custer has succeeded in publicly floundering in so much hot water as Smedley Darlington Butler.

Time then recounted highlights of Butler's career, emphasizing the controversies he had never shied away from and implying that they arose solely from the general's taste for publicity.

> Last month he told a Manhattan Jewish congregation that he would never again fight outside the U.S. General Butler's sensational tongue had not been heard in the nation's Press for more than a week when he cornered a reporter for the Philadelphia *Record* and New York *Post,* poured into his ears the lurid tale that he had been offered leadership of a Fascist Putsch scheduled for next year. . . .
>
> Thanking their stars for having such sure-fire publicity dropped in their laps, Representatives McCormack and Dickstein began calling witnesses to expose the "plot." But there did not seem to be any plotters.
>
> A bewildered army captain, commandant at the Elkridge CCC camp, could shed no light on the report that his post was to be turned into a revolutionary base.
>
> Mr. Morgan, just off a boat from Europe, had nothing to say, but Partner Lamont did: "Perfect moonshine! Too utterly ridiculous to comment upon!" . . .
>
> Investor Clark, in Paris, freely admitted trying to get General Butler to use his influence with the Legion against dollar devaluation, but stoutly maintained: "I am neither a

Fascist nor a Communist, but an American." He threatened
a libel suit "unless the whole affair is relegated to the funny
sheets by Sunday."

"It sounds like the best laugh story of the year," chimed
in General MacArthur from Washington. . . .

Though most of the country was again laughing at the
latest Butler story, the special House Committee declined
to join in the merriment. . . . "From present indications,"
said the publicity-loving New York Representative [Dick-
stein], "General Butler has the evidence. He's not making
serious charges unless he has something to back them up.
We will have some men here with bigger names than Butler's before this is over."

For those of its readers who might have found *Time*'s satirical
attack too subtle, the magazine helped them get the message by
its choice of photos to accompany the story. An unflattering
photo of Butler in civilian clothes, with his finger reflectively in
one ear, was labeled, "He was deaf to a dictatorship." The pose
subtly suggested that the general, as the copy broadly hinted, was
a bit daft.

In contrast, a jovial, laughing picture of that good-natured,
genial humanitarian, J. P. Morgan, looking like everybody's
grandfather, was labeled, "Moonshine provided the amusement."
And a stern, handsome picture of Colonel Grayson M.-P. Murphy,
dressed in a trim World War I colonel's uniform, hand dashingly
on hip, was captioned with this quote: " 'A fantasy!' "

The author asked McCormack in 1971 about *Time*'s fairness
in reporting the Butler hearing. The answer was a snort of disgust. "*Time* has always been about as filthy a publication as
ever existed," he said emphatically. "I've said that publicly many
times. The truth gets no coverage at all, just sensationalism,
whatever will sell copies."

Indignant on Butler's behalf, the New York City post of the
V.F.W. sent President Roosevelt a wire on December 7 pledging
their loyalty and support, and commending Butler for his courage
and patriotism in exposing the conspirators.

Ten days later McCormack announced that Albert Christmas
had returned from Europe and would testify in two or three

days in an executive session. Clark's attorney was not questioned, however, until the final day of the committee's life, January 3, 1935, after which no further investigatory action could be taken by the committee.

". . . and then the questions were limited only to money given MacGuire by the lawyer and Clark," Spivak noted. "Presumably because of the sacredness of lawyer-client confidences, no questions were asked about conversations or correspondence between an alleged principal in the plot and his attorney."

There was an interesting exchange, nevertheless, in the matter of $65,000 MacGuire testified that he had received for traveling and entertainment expenses:

> McCormack: So the way you want to leave it is there is $65,000 or $66,000 that Mr. MacGuire received from either you, or Mr. Clark, which he spent in the period between June and December of 1933 for traveling and entertainment expenses?
>
> Christmas: Yes, sir.
>
> McCormack: Did he return to you some time in August [1934] approximately $30,000 in cash?
>
> Christmas: No.
>
> McCormack: Do you know he testified he did?
>
> Christmas: The committee gave me some indication of such testimony at a previous session.
>
> McCormack: Assuming he has testified to that, that is not so?
>
> Christmas: I would say he is in error. He is mistaken.

So the committee found still another reason to doubt the veracity of MacGuire, who had denied, under oath, all the allegations of the Fascist plot in which he was the go-between, as alleged by General Smedley Butler.

13

Press coverage of what was obviously a startling story of utmost importance to the security of the nation was largely one of distortion, suppression, and omission.

"In the case of the Liberty League–Legion–Wall Street conspiracy to overthrow the United States Government," George Seldes declared in his book *1000 Americans*, "there was one of the most reprehensible conspiracies of silence in the long (and disgraceful) history of American journalism."

In his book *Facts and Fascism* he wrote, "Most papers suppressed the whole story or threw it down by ridiculing it. Nor did the press later publish the McCormack-Dickstein report which stated that every charge Butler made and French corroborated had been proven true."

The most sensitive revelations, as far as the press was concerned, were those touching upon connections with J. P. Morgan and Company and the powerful interests represented by the American Liberty League. Heywood Broun, the highly esteemed columnist for the New York *World Telegram,* once observed that the face of *The New York Times* was "black with the Morgan shoepolish." Speaker McCormack told me, "The *Times* is the most slanting newspaper in the world. I would not expect anything else from them. They brainwash the American people. It's an empire."

In fairness to *The New York Times* of today, however, I should quote their severest critic, George Seldes, who wrote me in October, 1971, "I find the press [today] more liberal, too, especially *The New York Times*. (And I have not grown mellow in my views, I think.)"

If the prestigious *Times* had distorted the Wall Street conspiracy story in 1934–1935, class-angling the news was obviously more pronounced in the heavily anti-Roosevelt, pro-big-business press of that day, much of which derived huge advertising revenues from corporations involved in the American Liberty League.

Van Zandt wrote Butler on December 26, "The next time I see you I will explain to you just how I became involved in the Nazi story. After I read your article in the paper the Commander of North Dakota and a few others asked me to give them the low-down which I did resulting that one of the boys carried the story to the newspaper; therefore, causing such article to appear in print, and, of course, misquoting me all around."

Butler replied on January 2, 1935, "I thought your statements on the Fascist story were darn good and served to stir up the lines. However, I can guess how it came about, but it did no harm."

14

The storm of controversy over his exposure of the plot led radio station WCAU of Philadelphia, Pennsylvania, to urge Butler to make broadcasts for them two to four nights a week. He agreed, and beginning on January 4 took to the airwaves with hard-hitting attacks on Fascist plotters. What he had to say was impressive enough to make small headlines in the back pages of newspapers sufficiently often to generate enthusiastic support from the nation's veterans.

On January 7 the Miami, Oklahoma, post of V.F.W. passed a resolution: "Major General Smedley D. Butler should be commended for his high type of patriotism in exposing the alleged plot to establish a dictatorship in the United States, and . . . Franklin D. Roosevelt, President, and citizens of the United States, should express their appreciation of this exposure."

A movement began within the V.F.W. to have each post

reaffirm its loyalty to the President and the Constitution. "This, in my opinion, would serve notice upon all plotters against our government," wrote Henry S. Drezner, V.F.W. official of a Brooklyn post, "that the Veterans will not stand idly by while an attempt should be made to destroy our form of government."

On January 31 a New Jersey veteran wrote Butler, "General, at this time I can say you have 95 percent of the New Jersey veterans in back of you in anything you do."

Two weeks later Dickstein declared that he intended to seek a new congressional appropriation to press a thorough investigation into Butler's charges.

"General Butler's charges were too serious to be dropped without further investigation," Dickstein insisted. "He is a man of unquestioned sincerity and integrity. Furthermore, in my opinion, his statements were not denied or refuted. I think the matter should be gone into thoroughly and completely and I intend asking Congress for funds to make such an investigation. The country should know the full truth about these reputed overtures to General Butler. If there are individuals or interests who have ideas and plans such as he testified to, they should be dragged out into the open."

On February 15 McCormack submitted to the House of Representatives the committee's findings in the investigation:

> In the last few weeks of the committee's official life it received evidence showing that certain persons had made an attempt to establish a fascist organization in this country.
>
> No evidence was presented and this committee had none to show a connection between this effort and any fascist activity of any European country.
>
> There is no question that these attempts were discussed, were planned, and might have been placed in execution when and if the financial backers deemed it expedient.
>
> This committee received evidence from Maj. Gen Smedley D. Butler (retired), twice decorated by the Congress of the United States. He testified before the committee as to conversations with one Gerald C. MacGuire in which the latter is alleged to have suggested the formation of a fascist army under the leadership of General Butler (p. 8-114 D.C. 6 II).

MacGuire denied these allegations under oath, but *your committee was able to verify all the pertinent statements made by General Butler,** with the exception of the direct statement suggesting the creation of the organization. This, however, was corroborated in the correspondence of Mac-Guire with his principal, Robert Sterling Clark, of New York City, while MacGuire was abroad studying the various forms of veterans organizations of Fascist character (p. 111 D.C. 6 II).

There was also corroboration of this point in French's testimony. The committee then cited an excerpt from the letter MacGuire had written to Clark and Christmas from France praising the Croix de Feu as a model veterans organization.

This committee asserts that any efforts based on lines as suggested in the foregoing and leading off to the extreme right, are just as bad as efforts which would lead to the extreme left.

Armed forces for the purpose of establishing a dictatorship by means of Fascism or a dictatorship through the instrumentality of the proleteriat, or a dictatorship predicated on racial and religious hatreds, have no place in this country.

This total vindication of Butler did not burst like a bombshell across the front pages of America. Instead, as Seldes noted, "Most newspapers again suppressed or buried or belittled the official verdict."

The New York Times made no mention of the plot in its head-lines on the committee's report, emphasizing instead the committee's proposal that all foreign propagandists—Fascist, Nazi, and Communist—be compelled to register with the State Department. In the fifth and sixth paragraphs of the story the *Times* briefly reported:

It also alleged that definite proof had been found that the much publicized Fascist march on Washington, which was to have been led by Major Gen. Smedley D. Butler, retired, according to testimony at a hearing, was actually contem-

---

* Italics are the author's.

plated. The committee recalled testimony by General Butler, saying he had testified that Gerald C. MacGuire had
tried to persuade him to accept the leadership of a Fascist
army.

And that was all.

15

John L. Spivak had been tipped off earlier by a fellow Washington correspondent that some of Butler's testimony had been deleted in the committee's November 26, 1934 report to the House
of Representatives, and not for national security reasons. Spivak
determined to get a look at the complete uncensored record of
the testimony given at the executive session.

He had asked for permission to see it, in order to follow up
leads on Nazi activities in the United States, but he had been
turned down on grounds that no one outside the committee and
its employees could see transcripts of testimony taken in executive session.

Other newsmen, however, joined him in pressing for a copy
of the Butler testimony. It was then that the defunct McCormack-
Dickstein Committee, possibly to quiet persistent rumors about
why it was being hushed up, decided to publish a 125-page
document containing the testimony of Butler, McGuire, and
others, on February 15, 1935. It was marked "Extracts," and the
last page explained why:

> In making public the foregoing evidence, which was taken
> in executive session in New York City from November 20
> to 24, inclusive, the committee has ordered stricken there-
> from certain immaterial and incompetent evidence, or evi-
> dence which was not pertinent to the inquiry, and which
> would not have been received during a public hearing.

Spivak's newshawk instincts did not let him fully accept this explanation, because he knew that the committee *had* published hearsay evidence. Like a terrier worrying a rag doll, he persisted in trying to find out what evidence had been cut. Other questions nagged at him. Why had the committee at first announced it would subpoena all those named by Butler, only to declare later that it had no evidence on which to question them? Was the clue to this abrupt change of mind to be found in the censored testimony?

A veteran Washington correspondent told Spivak that he had heard the deletions had been made at the request of a member of the President's Cabinet. The implication was that release of certain names could embarrass the Democratic party, because two had been unsuccessful Democratic candidates for the Presidency —John W. Davis, the Morgan lawyer, and Al Smith, governor of New York before Roosevelt.

Davis had been named in the committee's press release, but not Al Smith, the erstwhile "happy warrior" from the slums of New York who had become codirector with Irénée du Pont in the American Liberty League, and a bitter critic of Roosevelt's liberalism and New Deal reform.

Spivak tried everything to check out the story but found himself up against a brick wall at every turn.

He had been tipped off earlier that the House of Representatives intended to let the McCormack-Dickstein Committee expire on January 3, 1935, rather than renew it as the committee had asked in order to continue its investigations. And die the committee did.

About a week later, seeking to do a story on its accomplishments in exposing Nazi and anti-Semitic activities in the United States, Spivak won permission from Dickstein to examine the committee's official exhibits and make photostatic copies of those that had been made public. Dickstein wrote a letter to this effect to the committee's secretary, Frank P. Randolph, and added, "If necessary consult John [McCormack] about it."

Randolph, flooded with work involved in closing the committee's files and records, gave Spivak stacks of documents, exhibits, and transcripts of testimony that were being sent to the Government Printing Office. To Spivak's amazement, he found among these records a full transcript of the executive session hearings in the Butler affair.

Excited by this accidental stroke of luck, he compared it with the official extract of the hearings and found a number of startling omissions made from the testimony of both Butler and French, some of which could not be justified on grounds of hearsay evidence. Spivak copied down the censored material.

In 1971 I asked former Speaker McCormack if he could recall, after thirty-four years, the reasons for these omissions from the official record of the testimony at the hearings.

"I don't recall striking anything from the record," he told me, "but if I did, it was because I tried to be as careful as I could about hearsay evidence in open hearings. Executive hearings were different. We'd let people say anything there because we'd get lots of valuable tips to follow up that way. But in open hearings I insisted that all the evidence had to be pertinent, relevant, and germane—evidence that would stand up in a courtroom to the nth degree. I don't think all investigative committees follow this method, but they should. I wanted to be very careful about safeguarding the character of anyone who might be named, without hard evidence, by a witness in testimony at an open hearing, so if somebody gave hearsay evidence, I would say, 'Strike it out.'"

Omissions from the official record of some revelations from the testimony of Butler and French gave the American press, with a few minor exceptions, a legitimate excuse to keep silent about them. It was significant that none of the biggest newspaper chains or wire services saw fit to assign crack reporters to dig into what was obviously one of the biggest news stories of the decade.

John L. Spivak could not help wondering why MacGuire, the key to the plot, had not been compelled to testify on where and how he had obtained his advance inside information about Al Smith's plans, Hugh Johnson's firing, and the appearance of the American Liberty League; or why he had not been asked to reveal the sources of his information about the Morgan and Du Pont interests' involvement in the plot.

Worst of all, no one involved in the plot had been prosecuted. Spivak went to the Department of Justice and pointed out that MacGuire had denied essential parts of Butler's testimony, which the committee itself reported it had proved by documents, bank records, and letters. Did the department intend to file a criminal prosecution against MacGuire for perjury or involvement in the plot?

"I was told," Spivak reported, "it had no plans to prosecute."

Roger Baldwin, director of the American Civil Liberties Union, issued an angry statement on the curious apathy of the Justice Department in punishing any of the miscreants:

> The Congressional Committee investigating un-American activities has just reported that the Fascist plot to seize the government . . . was proved; yet not a single participant will be prosecuted under the perfectly plain language of the federal conspiracy act making this a high crime. Imagine the action if such a plot were discovered among Communists!
>
> Which is, of course, only to emphasize the nature of our government as representative of the interests of the controllers of property. Violence, even to the seizure of government, is excusable on the part of those whose lofty motive is to preserve the profit system. . . .

Powerful influences had obviously been brought to bear to cut short the hearings, stop subpoenas from being issued to all the important figures involved, and end the life of the committee.

The Philadelphia *Record*, which broke the story by French, had these observations in an editorial:

> General Butler deserves the highest praise for recognizing the significance of the offers made to him, and the menace they represent. "I'm a democrat, not a Fascist," General Butler says, "and I was sick and tired of being linked by rumor to this Fascist movement and that one. I believe in the right to vote, the right to speak freely and the right to write whatever one believes. . . . I am certainly not going to lead a movement to destroy the very principles in which I believe." General Butler performed a great public service

and showed himself a true American by taking his information to the McCormack committee.

The *Record* condemned phony "popular" movements like the National Economy League, a front for big business, and added:

> Some of the same interests behind the League, according to General Butler, are behind this effort to use him and his soldier following in defense of special privilege in America. The same people who succeeded in slashing aid to veterans would like to use those same veterans as their pawns in a war on democracy.
>
> The folk who want Fascism in this country are the same folk who made profit while others bled and who would rather see the veteran starve than unbalance the budget, i.e., add to the burden of taxes on great wealth. They did it in Italy. They did it in Germany. They did it in Austria. They will try to do it in America. . . . General Butler has nipped one such movement in the bud.

John L. Spivak had shrewd observations about the reasons the conspirators had failed dismally in their treason:

> The takeover plot failed because though those involved had astonishing talents for making breathtaking millions of dollars, they lacked an elementary understanding of people and the moral forces that activate them. In a money-standard civilization such as ours, the universal regard for anyone who is rich tends to persuade some millionaires that they are knowledgeable in fields other than the making of money. The conspirators went about the plot as if they were hiring an office manager; all they needed was to send a messenger to the man they had selected.

And with incredible ineptitude, they had selected the wrong man.

16

Was it possible that MacGuire had exaggerated to both Butler and French about the powerful and influential figures involved in the plot, in order to impress Butler into accepting the leadership of the Fascist putsch that MacGuire was in charge of planning?

It is conceivable that some of those named by MacGuire as under consideration for the role of dictator or subordinate positions of leadership had no knowledge of this fact, although Van Zandt reported that he, for one, had been approached. It is unlikely that Douglas MacArthur, as Chief of Staff and a stiff-necked hero with patriotic credentials as unchallengeable as Butler's, would have had any unsavory dealings with the plotters, however patrician his outlook.

As for involvement of the American Legion, MacGuire had obviously been influential enough in the organization to have been made chairman of the "distinguished guest committee" of its convention, on the staff of National Commander Louis Johnson, former Secretary of Defense and head of a large law firm in Clarksburg, West Virginia.

There is solid evidence that MacGuire had been able to use the Legion to do mutimillionaire Robert S. Clark's bidding and get the Legion to pass a resolution demanding a return to the gold standard.

MacGuire was certainly financed by Clark, Christmas, Walter E. Frew, of the Corn Exchange Bank, and others through the Committee for a Sound Dollar and Sound Currency, Inc., of which MacGuire was an official. And the McCormack-Dickstein Committee verified that he had been sent abroad to study Fascist organizations in Europe as models for creating one in America and had reported favorably to Clark and Christmas about the Croix de Feu.

MacGuire had outlined to Butler and French the conspirators' plans for a putsch, indicating it would easily succeed in just a few days because a "big fellow" organization—later identified by Butler and French as the American Liberty League—was behind it with money and arms.

He might have been boasting falsely about having had his headquarters while in Paris at the offices of Morgan and Hodges and about the involvement of the Morgan interests in the plot. The McCormack-Dickstein Committee failed to pursue this line of investigation, but a remarkable number of "coincidences" linked the Morgan interests to various facets of the plot.

Colonel Grayson M.-P. Murphy, MacGuire's boss who had supported his denial of Butler's charges by insisting, "I don't believe there is a word of truth in it with respect to Mr. Mac-Guire," was a director of a Morgan bank. Butler testified that Clark had implicated John W. Davis, attorney for J. P. Morgan and Company, as author of the speech Clark had given MacGuire to get Butler to deliver at the Legion convention. Davis was the same man from whom MacGuire had declared he could easily raise a million dollars for his Fascist army. MacGuire had also revealed to Butler that the same financial interests who had been behind the gold-standard propaganda were financing the plot to seize the White House.

The formation of the American Liberty League had been announced precisely at the time MacGuire had predicted the emergence of an organization of "big fellows" who were in the background of the Fascist putsch. Its treasurer had been none other than Colonel Grayson M.-P. Murphy. One of its financial backers was Robert S. Clark. Two of the largest contributors had been the J. P. Morgan Associates and the Du Pont interests. John W. Davis was a member of the National Executive Committee. Morgan and Du Pont men were directors. And MacGuire had told French that the putsch could obtain arms and equipment from the Remington Arms Company, in which the Du Ponts held a controlling interest, on credit through the Du Ponts.

The presence of ex-Governor Al Smith in the American Liberty League baffled many Americans who could not understand what the former poor kid from the Bowery was doing mixed up with

America's richest ultraconservatives. Few realized that following his defection from the Roosevelt camp, Smith entered private business as chairman of the board of the New York County Trust Company and joined in erecting the Empire State Building, of which he was corporation president.

His alliance with Raskob and the Du Ponts in the League brought charges that he had "forsaken the brown derby for the top hat." When he failed to stop Roosevelt's renomination in 1936, he stumped for Republican candidate Alf Landon, losing much of his former popularity in the process and speaking to dwindling, hostile audiences.

Were all the interlacing connections linking MacGuire, Clark, Colonel Murphy, and the Morgan and Du Pont interests to the plot only a series of remarkable coincidences? If so, another unique coincidence led the American Liberty League to subsidize such affiliated organizations as the openly Fascist and anti-Semitic Sentinels of the Republic and the Crusaders, who were urged by their leader, George W. Christians, to consider lynching Roosevelt.

One night when the President was scheduled to arrive in Chattanooga, Christians threatened to cut off the city's electric power and warned grimly, "Lots of things can happen in the dark!" This protégé of the American Liberty League was kept under surveillance by the Secret Service.

As Donald R. McCoy observed in his book, *Coming of Age: The United States During the 1920's and 1930's,* ". . . it was clear to most people that the organization [American Liberty League] was playing the same game on the Right as the radical groups were playing on the Left, to influence the [Roosevelt] administration and if unsuccessful to oppose it. As James Farley would later say, the American Liberty League 'ought to be called the American Cellophane League' because 'first it's a Du Pont product and second, you can see right through it.' "

Finally, one must consider the outlook of the conspirators against the background of the times. During the feverish atmosphere of the early New Deal days, big business was horrified by Roosevelt's drastic surgery on the broken-down machinery of the capitalist system. The savage hatred of "that cripple in the

White House" represented the most bitter animosity big business had ever manifested toward any President in American history.

Their hate campaign was echoed by the vast majority of newspapers, like the Hearst press, which had originally supported the President, then denounced him as a dictator. Roosevelt had been compelled to turn to "fireside chats" over the radio in order to communicate with the American people over the heads of the press lords.

In that emotional climate it was not at all surprising that some elements of big business should have sought to emulate their counterparts in Germany and Italy, supporting a Fascist putsch to take over the government and run it under a dictator on behalf of America's bankers and industrialists.

That it did not happen here could be credited largely to the patriotism and determination of one courageous American—Major General Smedley Darlington Butler.

PART
FOUR

Fallout

1

About seven weeks after Butler and French had testified, John Spivak asked McCormack for an interview, and it was granted. McCormack had no fear of talking to a reporter from the *New Masses*, for which Spivak was writing at the time. Communist-oriented or not, McCormack knew that the *Masses* was in the forefront of exposing Nazi and anti-Semitic activities in the United States.

Asked about the deleted testimony, McCormack at first suggested that Spivak was relying on gossip. When Spivak revealed and convinced McCormack that he had seen the transcript of the executive session, the congressman grew annoyed and canceled the interview. He agreed to let Spivak leave questions with him, however, and said he would reply to those he chose to answer within three days.

Writing Spivak a letter three days later, he gave no specific answers to questions about the American Liberty League, the American Legion's passage of the gold resolution, and the report that John W. Davis had written the speech that MacGuire and Clark had wanted Butler to make.

"The reason for certain portions of General Butler's testimony in executive session being deleted from the public record," he wrote, "has been clearly stated in the public record."

He went on to make a broad attack against the plotters and to suggest that the hearings had defeated them: "As a result of the investigation, and the disclosures made, this movement has been stopped, and is practically broken up. There is no question but that some of the leaders are attempting to carry on, but they can make no headway. Public opinion, as a result of the disclosures of the investigation, is aroused."

Spivak went to see Dickstein and asked him why Colonel Grayson M.-P. Murphy had not been called upon to testify. "Your committee knew," Spivak reminded him, "that Murphy's men are in the anti-Semitic espionage organization, Order of '76."

"We didn't have the time," Dickstein replied. "We'd have taken care of the Wall Street groups if we had the time. I would have had no hesitation in going after the Morgans."

"You had Belgrano, commander of the American Legion, listed to testify. Why wasn't he examined?"

"I don't know," Dickstein replied, and referred him back to McCormack for the answer.

2

Spivak decided to inform General Butler, who, he was sure, did not realize it, that portions of his and French's testimony had been omitted in the official report issued by the McCormack-Dickstein Committee. "If he knew and said so publicly," Spivak reasoned, "he would reach a vastly greater audience than was available to me through the *New Masses*."

Telephoning the general, Spivak announced that he was from the *New Masses* and wanted to see him about his testimony.

"Come on out," Butler said promptly. "Glad to see you."

The roads had not been cleared of a heavy snowfall of the night before, and Spivak trudged to the house in Newtown Square through knee-deep snow. His spartan march appealed to Butler, who welcomed him heartily with the approval he had always shown to soldiers who disregarded the foulest weather to push on doggedly with their assigned missions.

Spivak saw a slender man with receding hair, lined and sunken cheeks, thick eyebrows, furrowed lines between keen eyes, generous nose, and jutting underlip. He liked Butler instantly, and the feeling was apparently mutual.

During their talk Butler revealed that he was intensely preoccupied with the corporate exploitation of the military for profit. Anxious to arouse Americans to this spoliation, he now believed it might be done by a more sophisticated book of memoirs and reflections than *Old Gimlet Eye.*

"I think you're the man I've been hoping to run into to help me do an autobiography," he told Spivak. "There are things I've seen, things I've learned that should not be left unsaid. War is a racket to protect economic interests, not our country, and our soldiers are sent to die on foreign soil to protect investments by big business."

Spivak said regretfully that he felt compelled to continue investigating and exposing a more urgent and dangerous situation —Nazi activities in the United States. Butler agreed at once that this activity was more important and offered to help by opening any doors he could for Spivak.

During their discussion Spivak learned "things about big business and politics, sometimes in earthy, four-letter words, the like of which I had never heard." Butler spilled over with anger at the hypocrisy that had marked American interference in the internal affairs of other governments, behind a smoke screen of pious expressions of high-sounding purpose.

"We supervised elections in Haiti," he said wryly, "and wherever we supervised them our candidate always won."

Admiring Butler's candor, Spivak did not want to mislead him or sail under false colors. He reminded the general that he was from the *New Masses,* and in case Butler didn't know it, added, "It's supposed to be a Communist magazine."

"So who the hell cares?" Butler shrugged. "There wouldn't be a United States if it wasn't for a bunch of radicals. I once heard of a radical named George Washington. As a matter of fact from what I read he was an extremist—a goddam revolutionist!"

Because of his fierce anti-Fascist and anti-big-business views, Butler was sometimes Red-baited. He was scarcely unique in being made a target for this kind of attack by rightists and ultra-

conservatives. As George Seldes told me, "If you are saying anything in general about the fight against fascism in America, it
seems to me that a point to emphasize is that the entire Red-
baiting wave which culminated in the McCarthy era was successful in inundating the anti-Fascists by making every anti-
Fascist, whether liberal, socialist, or Communist, a Red."

Butler was shocked when Spivak showed him copies of the
portions of his and French's testimony that had been deleted
from the official report of the hearings. His scowl deepened as
Spivak revealed that Belgrano had been dismissed without being
asked a single question about what had happened at the "gold-
standard resolution" Legion convention in Chicago.

According to Spivak, upon learning that the committee had
reported to Congress that it had verified the authenticity of the
plot, yet no action had been taken about MacGuire's wholesale
denials under oath, Butler lost control of his volatile temper.

"I'll be goddammed!" he roared. "You can be sure I'm going
to say something about this!"

Spivak asked him to hold off long enough to let the tiny-
circulation *New Masses* break the story first. Butler agreed. When
the *Masses* appeared with the exposé, it was a sensational news
scoop, but none of the Washington correspondents dared touch
it or follow it up.

"Several expressed regret," Spivak related, "that the exposés
were appearing in the *New Masses*; when they quoted from one
of my stories—solely on its news value—their editors cut the
material out and advised them that quotes from 'that magazine'
might make readers say the paper was spreading Red propaganda. So great had the fear of communism and 'Red propaganda' become that even editors who did not swallow all of it
themselves went along because it was the popular attitude."

3

In his broadcast over WCAU on February 17, 1935, Butler revealed that some of the "most important" portions of his testimony had been suppressed in the McCormack-Dickstein report to Congress. The committee, he growled, had "stopped dead in its tracks when it got near the top." He added angrily:

> Like most committees, it has slaughtered the little and allowed the big to escape. The big shots weren't even called to testify. Why wasn't Colonel Grayson M.-P. Murphy, New York broker . . . called? Why wasn't Louis Howe, Secretary to the President of the United States, called? . . . Why wasn't Al Smith called? And why wasn't Gen. Douglas MacArthur, Chief of Staff of the United States Army, called? And why wasn't Hanford MacNider, former American Legion commander, called? They were all mentioned in the testimony. And why was all mention of these names suppressed from the committee report?
>
> This was no piker set-up. MacGuire, who was the agent of the Wall Street bankers and brokers who proposed this organization, told me that $3,000,000 was "on the line" and that $300,000,000—and that's a lot of money even today—was in view to put over this plot to bluff the government.

He kept up a running attack on the conspirators night after night, revealing facts that had been omitted in the official committee report. In another broadcast he lashed out at the American Legion with no holds barred:

> Do you think it could be hard to buy the American Legion for un-American activities? You know, the average veteran thinks the Legion is a patriotic organization to perpetuate the memories of the last war, an organization to

promote peace, to take care of the wounded and to keep green the graves of those who gave their lives.

But is the American Legion that? No sir, not while it is controlled by the bankers. For years the bankers, by buying big club houses for various posts, by financing its beginning, and otherwise, have tried to make a strikebreaking organization of the Legion. The groups—the so-called Royal Family of the Legion—which have picked its officers for years, aren't interested in patriotism, in peace, in wounded veterans, in those who gave their lives. . . No, they are interested only in using the veterans, through their officers.

Why, even now, the commander of the American Legion is a banker—a banker who must have known what MacGuire's money was going to be used for. His name was mentioned in the testimony. Why didn't they call Belgrano and ask him why he contributed?

Butler was incredulous when he read that Colonel William E. Easterwood, national vice-commander of the Legion, while visiting Italy in 1935, had pinned a Legion button on Mussolini, making him an "honorary member," and had invited the dictator to the next Legion convention in Chicago.

Why, Butler wondered, did the Legion membership stand for such an abuse of the organization in their name? Apparently an uproar of sorts did break out, because Mussolini's honorary membership was later canceled as "unconstitutional" on grounds that the Legion had no honorary members.

Representative Dickstein was given the job of replying to Butler's radio blasts in a broadcast over the same network. The fifty-year-old congressman gave the committee's version of the censored testimony:

> General Smedley Butler saw fit to employ this radio network to indulge in general criticism of the work done by the Congressional Committee on Un-American Activities and to cast aspersions on the character of such men as Alfred E. Smith, Louis Howe, General MacArthur and Hanford MacNider. . . .
>
> The committee felt it should hear General Butler and . . . follow out the "leads" which the general furnished to the

members of the committee. The testimony given by General Butler was kept confidential until such time as the names of the persons who were mentioned in his testimony could be checked upon and verified. The committee did not want to hear General Butler's allegations without giving itself the opportunity to verify the assertions made by him.

It did not feel like dragging into the mud of publicity names of persons who were mentioned by General Butler unless his statements could be verified, since untold damage might be caused to a person's reputation, by public discussion of testimony which could not be substantiated.

This accounts for the fact that when the results of the hearings were finally made public, references to Alfred E. Smith and others were omitted. They were wholly without consequence and public mention might be misinterpreted by the public.

The essential portions, however, of General Butler's testimony have been released to the public and his specific charges relating to the proposed organization of a "soldier's movement" have been thoroughly aired and passed upon by the committee. . . .

General Butler asks why Clark was not called before the committee. Well, the reason was that Mr. Clark has been living in France for over a year, as General Butler well knows, and naturally he could not be subpoenaed, but on the 29th of December, 1934, Mr. Clark was represented before the committee in the person of his attorney, and full information was given the committee. Mr. Butler didn't tell you this. . . .

4

For whatever additional light could be shed on the plot to take over the White House that he had helped to expose, I interviewed John W. McCormack on September 17, 1971. At seventy-nine, lean, bright, warm, and friendly, the former Speaker of the

House revealed a sharp, clear memory that enabled him to recall spontaneously many names and details of the hearings over which he had presided as chairman thirty-four years earlier.

I reminded him that the committee had said that it wanted to hear Clark's testimony, and Clark had stated that he would return from Europe to testify, but had not done so. Yet he had not called or subpoenaed Clark to do so. Why not?

"We couldn't subpoena Clark to testify at the executive session of our hearings because they were held outside of Washington," McCormack explained. "According to the law of that day, we had no power to subpoena anyone to executive sessions outside the Capital. I subsequently recommended changing the law to give congressional committees that right, and the change was in fact made." *

Asked whether he knew what the reaction of President Roosevelt or Louis Howe had been to the exposure of the plot, he replied that he did not.

Why had the Department of Justice under Attorney General Homer Cummings failed to initiate criminal proceedings against any of the plotters?

"The way I figure it," he replied, "we did our job in the committee by exposing the plot, and then it was up to the Department of Justice to do their job—to take it from there."

John L. Spivak was equally mystified by the lack of any action taken by the department against the conspirators. When I asked him about it, he replied, "I have no knowledge why the Attorney General did not pursue this matter except that most likely it was deemed politically inadvisable." He thought it possible that the decision might actually have been made in the White House on a basis of sheer pragmatism. As he speculated in his book *A Man in His Time*:

> What would be the public gain from delving deeper into a plot which was already exposed and whose principals could be kept under surveillance? Roosevelt had enough

---

* The hearings were probably held in New York rather than in Washington because the committee at the same time was investigating Communist infiltration in the fur unions of that city.

headaches in those troubled days without having to make a
face-to-face confrontation with men of great wealth and
power. Was it avoidance of such a confrontation? Was it a
desire by the head of the Democratic Party to avoid going
into matters which could split the party down the middle,
what with Davis and Smith, two former party heads, among
those named by Butler?

I asked McCormack what his own reactions had been to Mac-
Guire's testimony denying all of Butler's allegations.

"There was no doubt that General Butler was telling the truth,"
he replied. "We believed his testimony one hundred percent. He
was a great, patriotic American in every respect."

"In your considered judgment, Mr. Speaker, were those men
Butler named as involved in the plot guilty?"

"Millions were at stake when Clark and the others got the
Legion to pass that resolution on the gold standard in 1933,"
he answered. "When Roosevelt refused to be pressured by it, and
went even further off the gold standard, those fellows got desperate and decided to look into European methods, with the
idea of introducing them into America. They sent MacGuire to
Europe to study the Fascist organizations. We found the evidence
that Clark and [Colonel] Grayson Murphy, who underwrote the
American Legion with $125,000, were involved when we ex-
amined MacGuire's records and bank accounts."

I asked him about Colonel Murphy's role in the plot.

"Grayson Murphy was a number-one kingmaker in the Legion.
His firm had clients of great wealth. Those fellows were afraid
that Roosevelt would take their money away by taxes. They were
desperate and sought to take power and frighten Roosevelt into
doing what they wanted. But they made the mistake of approaching the wrong man to do the job."

"Had the plotters only wanted to take over the White House
to restore the gold standard, or were they also out to destroy the
New Deal and set up a Fascist dictatorship to run the country
through an American Mussolini?"

McCormack reflected a moment, then said, "Well, we were in
the depths of a severe depression, and we had a good man,

Roosevelt, in the White House, and he'd revived the hopes and confidence of the American people. The plotters definitely hated the New Deal because it was for the people, not for the moneyed interests, and they were willing to spend a lot of their money to dump Mr. Roosevelt out of the White House."

"Could you say definitely that the American Liberty League was the organization of 'big fellows' that MacGuire had described as being behind the plotters?"

"I don't know anything about the Liberty League," he replied in a crisp manner that did not encourage me to pursue any further interrogation along that line.

"Mr. Speaker, why were the plotters so insistent that General Butler accept their proposal that he be the one to head the Fascist march on Washington they planned?"

"They chose Smedley Butler because they needed an 'enlisted man's general,' not a 'general's general.' They had to have a colorful figure half a million or more veterans who had been privates and noncoms would follow. General Butler was the most popular one."

"If General Butler had been an ambitious man like Aaron Burr and had been willing to be the Man on the White Horse for the plotters, do you think their conspiracy to take over the White House, with all that money behind it, might have succeeded?"

"Well, if General Butler had not been the patriot he was, and if they had been able to maintain secrecy, the plot certainly might very well have succeeded, having in mind the conditions existing at that time. No one can say for sure, of course, but when times are desperate and people are frustrated, anything like that could happen."

"And we might have gone Fascist?"

"If the plotters had got rid of Roosevelt, there's no telling what might have taken place. They wouldn't have told the people what they were doing, of course. They were going to make it all sound constitutional, of course, with a high-sounding name for the dictator and a plan to make it all sound like a good American program. A well-organized minority can always outmaneuver an unorganized majority, as Adolf Hitler did. He failed with his beer-hall putsch, but he succeeded when he was better organized. The same thing could have happened here."

"How did it come about that the committee first approached Butler before he approached the committee?"

"Oh, we heard something about it and asked the general if he knew anything," McCormack replied. "He said he certainly did. He was giving the plotters a come-on and trying to get the whole story from them. When he had all the information on who was behind it, and what they were up to, he wanted to come to Washington, testify before our committee, and break the whole thing wide open."

Finally I asked him, "Then in your opinion America could definitely have become a Fascist power had it not been for General Butler's patriotism in exploding the plot?"

"It certainly could have," McCormack acknowledged. "The people were in a very confused state of mind, making the nation weak and ripe for some drastic kind of extremist reaction. Mass frustration could bring about anything."

He reminded me that the international smell of fascism had been very much in the air during the hectic days of the plot and that much undercover Fascist activity had been going on in the United States that the American people knew nothing about. The McCormack-Dickstein Committee had exposed Ivy Lee, the noted public relations expert ostensibly employed by the German dye trust, but actually on the payroll of the Nazi Government to help them win favorable publicity in the American press. The committee had brought about passage of the Foreign Agents' Registration Act to smoke out hidden Nazi and Soviet agents into the limelight.

This committee was not the headline-seeking, witch-hunting extravaganza that HUAC became under Martin Dies. "Its manner of investigation commanded special respect," notes historian Arthur M. Schlesinger, Jr. "McCormack used competent investigators and employed as committee counsel a former Georgia senator with a good record on civil liberties. Most of the examination of witnesses was carried on in executive sessions. In public sessions, witnesses were free to consult counsel. Throughout, McCormack was eager to avoid hit-and-run accusation and unsubstantiated testimony. The result was an almost uniquely scrupulous investigation in a highly sensitive area."

Schlesinger noted that the McCormack Committee had "declared itself 'able to verify all the pertinent statements made by General Butler' except for MacGuire's direct proposal to him, and it considered this more or less confirmed by MacGuire's European reports. . . . James E. Van Zandt, national commander of the Veterans of Foreign Wars and subsequently a Republican congressman, corroborated Butler's story and said that he, too, had been approached by 'agents of Wall Street.' "

I queried McCormack about one final point. One newspaper reporter had suggested that Butler had not himself taken the plot very seriously. "Oh, no, General Butler regarded the plot very gravely indeed," McCormack said emphatically. "He knew that this was a threat to our very way of government by a bunch of rich men who wanted fascism."

I also discussed this point with the Butler family. Smedley Butler, Jr., agreed with McCormack and explained why his father did not immediately go to Washington when he realized what the plotters were up to: "Dad was not stupid. He had no proof, and he could not name names, so he had to be careful about it."

In fairness to the American Legion today, it needs to be pointed out that the Legion leadership of our times is far different from what it was in the period during and preceding the Butler hearings, when so many former commanders and high officials were involved in the conspiracy and antilabor actvities dictated by big-business interests.

John L. Spivak explained why:

> A long struggle followed within the Legion between those who would use the members for their own business and political interests and those who wanted the organization used for the benefit of former servicemen. The latter won. At the time of the plot, the cleavage between the rank and file and the Royal Family seemed—as it indeed turned out to be—a permanent one. In the generation that followed, the

Legion underwent drastic changes and a mellowing. . . .
Members now rarely participate in antilabor activity. In
fact, many Legionnaires are themselves loyal union men.

5

To carry his warnings further to the American people, Butler
began touring the country in a series of lectures. On the podium
he held audiences fascinated not only by his vigorous exposés
of big business, war-makers, the American Liberty League, and
the American Legion "Royal Family," but by the sheer dynam-
ism of his personality.

As he grew more and more heated, he would roam the stage,
gesticulating vigorously as he made his points, often extempo-
raneously, in salty, sometimes ribald, always blunt language.

He was flooded with requests for appearances at huge veterans' bonus rallies staged by the V.F.W. all over the country.
In his speeches to veterans he would growl at their naïveté as
"dumb soldiers" because they didn't organize politically to fight
for veterans' benefits due them. They would grin and applaud
enthusiastically, knowing that behind his gruff manner was a
genuine fondness and concern for their welfare.

Acknowledged as the spokesman for the "forgotten veteran,"
he was besieged with requests for help in getting adequate pensions for disabled veterans, and through the V.F.W. put pressure
on the Veterans Administration in hundreds of cases.

The worshipful attitude of veterans toward Butler was expressed in a typical letter to him in March, 1935, by a veteran
who wrote, "We all know that you speak our language, and that
the Vet is about as close to your heart as anything else in the
world."

There was no generation gap between the fifty-four-year-old
general and youth leaders of that period, who were organizing

the American Student Union to fight "against war and fascism." They felt a close kinship with the war hero who hated wars, and hated the men who had sent him to fight them. Now constantly proselytizing against war in the hope of stopping any new ones, Butler also wrote magazine articles condemning Marine intervention in the affairs of China.

Speaking to a Y.M.C.A. in Coatesville, Pennsylvania, in February, he accused the big industrialists of America of fattening on the blood of soldiers. He pointed out that the average profit of the Du Ponts from 1910 to 1914 had been only $6 million, but had soared to $58 million between 1914 and 1918. The jump in the same periods for Bethlehem Steel had been $6 to $49 million; for International Nickel, $4 to $73 million.

"It makes you feel proud," he said bitingly. "A lot of the stockholders are members of the National Economy League, and, after I complete my investigation, I will probably find they are also members of the American Liberty League."

On February 25 *Time* magazine ran a two-column photo showing Butler and comedian Jimmy Durante, who attended a dinner in Pittsburgh where the general was speaking, facing each other "nose to nose" in a light moment for the photographer. The caption read "SCHNOZZLE, GIMLET EYE. Fascist to Fascist?"

In a tiny footnote at the bottom of the page, in five-point type that could barely be read, *Time* informed those of its readers with 20-20 vision, "Also last week the House Committee on Un-American Activities purported to report that a two-month investigation had convinced it that General Butler's story of a Fascist march on Washington was alarmingly true." This was *Time*'s microscopic amends for its lengthy page-one ridicule of the plot a dozen weeks earlier.

In March, 1935, Butler began lecturing to mass meetings called by the V.F.W., speaking on behalf of the Patman Bonus Bill. He lost no opportunity to warn veterans also against those big-business interests who favored war and fascism. His convictions were strengthened by a new book based on the Nye munitions investigation, *The Road to War*, by Walter Millis.

He wrote a small antiwar book of his own that year, based on an earlier magazine article in which he favored a foreign

policy of strict neutrality. In *War Is a Racket* he advocated an
"ironclad defense a rat couldn't crawl through," but only to
defend the United States against attack. The job of the armed
forces, he insisted, was only to protect democracy at home—not
waste lives on foreign soil to protect American investments
overseas:

> [War] is conducted for the benefit of the very few at the
> expense of the masses. Out of war a few people make huge
> fortunes. . . . How many of these war millionaires shouldered
> a rifle? . . . Newly acquired territory promptly is exploited
> by the . . . self-same few who wring dollars out of blood
> in the war. The general public shoulders the bill. . . . Newly
> placed gravestones. Mangled bodies. Shattered minds.
> Broken hearts and homes. Economic instability. Depression
> and all its attendant miseries. Back-breaking taxation for
> generations and generations.
>
> For a great many years, as a soldier, I had a suspicion
> that war was a racket; not until I retired to civil life did I
> fully realize it. Now that I see the international war clouds
> again gathering, as they are today, I must face it and speak
> out. . . .
>
> There are 40,000,000 men under arms in the world today,
> and our statesmen and diplomats have the temerity to say
> that war is not in the making. Hell's bells! Are these
> 40,000,000 men being trained to be dancers? . . . [Mus-
> solini is] ready for war. . . . [Hitler] is an equal if not greater
> menace to peace. . . . The mad dogs of Europe are on the
> loose. . . .
>
> Yes, they [munitions makers, bankers, ship-builders, manu-
> facturers, meat packers, speculators] are getting ready for
> another war. Why shouldn't they? It pays high dividends.
> But what does it profit the masses . . . who are killed?
> [American boys in past wars] were made to . . . regard
> murder as the order of the day. . . . We used them a couple
> of years and trained them to think nothing at all of killing
> or being killed. Then suddenly, we discharged them and told
> them to do their own readjusting. . . . Many, too many, of
> these fine young boys were eventually destroyed mentally. . . .
>
> The soldiers couldn't bargain for their labor. . . . By de-
> veloping the . . . medal business, the government learned it

could get soldiers for less money. . . . We gave them the large salary of $30 a month!

All they had to do for that munificent sum was to leave their dear ones behind, give up their jobs, lie in swampy trenches, eat canned willy [when they could get it], and kill and kill and kill . . . and be killed. . . .

But there is a way to stop it. You can't end it by disarmament conferences . . . by resolutions. It can be smashed effectively only by taking the profit out of war.

The only way to smash this racket is to conscript capital and industry and labor before the nation's manhood can be conscripted. . . .

Let the officers and directors and the high-powered executives of our armament factories and our steel companies and our munitions makers and our ship-builders and our airplane builders . . . as well as the bankers and the speculators, be conscripted—to get $30 a month, the same wage as the lads in the trenches get.

Let the workers in these plants get the same wages . . . yes, and all generals and all admirals and all officers and all politicians. . . . Why shouldn't they? They aren't running any risk of being killed or having their bodies mangled or their minds shattered. . . .

Give capital and industry and labor thirty days to think it over and you will find, by that time, there will be no war. That will smash the war racket—that and nothing else.

Industrialists and financiers were shocked by Butler's "radical" notion. But if they had checked the Oxford Dictionary, they would have found as one definition of conscription: "taxation or confiscation of property for war purposes to impose equality of sacrifice on non-conscripts."

6

Butler's speeches at bonus rallies and over the air helped put pressure on Congress to pass the Patman Bonus Bill. As it went to the White House, Butler urged the President to sign it into law, pointing out that it was one way the nation could make amends to the veterans for their exploitation by big business in America's wars of the twentieth century. In a radio broadcast on May 9 he urged his listeners to deluge Roosevelt with a million wires and letters supporting the bill.

But the President vetoed it. On May 21 Butler conferred with Senator Elmer Thomas, of Oklahoma, in Washington on tactics to get Congress to override the veto. Afterward he declared his hope of organizing a large-scale political movement of veterans to press for the bonus.

"My idea," he told the press, "would be a mammoth organization like the Grand Army of the Republic, which would bring political pressure to bear to take care of the soldiers."

Now he criticized not only the American Legion but also the V.F.W. for avoiding the political arena: "They're no good. They've got provisions in their bylaws which say they can't engage in political action. The politicians put them to sleep. . . . If the soldiers don't get theirs now, they'll organize and get it. There'd be about five million of them."

He was asked who would head the new organization.

"I don't know who we'd get to lead it," he replied.

He was instantly besieged with requests from various veterans groups that he take them over as the nucleus for his battle for the bonus and veterans' pensions. Morris A. Bealle, publisher of *Plain Talk* magazine, wrote Butler on May 24 that he had already begun such an organization, calling it the Iron Veterans. He urged Butler to assume its leadership.

"You may be interested to know that Bill Doyle tried to finance this organization for us," Bealle wrote, "but acted so suspicious[ly] at Miami that I thought he was trying to take it over for the Royal Family of the American Legion, and declined to do business with him." This was the same Doyle who had accompanied MacGuire in the plotters' first contact with Butler. Bealle added, "A few weeks later I discovered to my horror that he was trying to take it over for the House of Morgan."

But Butler, made wary by the Fascists' plan for a veterans' "superorganization," began to have second thoughts about the wisdom of any attempt to organize a national veterans group for political purposes.

"To attempt a national association in the beginning," he wrote to the organizer of the American Warriors in Iowa, "would only lead to great financial expense and exploitation of the veterans by chiselling professionals. . . . While it might be possible to find those who would contribute the necessary funds, it would put the veterans under obligation to the contributors."

His fight for the Bonus Bill, and his bare-knuckled attacks against the establishment, led to cancellation of his radio broadcasts as of July 3. A month earlier, when Van Zandt urged him to come to Montana to speak for the soldiers' bonus at a V.F.W. rally there, Butler declined.

"Such a trip would be a very heavy drain on my pocketbook," he explained. "And as long as I am being put off the air for being too noisy in my criticism of this administration and for taking the part of the soldiers, I more or less shall have to conserve my resources."

But he was determined to get the truth as he saw it out to the American people and undertook a new lecture tour that would cover the country. Roosevelt had not been able to get the press to carry his message to the people, so he had turned to national radio. Butler had not been able to get national radio to carry his message, so he turned to town-hall meetings all over America.

On June 12 the American League of Ex-Servicemen asked him to speak at a rally in favor of the bonus with American Labor party Congressman Vito Marcantonio. Butler agreed, with the understanding that he spoke as an individual only, not as a representative of any group. The League adjutant quickly agreed, adding, "Millions of rank-and-file veterans have always looked to you as a champion of their cause in fighting for their rights and to receive justice from the government."

Meanwhile a vigorous debate was taking place in Congress, sparked by the Nye Committee revelations and the weakness of the League of Nations, over the Ludlow Resolution calling for a national referendum before war could be declared. The resolution failed, but on August 31 Congress passed the First Neutrality Act. It forbade transportation of munitions to any belligerents after the President had declared a state of war to exist between them and authorized the President to prohibit travel by American citizens on the ships of belligerents.

Butler regretted the failure of the Ludlow Resolution to pass, because he saw it as a way to prevent powerful men from making decisions that could drag the country to war. He praised Congress for passing the Neutrality Act, however, believing that it would help take the profits out of war for American munitions-makers, and also make it difficult for them to embroil the United States in a foreign war by stirring passions over Americans lost at sea in naval attacks.

When a book by Senator Huey Long appeared, hopefully called *My First Days in the White House*, it listed as members of Long's mythical cabinet Franklin D. Roosevelt and Herbert Hoover, with Smedley Butler as Secretary of War. On September 15, one week after Long was assassinated, Butler was interviewed in Atlanta. He was asked how he felt about his inclusion in the late senator's proposed cabinet.

Characterizing it as "the greatest compliment ever paid to me," Butler smiled, "I certainly felt in good company."

Asked about his own political ambitions, Butler shrugged, "I'm just a gentleman farmer now." Reporters then asked him to comment on the government's transfer of veterans who had been lobbying for the bonus from Washington to Florida, where some had been killed in a violent hurricane.

"What I'm interested in," Butler replied, "is who approved the order to send them down there. They were in Washington, lobbying or pleading under their constitutional rights, when they were sent down to the sandspits. There are other lobbyists in Washington. Why not deport them, too?"

On October 5, when Mussolini invaded Ethiopia, the Senate Foreign Relations Committee invoked an arms embargo against both countries under the Neutrality Act. Although Butler sympathized with Ethiopia, he approved of Congress's determination to keep clear of involvement in any foreign war.

On Armistice Day he spoke to a crowd of ten thousand in Philadelphia at a peace rally held by the Armistice Day Celebration Committee and the Women's International League for Peace and Freedom. Deglamorizing the first war he had fought in, the Spanish-American War, he shouted, "That war was caused by the newspaper propaganda of William Randolph Hearst, and he's been trying to get us into another war ever since. Don't let the man you send to Washington get you into another war . . . that is surely coming along." Urging an even stronger neutrality law to keep America at peace, he declared:

> My interest in peace is personal. I have three grown sons[*] and I'll be damned if anybody's going to shoot them! . . .
> We pay the farmers in the West not to grow corn. We pay other farmers not to raise hogs . . . not to grow cotton. Let us pay the munitions makers not to make munitions! . . . We must work against war now. Wait until the war drums beat and you'll go half crazy. You'll march up Broad Street and raise Liberty loans to help Europe pay off its debts to the House of Morgan. . . .
> The present man in the White House, Mr. Roosevelt, says he will do his utmost to keep us out of war. That language isn't strong enough for us. We want him to say we *won't* have war!

He told a Y.M.C.A. audience that Mussolini was invading Ethiopia to get oil because the nation was bankrupt:

> The only way out for Mussolini is to declare war on somebody. That's the regular way of dealing with such situations.

---

[*] He included his son-in-law, John Wehle.

If this country ever gets busted, you can look for a war in about six months. Before he started it, Mussolini called a conference with England and France . . . and he thought he had everybody's permission to go ahead. Diplomacy is reeking with rotten politics. None of the representatives of any of the nations is sincere. I wouldn't trust any of them anywhere.

Interviewed on an N.B.C. radio program, he reported:

After the war I began visiting the veterans' hospitals, where I saw the ghastly, human wreckage of that war. . . . What right have we to send men away from their homes to be shot? I'd limit the plebiscite to those who are actually going to do the fighting and dying, to the men of military age. . . .

Do you want *your* son to go? Do you want your son to leave his home and lie down on the ground somewhere on the other side of the world with a bullet in him, cut down like a stalk of wheat? Oh, no, not *your* son! I've got three sons and I know! I've just come back from a 9,000-mile trip around the country and I know this, too. None of the American men I spoke to want to nominate their sons for the Unknown Soldier of the future!

Seeing the war clouds gathering over Europe, he grew worried that Americans would once again be fed slogans and half-truths to distort their judgment, and fall victims to professional propagandists for those who would urge war in support of one favored country or another. He sensed the President's growing internationalism and joined other liberal pacifists in demanding that Roosevelt stick to implementing the New Deal and steer clear of any foreign adventures.

Addressing the Third U.S. Congress Against War and Fascism in Cleveland on January 3, 1936, he urged strict neutrality:

Every indication points to a second World War. . . . The nations of Europe and Asia are spending billions of dollars each year in military preparations. . . . These nations are bound to go to war because the men in charge of the governments of some of them have worked their people into a fanatical frame of mind. . . . Now that their people are getting out of control, these so-called leaders must attack some foreign objective if they are to remain in control. With many of them it is a question of a foreign war or being overthrown. None of these dictators is willing to cut his own throat, hence this war. . . .

If we pass a single, tiny thread of help to these leaders gone insane, these same leaders will pull a bigger line after the little one until the rope is so big they can drag us in with it. . . . When you take sides, you must eventually wind up by taking part. . . .

See that our Congress writes into law a command that no American soldier, sailor or Marine be used for any purpose except to protect the coastline of the United States, and protect his home—and I *mean* his home—not an oil well in Iraq, a British investment in China, a sugar plantation in Cuba, a silver mine in Mexico, a glass factory in Japan, an American-owned share of stock in a European factory— in short, not an American investment anywhere except at home! . . . Let Congress say to all foreign investors: "Come on home or let your money stay out of the country—we will not defend it."

As the nation grew increasingly polarized between anti-Fascist interventionists and antiwar isolationists, Butler's uncompromising stand against war was sometimes confused with the right-wing propaganda of pro-Fascists who wanted no American help given to the victims of Mussolini and Hitler.

In April, 1936, the Tacoma *News-Tribune* published an editorial on his antiwar speeches, intimating that he was "credited with fascist leanings." The Olympia, Washington, post of the United Spanish War Veterans immediately passed a resolution protesting this libel. Demanding a retraction, they pointed out, "Less than three years ago he stifled an incipient fascist rebellion in the eastern United States, an accomplishment due solely to his own prompt initiative, thereby demonstrating once more his stalwart Americanism."

While Butler had become an isolationist out of disillusionment

with the motives of those who had engineered armed U.S. intervention in other countries, he hated fascism as fervently as he
hated war. He warned angrily that the Fascist fifth column in
America was so active that one in every five hundred Americans
had become "at heart a traitor to democracy."

One of his long-fought crusades ended in triumph in January, 1936, when Congress, under heavy pressure from the nation's veterans aroused by Butler, Senators Patman and Thomas,
and the V.F.W. bonus rallies, finally passed the Patman Bonus
Bill over Roosevelt's veto.

Many veterans groups now urged him to throw his hat into
the presidential race of 1936. A realist, he declined, explaining,
"I am too ignorant to be President of the United States and have
not a definite plan for curing our present ills. I am doing the
best I can to educate myself, but feel that no man should invite
others to follow him unless he has a definite objective, and has
the course marked out, day by day. I, of course, learned the
above from my military life."

He devoted all his energies to keeping America out of the
war he saw coming. Preoccupied with writing and speaking
against it, as well as reading to learn more about it, he had no
time for the theater, radio, or tennis, which he loved and played
brilliantly. At the dinner table at home and elsewhere, guests
listened to him spellbound in complete silence. He was kept
talking so much that he frequently left the table without having
had more than a mouthful of food.

A thoroughgoing extrovert, he was not ostensibly an egotist;
it simply came naturally to him as a Marine general to be in
command of any situation. His children could not recall any
gathering at which their father did not hold forth, less because
he wanted or needed to, than because he was urged on by a
barrage of interested questions. People were fascinated by his
views and experiences.

He was not, however, among the honored guests when the
American Liberty League, in January, 1936, organized a banquet
for two thousand of its members at the Mayflower Hotel in
Washington. The principal speaker was Al Smith.

7

In his speech Smith warned Americans that they faced a choice between "the pure air of America or the foul breath of Communistic Russia." The New Deal, he charged, was taking the nation into communism. The press, 80 percent anti-Roosevelt, warmly applauded his attack. Militant C.I.O. labor leader John L. Lewis growled that Smith had undoubtedly been "well paid" by his present employers for what he had said. New Deal partisans denounced Smith as a tool of Wall Street.

"I just can't understand it," Roosevelt told Secretary of Labor Frances Perkins. "All the things we have done in the Federal Government are like the things Al Smith did as governor of New York. They're the things he would have done as President. . . . What in the world is the matter?"

The American Liberty League banquet marked the opening of their hate campaign of propaganda to defeat the reelection of Roosevelt in 1936. The Scripps-Howard press and its United Press wire service, an exception to the rabidly anti-Roosevelt newspaper chains, rushed to the President's defense.

Following through on Butler's exposé, their papers carried a story headlined: "Liberty League Controlled by Owners of $37,000,000,000." Directors of the League were identified as also being directors of U.S. Steel, General Motors, Standard Oil, Chase National Bank, Goodyear Tire, and Mutual Life Insurance Company. Liberal senators joined the attack.

On January 23 Senator Schwellenbach denounced "J. Pierpont Morgan and John J. Raskob and Pierre du Pont and all the rest of these rascals and crooks who control the American Liberty League." Senator Robert M. La Follette, Jr., pointed out that the League's biggest contributors were the Du Ponts, A. P. Sloan, the Pews, E. T. Weir, Sewell Avery, and John J. Raskob, and declared, "It is not an organization that can be expected to defend the liberty of the masses of the American people. It speaks for the vested interests."

The attacks on the League, plus Roosevelt's reelection in 1936 over its desperate and expensive opposition, destroyed the organization as an effective force of reaction in America. It was disbanded soon afterward with a brief announcement to the press that the purposes for which the League had been formed had been served, and that it was therefore no longer necessary. But affiliates financed by the League, like the Sentinels of the Republic, the Crusaders, and other pro-Fascist and far-right organizations, continued their agitation.

Butler continued to stump the country through 1936 warning against involvement in the coming war he foresaw. He was gratified on February 29 when Congress passed the Second Neutrality Act, amending the original act to prohibit either loans or credits to belligerent nations.

He was disturbed, however, when the Spanish civil war broke out in July. The Neutrality Act imposed a boycott of aid to the Loyalist Government, while it was apparent that Mussolini and Hitler were supplying both money and military assistance to Franco. But by this time Butler was so passionately opposed to the loss of another American soldier on foreign soil, he felt only strict neutrality could prevent it.

He shocked a meeting of the American League Against War and Fascism, which was trying to raise funds for the Loyalists, by asking them, "What the hell is it our business what's going on in Spain? Use common sense or you'll have our boys getting their guts blown out over there. Americans en masse never did a wrong thing. Mind your own business. Have faith in your own country." He considered the argument that Hitler and Mussolini had to be "stopped now before it's too late" the kind of sophistry that had plunged America into World War I with frightening warnings about the Kaiser.

In September he endorsed the candidacy of Representative Vito Marcantonio, of the left-wing American Labor party, for his antiwar, anti-Fascist stand. Butler's detractors assailed this endorsement as "proof" that he was some kind of Red, ignoring the fact that two weeks earlier Roosevelt had accepted the invitation of the A.L.P. to become its candidate, as well as the candidate of the Democratic party.

The growing isolationist movement in America now resulted in more prominence being given to Butler's antiwar speeches in the press. On September 17 when he delivered a slashing attack on war makers before the V.F.W. in Denver, it was carried in part on the wires of the Associated Press:

WAR IS CALLED 'HELL'
AND 'BUSINESS RACKET'

Gen. Butler and Senator Bone
Warn Veterans of Foreign
Wars of the Future

Men who fought America's foreign wars cheered violently today as a major general and a Senator called warfare "a business racket." Major Gen. Smedley D. Butler, retired, used blunt language as he told the Veterans of Foreign Wars that "war is hell." . . . "But what in the hell are we going to do about it? I've got something for you to do about it. I'm going to tell you in simple language so all of you can understand. Let the world know that hereafter no American soldier is going to leave the shores of this country! . . . Soldiers never leave the country except to protect the moneyed interests."

One enthusiastic veteran who applauded him afterward wrote to President Roosevelt urging Butler's appointment as Secretary of War to replace retiring George H. Dern:

This man is the most popular Military figure with the Vets as a class. Pershing hasn't one tenth of one percent his color and personality. He's a Quaker, and a helluva good one, i.e., not the Hoover type. . . . If you asked him to fill Dern's place, the army and the Republicans would holler but the common people would understand, and so would the rank and file of the veterans. Of course, the slap at Liberty Leaguer Dupont would cost their family's votes. P.S. You won't get many anyhow!

The Du Ponts supplied more grist for Butler's antiwar mill in September, when the Senate Munitions Investigating Committee revealed that the munitions industry, led by the Du Ponts, had sabotaged a League of Nations disarmament conference held at Geneva.

"After the whole conference was over and the munitions people of the world had made the treaty a satisfactory one to themselves," reported Chairman Gerald Nye, "we find that Colonel Simons [of the Du Ponts] is reporting that even the State Department realized, in effect, who controlled the Nation."

On October 19 Butler used his popularity with the dry forces, who remembered him affectionately from the Volstead Act days in Philadelphia, to appeal to the Women's Christian Temperance Union to join the peace movement. Six days later the mood of the nation grew more apprehensive, however, as Hitler and Mussolini signed the Rome-Berlin Axis pact and the following month were joined by Japan, which signed an Anti-Comintern Pact with Germany.

Roosevelt's landslide reelection strengthened his hand against the isolationists, and there were signs that the White House intended to take a tougher stand against the Axis powers. Butler grew increasingly worried that the President might be starting the nation down the road to war.

Speaking at an Armistice Day dinner for veterans, Butler announced firmly that he, with a record of thirty-three years of military service, would never again shoulder arms except in defense of America's own shores.

8

Attacking congressional attempts to put loopholes in the Neutrality Act, Butler warned in a subsequent speech that once the United States was lured into shipping supplies to a belligerent,

Americans would soon hear the old cry—"the American flag insulted, American property destroyed . . . same old thing over again, just as it was in the World War." America, he said, best served itself and the world by staying at peace:

> Help them to bind up the wounds when the distressed world has fought itself to exhaustion and has overthrown its false and selfish leaders. I am firmly convinced that every government which hurls its loyal but dumb masses into this coming war will be overthrown, win or lose. I am also firmly convinced that another universal war will make man into a savage, ready to take by force what he wants, law or no law.

His tone grew acrid and resentful when Roosevelt won congressional consent to amending the Neutrality Act in May, 1937, authorizing the sale to belligerents of some commodities on a cash-and-carry basis. Since a national poll showed that 73 percent of Americans favored some kind of popular referendum before the United States could declare war, Butler felt that the President was ignoring the will of the people and seeking to tie their fate to that of England and France.

On July 12 he warned a thousand veterans at Paterson, New Jersey, that unless the nation's veterans banded together to demand peace, America would be at war again in a short time. He urged them to demand that U.S. armed forces be kept within their own borders and that the use of the American flag be restricted to government-owned ships.

Speaking to a Writers' Union meeting in Philadelphia, he described how the United States might be dragged into the next European war. A European ship would stop a U.S. ship carrying munitions to a potential enemy. The American captain would radio William Randolph Hearst that the flag had been insulted. Orators would begin demanding that Americans avenge the insult. Ministers would discover that they were "transmitters from God" and encourage a holy crusade. Arms manufacturers would bring pressure to bear on Washington. And we would go to war.

A July speech he made to the Institute of Public Affairs at the University of Virginia in Charlottesville was broadcast:

> Wars do not occur. They are made by men. . . . There will never be a congressional investigation into the steps taken or the methods adopted which saves us from a war. . . . Lying propaganda is almost certainly necessary to bring nations to the pitch where men kill and women give their men and boys to be killed. . . .
> The object of war is to get something for nothing. . . . When we have announced what we intend to defend, let us put our national flag over it and forbid the flying of our flag over anything else; then we will avoid insults to our flag, the most popular cause for our wars. . . . We Americans who love and protect our flag should certainly have a voice in where it is flown.

With Japanese troops sweeping through China and seizing the coastal cities, Butler addressed the V.F.W. convention in September urging that all American forces be withdrawn from China. Three months later Japanese airmen sank the U.S. gunboat *Panay* in Chinese waters. A poll showed that 53 percent of Americans agreed with Butler's demand for withdrawal of all United States forces. But instead Washington demanded indemnity from Tokyo.

Butler was convinced that a continued American presence in Asia could only lead to eventual war with an aggressive Japan bent on becoming the dominant power in the Orient. He saw confirmation of his belief that war was a business racket when Washington continued to permit American corporations to sell scrap iron and oil to Tokyo for its war machine. He also knew that there were over two billion dollars in American investments in Germany, which was being goaded by British diplomacy into attacking the Soviet Union.

If these facts seemed to him more immediately menacing than the steadily escalating aggression of the Axis powers, he was not alone among liberal and left-wing Americans in this myopia. In January, 1938, John Chamberlain, Alfred M. Bingham, Dwight

MacDonald, Bertrand Wolfe, and Sidney Hook were among those who opposed any strong action against Japan, or any of the other Axis powers, arguing, "We believe that the first result of another War to Make the World Safe for Democracy will be the establishment of virtual fascism in this country."

By now the country was almost evenly divided between isolationists and those who advocated anti-Fascist alliances. In late January Roosevelt asked Congress for appropriations to build up the Army and Navy for "national defense."

Interviewed on February 28, 1938, on a national radio program, Butler had strong doubts about F.D.R.'s plans:

> Now is the time to keep our heads better than we ever kept them before. . . . We ought to agree on a definition of the word "national." If it means defense by our Army and Navy of every dollar and American person anywhere they may happen to be on the surface of the earth, then, just as sure as I'm standing here, we'll be fighting a foreign war.

He was asked how long he estimated it would take to train a man to fight. "Well," he replied, "if you want to send him three thousand miles away to fight, at least six months' training will be needed. If he was defending his home, it would take about an hour."

9

On April 9 Butler was called to testify before the Senate Committee on Naval Affairs on a billion-dollar naval construction bill. Urging defeat of the bill, he called it unnecessary for the real defense of the United States. In the event of war, he told the committee, he favored abandoning Alaska, the Panama Canal, the Virgin Islands, and Puerto Rico. The Canal, he asserted, could be destroyed by "a handful of bombs." He also insisted that all mercantile ships operated for profit should fly commercial flags, not the American flag.

He explained that since his retirement he had visited twelve hundred cities and towns and "talked to all kinds of people in all parts of the country." He said, "I have a feeling that this bill does not represent a consensus of opinion among naval officers. I have a feeling that it is a grand bluff. Furthermore, I believe that the American people will turn against this bill before any of the keels provided are laid. I cannot prove it, but I believe it is proposed for the purpose of doing somebody else's business."

He had used up fifteen years of his life, he growled, "going about the world guarding Standard Oil tins" and had participated in twelve expeditions outside the United States which he considered missions largely in the interest of Wall Street. "The whole thing is a racket," he added, "and the American people are going to catch up with it."

The committee chairman asked if he considered the existing Navy adequate to defend the continental United States. He did, he replied, and hoped that Congress would fix a defense line beyond which the Navy would not be allowed to operate.

"Suppose Japan tried to invade the United States?"

Her forces would be so weak by the time they reached the Pacific Coast, Butler replied, that "we could knock her over with a feather." He recommended a force of twenty-thousand-ton battleships that would hug the coasts and, with the aid of submarines, aircraft, and coastal defenses, would be able to stand off any hostile forces that came within striking distance.

"I am a friend of the Navy," he declared, "and I have an anchor tattooed on my chest, but if we go to building up the Navy as proposed in the bill, and loading down the people with the cost of it, the people will turn on the Navy as they did in the eighties, and not a ship will be able to leave port, for there just won't be a dollar appropriated for the Navy."

He was joined in opposing the Navy construction bill by eighteen peace organizations, including the American Friends Service Committee, the Federal Council of Churches of Christ in America, the National Council of Jewish Women, the Conference on World Peace of the Methodist Episcopal Church, the National Council for the Prevention of War, the Church Peace Union, and the National Student Federation. But Congress turned a deaf ear, and in May it passed the Naval Construction Act, authorizing a billion-dollar expansion program.

Butler's raging hatred of war led him into the same errors of judgment that ensnared the isolationists of America. Like them, he approved of Prime Minister Neville Chamberlain's efforts to buy "peace in our time" at Munich. Confident that the Nazis could not get through the French Maginot line, he also believed that every Frenchman would fight fiercely to protect his own plot of land against any invasion.

The Stalin-Hitler nonaggression pact of August 23, 1939, followed by the invasion of Poland, made it clear that the world was tottering on the verge of another great war. On August 31 Butler joined Senator Henry Cabot Lodge, Jr., in appeals to keep America out of it, at a V.F.W. convention in Boston.

"There are only two things for which Americans should be permitted to fight," Butler shouted over the whistles and cheers of veterans. "Defense of home and the Bill of Rights. Not a single drop of American blood should ever again be spilled on foreign soil. Let's build up a national defense so tight that even a rat couldn't crawl through!"

Three days later Great Britain and France declared war on Germany. On the same day the British passenger liner *Athenia* was torpedoed and sunk without warning off the Hebrides, drowning thirty American passengers. That night, in a fireside radio chat to the American people, Roosevelt declared, "This nation will remain a neutral nation, but I cannot ask that every American remain neutral in thought as well."

In November Congress passed a new neutrality act that legalized the sale of munitions to belligerent nations on a cash-and-carry basis. The news filled Butler with dismay.

"This country," he protested, "did not have one solitary blessed thing to do with the making of this mess over there, and there is no possible sane and logical reason why we should feel any impulse to take a hand in it."

10

A spiteful rumor that Butler had become a spokesman for Father Coughlin's Christian Front led some Jewish groups to threaten cancellation of speeches he was scheduled to make to them in November.

"I couldn't believe there was a word of truth in this," wrote Mildred Smith, executive secretary of the Open Forum Speakers Bureau, "but I dared not say an official 'no' without direct word from you on this matter."

He wired back indignantly, "Have never spoken for the Christian Front. I am a Quaker and am preaching tolerance and am not connected nor will I have anything to do with any movement or organization advocating intolerance or the entrance of this country into any foreign war."

His hatred for war did not cause any diminution in his hatred for fascism, but he refused to sanction one to fight the other except in absolute self-defense. Once he was visited by a female cousin who had married a German and brimmed over with praise for the Nazis. Butler's face grew taut as she babbled on, but he said nothing until it was time to say good-bye.

Unable to contain himself any longer, he rasped at the door, "Nellie, if Hitler comes over here, thee can be sure I will be on the beach at Atlantic City to kick the everlasting hell out of him!"

His taste in books increasingly reflected both his antiwar and his anti-Fascist convictions. In his library during his last years were *Sawdust Caesar*, by George Seldes, *The Road to War*, by Walter Millis, and *Johnny Got His Gun*, by Dalton Trumbo. *Europe Under the Terror*, by John L. Spivak, was inscribed to him as "one of the best fighters against Fascism in the country, with the respect and admiration of J.L.S."

In 1939 he wrote an antiwar piece for a book edited by Paul Comly French, *Common Sense Neutrality—Mobilizing for Peace*. Sharing the covers with him were such contributors as Eleanor Roosevelt, Charles A. Beard, Dr. Harry Elmer Barnes, Senator William Borah, Norman Thomas, Sumner Welles, Herbert Hoover, Senator Robert La Follette, Jr., John L. Lewis, and Elliot Roosevelt.

But as the Nazis swept through Belgium and the Netherlands on May 10, 1940, bypassing the Maginot line and imperiling France, millions of Americans grew alarmed. A Committee to Defend America by Aiding the Allies was organized by William Allen White to rout the isolationists.

In a mood of black despair Butler delivered his last antiwar speech on May 24 at Temple University. Hating Hitler and Nazism, he nevertheless could not shake off the dread specter of one or two million dead American youths strewn over Europe's battlefields. He decried fears of a German invasion of the United States as alarmist, playing into the hands of war profiteers.

From the comfortable vantage of hindsight, it is easy to fault Smedley Butler as having been woefully shortsighted in his stubborn view that the best interests of Americans were served by persisting in a policy of neutrality. But thirty years in uniform, seeing active service in every war and campaign since the Spanish-American War, had convinced him that war was nothing but a cruel and bloody swindle of the people.

His suspicions were not eased by observing industrialists and bankers entering trade cartels with America's potential enemies, Germany, Italy, and Japan, while U.S. arms manufacturers made huge profits selling munitions to both sides and pressed Congress to spend new billions on "defense" to keep up with the "arms race" they themselves had promoted.

In his disillusionment he saw little difference between World War I and World War II. Ever since he had been a starry-eyed Marine recruit of sixteen, American administrations had persistently cried wolf in order to use him and the youths under him in order to protect and augment foreign investments wrapped in the flag. It was now impossible for him to believe that the shouts of wolf he heard once more were any more genuine than all those he had heard at regular intervals since 1898.

Worn out by his strenuous speaking tours, discouraged as he saw the United States slipping step by step into another blood-bath, he fell ill with exhaustion. His doctor ordered him to enter the Naval Hospital in Philadelphia for a rest and examination.

"As soon as I get out," he promised Ethel Butler, "I am going to take thee to Europe for the vacation I've never managed to find time for. Thee deserves it for thy patience!"

During his four weeks in the hospital, however, he lost weight rapidly and guessed that his ailment was more serious than the doctors were letting him know.

On June 10 Italy declared war on Britain and France. Roosevelt promptly called for "full speed ahead" in the promotion of national defense and for the extension of material aid to "opponents of force." The next day Congress voted another $3.2 billion in military appropriations.

On June 14 Butler's gloom plunged to new depths when Germany invaded France unopposed. Four days later Admiral Harold R. Stark, Chief of Naval Operations, asked Congress for a two-ocean navy in a $4-billion expansion program.

During a visit by his son Smedley, Jr., Butler reflected glumly on the futility of his long fight to keep his country from getting involved in another war. "I think," he said ruefully, "that I should have stayed with my own kind." He meant Quakers and Marines, rather than politicians.

On June 21, 1940, hours before France was scheduled to surrender officially to Adolf Hitler, Smedley Darlington Butler died in the hospital of an abdominal ailment suspected to be cancer.

11

Although the paths of President Roosevelt and Smedley Butler had diverged sharply over the questions of war and peace, the President sent a wire to Ethel Butler: "I grieve to hear of Smedley's passing. I shall always remember the old days in Haiti. My heart goes out to you and the family in this great sorrow."

Among others who sent condolences were former Secretary of the Navy Josephus Daniels, then ambassador to Mexico, and Major General Thomas Holcomb, commandant of the Marine Corps. A simple funeral service was held at the Butler home in Newtown Square, followed by burial in West Chester, with attendance limited to close friends and immediate members of the family. Ethel Butler knew that elaborate formal ceremonies would be a violation of the principles of her husband, who had always detested phony pomp and circumstance.

The general who could have had all the wealth and power he wanted as dictator of the United States died leaving an estate that totaled two thousand dollars.

The New York Times now hailed him as "one of the most glamorous and gallant men who ever wore the uniform of the United States Marine Corps. . . . a brave man and an able leader of troops. . . . He laughed at danger, and he set an example to his men that helped them to carry out the traditions of the Marine Corps." Calling him also "often a storm center," the *Times* added, "It was when he ventured into public affairs that his impetuosity led him into trouble."

In an editorial obituary on June 23 the New York *Herald Tribune* had no cautious reservations:

> It is as a great "leatherneck" that Gen. Smedley D. Butler will be remembered. He was an admirable officer, as tough

in his speech as in the fiber of his body and soul. He came of Quaker ancestry, but no Quaker more dearly loved to be belligerent. . . . Because he was utterly unafraid, brave and unselfish, he earned the characterization of being the ideal American soldier, and, to use the words of an official citation of the Navy Department, of being "one of the most brilliant officers in the United States."

Thirty years later Tom Dick Butler told me wistfully, "Dad's experiences were an important part of our lives. He was always 'where it was at.' We miss him tremendously."

When the war that Smedley Butler had dreaded and sought to prevent came to his country out of the clouds over Pearl Harbor, eighteen months after his death, an American destroyer was named the U.S.S. *Butler* in his honor. Converted to a high-speed minesweeper, it saw distinguished service during the war.

That would not have seemed inappropriate to the fighting hero who hated war as a racket, yet who had once declared, "I am a peace-loving Quaker, but when war breaks out every damn man in my family goes." Both his sons entered the service, Smedley, Jr. in the Marines, Tom Dick in the Navy.

A hell-for-leather Marine officer who drove himself as hard as his men, he had won their enthusiastic admiration and loyalty. He, in turn, had been passionately and stubbornly devoted to them, in service and out of it. Former Marine Commandant David M. Shoup, who served under Butler in China, told me that he and all the men in the command had respected Butler as "one helluva fine soldier."

During World War II Butler's old newspaper friend, E. Z. Dimitman, interviewed Douglas MacArthur in the Pacific as a war correspondent. Noting a resemblance between MacArthur's commander of the 32d Division, General Robert L. Eichelberger, and Old Gimlet Eye, Dimitman mentioned it to MacArthur and suggested that Eichelberger might prove another Butler.

"Never in a million years," MacArthur replied emphatically. "There's only one Butler. He was one of the *really* great generals in American history."

12

Although Butler may have been the first high-ranking Marine Corps general to challenge establishment policies, he was not the last. Significantly, as early as January, 1966, another distinguished Marine general, former Commandant David M. Shoup, went before the Senate Foreign Relations Committee to warn the American people that President Lyndon B. Johnson's escalation of the war in Vietnam was a tragic mistake.

It might also be noted that before the explosion of the Pentagon Papers, two Marine Corps colonels wrote books denouncing the intervention in Vietnam as genocide against a people caught up in a civil war, in support of a corrupt Saigon dictatorship.

Perhaps the elite fighting team of the United States produces high-ranking dissenters like Butler, Shoup, and the two colonels because many men who choose careers as Marine Corps officers tend to be strongly motivated by patriotism and idealism. When there is an American military intervention overseas, it is usually the Marines who spearhead it, do the fighting, get an accurate picture of the real situation, and observe who is being politically supported or suppressed, and why.

All too often these officers have been disillusioned by the use of the Marines to suppress social change in small countries, on behalf of dictators, an elite military and business class, and American commercial interests. This realization outrages their idealism. They resent the expenditure of the lives of Marines under them for sordid motives in power games of dollar diplomacy and international politics.

Hence the most intelligent and high-principled Marine staff officers may become the bitterest critics of American administrations that misuse the Corps. The war records, motivation, and integrity of such generals as Butler and Shoup make it impossible to dismiss their testimony expressing dismay at the way United States expeditionary forces have been deployed in the name of national defense.

Although Butler had considered himself basically a pacifist who hated war, he had placed duty to his country above all other considerations and had spent thirty-three years of his life carrying out orders to defend it. His gradual disillusionment with those orders, and the men who gave them, had led him to speak out abrasively against the use of the military on behalf of American vested interests.

No matter whose corns he trod on, or the cost to his career, he had habitually said and did what he thought right. His bluntness had made him unpopular with some Presidents, Secretaries of State and Navy, and the highest-ranking generals and admirals in Washington, who considered him a military firebrand as irrepressible as Generals Billy Mitchell and George S. Patton. But it was just this quality in Butler that had given him the courage and integrity to face public ridicule to expose, in the name of service to his country, what John L. Spivak called "one of the most fantastic plots in American history."

"What was behind the plot was shrouded in a silence which has not been broken to this day," Spivak wrote. "Even a generation later, those who are still alive and know all the facts have kept their silence so well that the conspiracy is not even a footnote in American histories. It would be regrettable if historians neglected this episode and future generations of Americans never heard of it."

In 1964 Speaker of the House John W. McCormack referred to the plot in his speech before the Democratic convention in Atlantic City, when he warned against right-wing extremists in the Barry Goldwater camp. But he did not give any details, and only a knowledgeable handful of Americans understood the full implications of what he was talking about.

The conspiracy unquestionably inspired the novel *Seven Days in May*, made into a successful film, which portrayed a Fascist plot by high-placed American conspirators to capture the White House and establish a military dictatorship under the pretext of saving the nation from communism. Few of the millions of Americans who read the novel or saw the film suspected that it had a solid basis in fact.

It would seem time that school textbooks in America were revised to acknowledge our debt to the almost forgotten hero who thwarted the conspiracy to end democratic government in America.

If we remember Major General Smedley Darlington Butler for nothing else, we owe him an eternal debt of gratitude for spurning the chance to become dictator of the United States— and for making damned sure no one else did either.

Index

Index